TABLE OF CONTENTS

Will Booher

THE TABLE

WILL BOOHER

BLUE HANDLE PUBLISHING

This book is a work of fiction. Any references to historical events, people, or places are used fictitiously. Other names; characters, places, and events are products of the author's imagination, and any resemblance to actual events, places, or persons, living or dead, is entirely coincidental.

For information, address:
Blue Handle Publishing
2067 Wolflin Ave. #963
Amarillo, TX 79109

For information about bulk, educational, and other special discounts, please contact Blue Handle Publishing, www.BlueHandlePublishing.com.

To book Will Booher for any event, contact Blue Handle Publishing.

Cover and interior design: Blue Handle Publishing

Editing: Book Puma Author Services, BookPumaLive.com

ISBN: 978-1-955058-25-4

To everyone who has ever doubted my intellect
or intelligence due to my size and stature . . .
HAHAHAHA! I AM AN AUTHOR!
NANA NANA BOO BOO!

BOOK ONE

THE TABLE

1

THE RIVER

When Aaron was on the river, he was invincible. If you are not seen, no one can get mad at you.

Summer had always been the ten-year-old's favorite time of year, even with the scorching southwest Texas heat. He could explore the wilderness and escape from the pressures of school, the world . . . and home. Time in class brought bullying for his size; he was heavy-set, but still athletic. Time at home brought bullying from his angry tyrant of a stepfather. So, Aaron snuck off to the river any chance he could.

Aaron woke up around six o'clock on another lonely Saturday, well before his parents and three older siblings. His mom worked long hours trying to make ends meet and liked to try to sleep in a bit on the weekends. Rick, his awful stepdad, never wanted to be bothered, so it was just better if Aaron was not around. He rubbed his eyes and ran his fingers through his sandy-brown hair. "Yes! I can sneak out for some fishing without talking to anyone."

Okay, first things first: What to wear? He scanned the room, wincing as his eyes land on his muddy fishing pole. Yesterday's run-in with the local bullies on the road to the river was the exact reason Aaron usually took a different path.

"Oh, look. It's Fatty McFatts," Chuck yelled in his direction.

He knew the voice without taking a look. Aaron was loaded down with his fishing gear, so he didn't have a way to defend himself. He kept walking without turning to face them.

"What an idiot," added one of Chuck's cronies.

"Just a dumb oaf," replied another.

When he finally thought he was in the clear, they rushed up and shoved him down into the mud. They're lucky that I didn't have my hands free, Aaron thought.

As Aaron tried to wipe the mud from his hands and chest, Chuck and the boys just laughed.

"Look, he won't even do anything. He must have eaten all the food in town to get that big, and now little piggy is sad!" The horrible things Chuck would yell at him rang through his head.

Chuck was an awful child who was mean to everyone who crossed his path, and yesterday wasn't that different than many other days before it. If the jerk didn't get his way, he would scream and throw a tantrum until he did. His family was well-off, so no one bothered to stand up to him; there was no point. If Aaron was asked to name his mortal enemy, it would be Chuck.

Chuck didn't always win, though. One of their

wildest encounters happened the day before summer break as Aaron was walking toward home across the football team's practice field. The Butthead Club started in with their usual fatty lines, but Aaron had reached his breaking point.

The bullies stopped their laughing and pointing once Aaron closed in on their bleachers hangout spot. "Shut up, idiot! Don't call me fat!"

"Oh sorry, Aaron," Chuck teased. "Don't call you what? Fat? But why? I mean, look at you. You are—"

As the words left his lips, Aaron's balled fist smashed into Chuck's stomach.

"Oof!" Chuck fell to the ground in pain, gasping and clutching his belly.

Aaron looked up to see the rest of the club in shock, hidden and staring from behind the bleachers. Not wanting to take five-to-one odds, he took the chance to flee before they figured out what just happened. He took off running toward home, knowing this war wasn't over yet.

No, let's not think about The Butthead Club today. We just need to get to the river and everything will be great. He quietly tossed on his dark blue swimming trunks and his lucky hat, a simple John Deere one he found in an old shed, and crept to the front door for his shoes. He contemplated the best path out of the house, immediately dismissing the front door with its squeaky screen. *If I use the back door, in the kitchen, I can grab some cheese and bread for a snack on the way.*

The kitchen exit had its own pitfalls, too. The loud floorboards of the old parsonage could disturb the sleeping troll, who would sound the alarm if awoken. Most would refer to the troll as Stacey, his sister who was asleep on the couch, but this was more fun.

Effortlessly and silently, he slowly tiptoed past the slumbering beast and into the kitchen with one last slide across the floor. As he opened the fridge, it slipped out of his hand and . . . *SMACK!* It hit the wall connected to the bedroom where his horrible stepfather was sleeping. Aaron couldn't breathe. He stood silent as a statue, waiting to hear the stomping and grumbling from the master bedroom. There were none. He snatched a few slices of wrapped American cheese as quickly as he could and inched the fridge door shut again.

"Okay, almost out," he whispered. "Just need some bread."

The loaf was across the room, already next to a box of Ziploc bags. Lucky! Aaron dropped to his knees and continued his treacherous journey through the troll's habitat. At the counter, he put his back to the cupboards to keep an eye out and reached his left hand up above to feel for the wheat bread. He felt the plastic of the bread bag and the cardboard of the bags' box and pulled them down to him. Supplies secured, he had just a foot to go for his escape out the wooden door.

2

THE ESCAPE

"Aaron! What are you doing?" The bellowing of his sister surprised the intrepid adventurer as he pulled on the escape hatch.

Oh no! The troll is awake. Not only did Stacey glare at him, but she made sure to yell loud enough to wake the entire house. Panicked, Aaron grabbed the food and bolted out the door. "Why do you have to suck so much, sis?"

The screen door slammed shut behind him as he grabbed his fishing gear from beside it. As he was running, he could hear his stepdad yelling and some '90s teen drama his sister turned on. The smile on Aaron's face grew as he closed in on the woods.

No one else ever cared to join him on his trips, so the fishing spot was sacred to him. He spent his days dreaming of an epic destiny, of pulling the sword from the stone, or taking on a quest where he was the key to greatness. Really, he just wanted to feel like he was cared for and important.

Most people take the highway alongside the parsonage to reach the river and swim at the bridge, but not Aaron. It wasn't just because of The Butthead Club. He had gone down there a few times, but the solo visitor felt like he was intruding on other families' time together. He took the backwoods to his paradise, down a path he had worn through the field, then along the river's edge to the crooked tree that hung out over the water.

He crawled out onto its trunk and laid there for a few minutes, just watching the fish swim and play. It was his way of saying hello to the river. After finishing his sandwich at that old tree, he took a right and continued down the bank, greeting the creatures he saw along the way. Aaron had spent so much time in the West Texas wilderness that he knew to respect the animals and that they would respect him if he kept his distance. There were also so many types of birds that he couldn't name them all. A day in his oasis could include spotting deer, armadillos, rabbits, and others. Every inch of it was beautiful, and he cherished it.

Aaron found a spot that looked good for fishing and got his rod ready. He tied the hook up a little higher and the weight at the bottom so he could bob the line up and down from a branch above the water. He scraped back the earth's top layer of oak leaves and silt to reveal giant earthworms that were perfect—and free—bait. He fished for the next hour or so like he had hundreds of times before, but there were not many bites this time. As he considered moving to another spot, it started to sprinkle.

"It's just a little mist," he told himself, not worried about melting. But as soon as he could finish that thought, that sprinkle turned into sheets and the wind sped up with a fury. Aaron gripped the tree with all his might as branches swung wildly in the wind. He couldn't see two feet in front of his face.

KABOOM! Thunder crashed in Aaron's ears, scaring him so much he lost his grip and fell into the water. He had swum in this river more times than he could count, but not like this. The now-rushing water shoved him down and sent him tumbling over rocks. He was gasping for breath, trying to make out anything other than blurry water, mud, and rocks. Finally, there was only darkness.

3

"WHERE AM I?"

Aaron opened his eyes and spat out the water and mud from his mouth. His mind was racing as things came into focus. *I can't breathe! Where am I? What is happening? Why is the ground so cold?*

His body ached, but he didn't see any blood, cuts, or broken bones. Somehow, his lucky hat made the trip safely, too. He carefully sat up, taking in the dark cave around him. A crack in the wall let in a bit of light that showed a small path forward.

"I definitely haven't been in here before. What is this place?" He noticed the cave had a small pool, but no openings other than the illuminated path. "I bet I just need to swim under and out!"

In an excited panic, he cannonballed into the water to head for home. *SMACK!* Standing up slowly, Aaron came to the painful realization that the pool was only a few feet deep. "Welp, only one way I can go now," he lamented. He stomped out of the water and down the path.

The trail was quite narrow, from what Aaron could see in the darkness. The light faded the farther he walked until all he could do was feel the way with his hands. Aaron followed the wall on his left, trying to find any source of light or the outside world. At the corner, he grabbed onto what felt like a root—or something worse.

"A snake! Ahh!" He threw whatever was in his hand away in terror, but it smacked him in the face a split-second later. Scared out of his mind, his wild swinging and grabbing ended with a hard tug. "My eyes!"

The cave was showered in light like someone turned on the stadium lights for Friday night football. Aaron could now see what he was fighting—a rope. The cave walls were a gorgeous black stone. His eyes adjusted to the new light, and he could now see it was coming from a chandelier of wood and glowing mossy greens. It was hard to pull his attention from the fascinating space, but Aaron managed to spot an opening in the wall he hadn't seen or felt before. *I don't think that was there a minute ago.* He peered inside, but could only see darkness. "No other way but through, I guess."

Curtains of grass and moss enveloped his face and body, making it difficult to see and move forward. Aaron persisted and, with one last push, he stumbled into the light. The cobblestone street at his feet was perplexing, but the massive cavern he found when he looked up was mind-blowing. The roads were marked with street signs and went into and out of cave walls like an intricate highway system. "Okay, I've *definitely* never been here before. Is this place even real?"

"Ahh! What are you?" a deep, booming voice shouted to Aaron's left. "Stay away! I'm warning you!"

The frightened ten-year-old turned to find a giant

of a boy attempting to hide behind one of the tiny sign poles. Aaron jumped behind a different sign—it covered more of him than the giant boy, but not by much. "What do you mean what am I? What are you?"

Both boys stayed silent for what felt like forever, until Aaron looked down and realized he was covered in mud and sticks, probably looking a bit insane. "You are huge," Aaron squeaked out.

"No, you are small," the giant said timidly. More silence followed as they eyed each other.

"Well, hi. I'm Aaron, and I am lost. I fell in the river . . . and now I'm here."

The giant boy pondered for a moment before responding. "Hi! I'm Steve, and I was just finding some cool rocks." After pointing to his pile, Steve moved from behind his sign and stood up tall so Aaron could see his full size. Wearing a neon pink ballcap turned backward and a bright green "Radical!" T-shirt with some shorts and Converse, his new friend was probably eight feet tall. He looked a bit pudgy and scarred, but seemed kind and gentle.

All of this was a lot for Aaron to take in. "Hello, S-Steve. Nice to meet you. I have n-never seen anyone like you before."

"I haven't ever seen anything like you before, either!"

"I know I look weird, but I am normal," Aaron assured him. "It's just a bunch of mud and sticks. I just need to shower, and you will see. Where, umm, are we?"

"Well, this is Eighth Street, that over there is Ninth Street, and that one over there, you can probably figure out, is Seventh Street!"

Aaron scratched his head. "But where do all these streets go? Is this, like, an underground town or something where people grow bigger than normal? I don't know how I got here or how I am going to get home. Do you know anyone who can help—"

"I'll show you!" Steve shouted, grabbing Aaron by the hand and practically dragging him to a door. With a wide goofy smile, the giant opened it. The visitor couldn't even register what they were seeing.

4

THE SAME, BUT DIFFERENT

W*OOSH* went a car speeding past. *HONK!* The pair stood on a bridge overlooking a huge city sprawling before them. The view reminded Aaron of New York City in movies, except inside a massive domed cavern with huge stalactites hanging from the glowing, moss-covered ceiling.

HONK! A passing car snapped Aaron out of his daze. "What?! This can't be real!"

Steve motioned for Aaron to follow him across the bridge. On the other side, stairs led down to what looked like a normal sidewalk. Aaron stumbled at the bottom, still trying to take everything in. Questions raced through his head faster than he could process them.

"So, you said you are lost?" Steve's words cut into Aaron's thoughts.

"Umm, yeah, I guess."

"Okay, well, let's get you home," Steve said with a smile. "Where are you from?"

Aaron paused, looking at the people around them. Everyone was dressed normally, but they weren't . . . people. To his left was a huge, hairy dude in a tank top and shorts, but with the head of a bull. *That has got to be some sort of costume.* To his right was a man about four feet tall in a full suit of black armor, wielding a pickaxe and a pager.

Creatures from television and books seemed to be all around him, causing his head to whip back and forth trying to take it all in. His frizzy hair flopped all over as his mind reeled.

"Are you okay?" Steve's voice paused Aaron's thrashing.

"No . . . I don't know. I think so," Aaron mumbled.

Steve was worried about the unusual visitor. "Hmm, how about we head to my house? It's right down the road, and maybe my parents can help you."

"Yeah, that is probably the best idea."

Steve smiled and headed down the street to their left. "So, what are you?" he asked as they walked.

"I am . . . human."

"Huh. Never heard of it!"

"You've never heard of a human?" Aaron was stunned, again.

"Umm, no. Is that weird?"

Yeah, of course, Aaron screamed in his head. He didn't want to offend Steve, his only friend in this place, though. "Sorry . . . I am just really confused and scared and I don't know—"

"Well, I don't know anything about—how did you say it?— hoomans, but my parents are super smart. I am sure they can help us. We are almost there!"

Everything was a dizzying blur for Aaron, from almost dying to finding an underground city, and he just found himself continuing behind the giant boy.

"Yup, this is us!" Steve yelled, gesturing across the street.

Aaron looked around at the looming apartment buildings, almost identical to those seen in big cities. The only difference was the people. "Hey, Steve, what is this place called?"

"Oh this?" He gestured to the city around him as if presenting a show. "This is The Table."

"Why The Table? That doesn't sound like the name of a city."

"It's not," Steve replied. "It's the name of the entire area, and it has to do with the founders or something. All I know is they wanted a place everyone was welcome or something. I'm not really sure, but I think it's a pretty cool place."

Steve opened the door to the dilapidated tan and stone building and ushered Aaron in. As he stepped into the lobby, it was finally sinking in that he wasn't in Texas anymore.

DING! The elevator arrived, and Steve shuffled inside. The giant jabbed the button for the seventh floor, and the doors closed.

5

WHO DECORATED THIS PLACE?

The seventh floor looked like any other high-rise hallway. Maroon carpet, off-white walls, and rows of doors with gold-painted door knockers and numbers.

"We are in 7C, three doors down on the left," Steve said as he led his new pal in that direction. "Let's get you some answers."

Aaron walked toward the door more overwhelmed than ever, but hopeful that whoever was on the other side had some answers and a way home.

BOOM, BOOM, BOOM! Steve pounded on the door after trying the knob. "Hey, sis! The door is locked," he bellowed loud enough that everyone in the complex knew it.

"Quiet, Steve!" they heard from inside the apartment. "Remember to use your inside voice." The voice was feminine, strong, and direct with the distinct aura of older sister to it. The door unlocked to reveal a looming dragon lady with a fire mohawk. She was at least seven feet tall, with a body similar to a human female but with the skin of a dragon. After remembering to blink, Aaron realized her hair wasn't on fire; it was just shades of red, yellow, and orange.

Steve pushed past her. "This is my new friend, Aaron, and he doesn't know how to get home. I found him over in the tunnel intersections between Eighth and Ninth streets. Aaron, this is my sister, Vee." His voice turned to a whisper. "It's short for Venus, but don't call her that. She hates it."

Aaron was not sure what he was expecting, but it was not a dragon lady. Steve noticed Aaron's awkward expression. "Oh yeah, I forgot to tell you I am adopted."

Aaron wanted to ask more questions, but sensed the time wasn't right. He stepped forward, took off his lucky hat, and extended his trembling hand. "Nice to meet you, Venus . . . I mean Vee."

"Vee, I was hoping we could help Aaron get back home," Steve added. "I told him that Mom and Dad are the smartest people I know and that if anyone can help, it's them."

Vee looked Aaron up and down questioningly, eyeing the mud and sticks. "Well, come on in, I guess."

Stepping into the apartment felt like entering a 1970s sitcom. The walls were trimmed in some sort of twisted wood Aaron had never seen before, and the shag carpet bathed the room in yellow. The furniture and decor kept the style, except the electronics. A big-screen color television dominated the living room, and the kitchen appliances were top of the line.

Vee motioned for Aaron to have a seat on a twisted wood chair. Steve plopped down beside him with a thud on what looked to be a normal cream-colored sofa, but much larger. She glared at him.

"We talked about this. Mom and Dad don't want

another broken couch. Remember your size, bud."

"Sorry," Steve replied.

"Whatever," Vee replied, rolling her eyes. She turned to Aaron and sighed. "Now tell me what's going on." Aaron recounted the day's journey and meeting Steve, embellishing in a few spots to sound tough.

"And he says he is a hooman," Steve interjected. "I think that's how you say it."

The second the word left her brother's lips, Vee's face turned ghost white. "You brought a *human* here?!"

Steve nodded happily, stopping abruptly when he noticed her bubbling anger. "Is that bad?"

"Yes, it's bad!" she shouted as color returned to her face.

"Hey, why are humans bad?" chimed in a somewhat-defensive Aaron.

Vee grabbed Aaron with her tail, coiling it around him so tightly he could barely breathe. Aaron gasped for air as Steve screamed at her to stop.

Vee yelled over the noise with a hiss: "Remember that I can do this any time I need to, human. Do you swear that you will not try to harm anyone that lives here?" She stormed down the hallway, her grip tight as ever. "Swear it or else!"

Aaron whispered out an "I swear," and was abruptly dropped in a sparse room with no windows. Losing consciousness, he could vaguely see Steve rushing to check on him. Vee stopped him and slammed the door. Once again, Aaron could only see darkness.

6

ARE HUMANS BAD?

Aaron jerked awake on the bed in the windowless room, slowing recalling how he got there. Food and water had been placed next to the bed, and the door had been opened. He tried to get up, but sharp, shooting pain in his lower back and rib cage sent him back to the mattress. Bandages with a minty ointment had been wrapped around his middle.

With tremendous effort, he sat up on the edge of the bed. Still confused and wobbly, Aaron slowly made his way out of the room and into a hallway leading back to the living room. He wasn't sure what his next step was, but knew he wanted to get home and out of this building.

As he moved closer to the living room, he could hear low hissing voices. "Vee! What were you thinking, attacking someone like that?" a new feminine voice asked.

"But, Mom, he is a *human*! Aren't they evil?" she replied.

"Shhh, keep your voice down," a male voice added. "But, yes, from what we know they are. That doesn't mean you can try to suffocate them and break their ribs!"

Aaron reached down to the bandages. *Just what I needed to add to this chaos . . . broken ribs.*

"Okay, but what do we do with him now?" Vee replied.

"Didn't Steve say he came from above?" the female voice asked.

"Darla, you know we can't keep him here!" the man said.

"Oh, Phil, I know the rules. But did you see him? He looks like a young one, and he seems harmless. I mean, Vee choked him out like it was nothing. He said he was lost, and he was kind to Steve. I think we should hear him out."

From directly behind Aaron, Steve attempted to whisper. "What are we listening to?"

Aaron yelped and jumped into the living room to the shock of the three dragon people there. *I remember Vee, but the other two look older. Are these the parents?*

"Please don't kill me!" he shouted.

"Oh no, honey! We aren't going to kill you," Darla assured him. "Right, Vee?"

"Yeah, I guess," Vee shrugged.

The conversation did little to relieve Aaron's fear. Vee had crushed him until he passed out, so what could the adults do to him? Aaron began bawling, and collapsed in a heap. "I just want to go home. That's all. I don't know how I got here. I don't even know where *here* is."

Darla moved over him, with her kind, blue eyes showing warmth and concern. He got lost in them, and for a few moments everything was okay.

"You okay, buddy?" Steve boomed, snapping Aaron out of his trance. Aaron turned to look at his friend, then curled away from the dragon lady.

"Hi, I'm Darla. I am their mother, and I am truly sorry for her behavior. That was a terrible way to greet a guest."

Aaron surveyed the room, noting Vee, Steve, Darla, and another dragon person looking back at him. That one looked just like the other two, but a little taller and definitely older. His shaggy brown hair and his goatee had some streaks of gray.

"We will not harm you again," Darla continued. "I mean, let's begin again. That is my husband Phil, and you have met Venus and Steve. Just to confirm: Are you human, Aaron?"

Aaron was taken aback by the question. "Umm, yeah. What else could I be?"

Darla sighed, straightening the long brown braids that laid on either side of her face. Phil let out a small groan.

"Can someone just tell me what is so bad about being a human? And how there is a city under the river with all these creatures, but it looks kind of like where I am from?"

As Aaron continued babbling, Darla hugged him. "It will be okay. We will explain everything. Just know you are safe."

He slowly calmed down, enjoying the most warm and safe embrace he had ever felt. It was like being wrapped in a warm blanket. As he opened his eyes and raised his head, he noticed there was no blanket. *They have wings!*

Aaron jumped out of her grasp and pointed at the wings. "Oh, yes those . . . sorry, sweetheart," Darla said. "I know it's a lot to take in. Just try to take it one step at a time, okay?"

Phil walked over to Darla and put his hand on her shoulder as her wings dropped back down and closed behind her. "As she said, we want to help you understand some things. So you mentioned how crazy it is that there is an underground city no one above-ground knows about. You are not wrong, but we down here know of y'all up there."

Steve and Aaron stared wide-eyed at Phil. "This makes no sense," the visitor said.

"Yeah, what?" Steve added. "I've never heard of no hoomans."

"Remember when Darla asked you to confirm if you were a human? You seemed a bit confused because you clearly look human," Phil continued. "You see, a lot of the races here at The Table look human. That is to say, they have the same form. We use some of them to gather information on the human race, technological advancements, fashion trends, and such.

"Some of them live up there full-time and talk with us through the internet. One of the most identical-looking races is the shimmers. They look completely human, but they have a shimmer to them in a certain light. They can also breathe underwater. That is why no one questioned you on the walk over.

"Our world here is very similar to yours because we based it off yours hundreds of years ago. When you look at your history, they talk of dragons and these large mythical creatures in stories as fantasy or imagination. Aaron, every story ever told starts in a place of truth."

Darla jumped in. "That is where the people of The Table come from. They are not one specific race—everyone is welcome at The Table. Yes, we have laws and a justice system very similar to the ones you know, but the difference here is we accept each other for who we are and what we look like. Unfortunately, your world does not and did not in the past. Long ago, back in the time when knights and kings ruled, we all lived in the overworld together despite tension between the humans and other races.

"A giant war took place, and the humans pushed all other races into the shadows," she said. "Our ancestors got frustrated with fighting just to survive. The four originals, as they are called, started The Table. They devised a plan where people of all races could be free to walk the streets and become whatever they wanted in life. That was not an option in the overworld. They broke ground in this cavern, almost what . . . seven hundred and fifty years ago, Phil?"

"Yep," he replied. "That reminds me—The Originals Festival starts tomorrow!"

"Oh heck yes!" Steve shrieked. "Aaron, the festival is so much fun!"

Aaron had been still and silent through the explanation, bewildered with all that had unfolded.

"You okay, son?" Phil asked, placing a hand on his shoulder.

Aaron glanced back at him, clear-eyed for the first time that day. "Yeah, I think so. So basically, humans were jerks to your ancestors and forced them all to move here and create this?"

Phil and Darla nodded.

"Okay, then why did Vee attack me thinking I would hurt her?"

"Again, very sorry about that," Phil said apologetically. "The humans would throw rocks and sometimes try to burn us at the stake, claiming we were evil. It was a terrible time for our ancestors, and they didn't want the children of the city to have any desire to look for the overworld. It was instilled in them and future generations that humans were dangerous."

That made sense to Aaron. "You said y'all send people up to the overworld all the time, so where is the bus stop or whatever? I need to get home."

The parents exchanged glances. "Well, yes, I did say that," Phil replied. "However, not all the people here are as understanding as our family. I am worried that if word gets out that you are human, it will not go well for us or for you."

Aaron's stomach flipped. "Then what do we do? I have to get home! I am sure my mom will be looking for me."

"That is the other thing about The Table," Phil said calmly. "Time works differently down here. For what feels like twenty-four hours here, only two hours pass in the overworld. You've only been gone about a couple hours."

Relieved but overwhelmed, Aaron's eyes welled up again. Darla swooped over and hugged him.

"I will do everything I can to help once I get to the office tomorrow," Phil promised. "I will see if we can figure something out."

"Oh, do you work in the government or something?"

Phil chuckled awkwardly. "No, I am a sanitation specialist."

"How is that going to help?" Aaron's tone sounded ruder than he intended.

"The sanitation workers know every inch of this city and its exits and entrances. That includes all the ones some others don't know about. I would argue that it's a better option than some fancy government person!"

"Okay, okay, let's all just calm down," Darla interrupted. "Aaron, it looks like you are here for the night, so we need to get you some dinner. Vee, show Aaron back to his room and where the shower is. No offense, but you don't smell great."

Aaron's cheeks turned red. "A shower would probably feel good, and it will be nice to get the rest of this mud off." Vee headed down the hall, with Aaron and Steve following.

Darla looked at Phil, concerned. "What are we gonna do? If anyone finds a human here, we are in so much trouble."

"I know, but the kid needs our help. Remember when we found Steve? A lot of people told us we shouldn't adopt a child of a different species because they can be 'a lot to handle,' " Phil reminded her. "Look at how amazing Steve is and how much happier we all are because he is here with us."

"That's true, and Aaron seems like a genuinely nice kid. It's hard not to worry about the human side of him, though. We don't know what he was taught or what his people are like. Still, my heart tells me we should give him a chance."

"Okay, I will talk to Bob tomorrow when I get to dispatch and see what he thinks. I think we can get the kid back home, but it's not going to be easy."

"When we're filling Aaron in on how things work, let's not tell him about the Blackwings just yet," Darla added. "I don't want to traumatize him any further. He is already a mess."

"Agreed."

7

DINNER IS SERVED

All cleaned up and dressed in some of Steve's old clothes, Aaron stared at the guest room wall wondering when he would get home and whether anyone noticed he was missing. *The Dimeters seem like good people, so I bet they can help. Vee seems calmer now, and Steve is really cool. I wish things were this nice at home. Is anyone even looking for me yet? I doubt it.*

His thoughts were interrupted by Steve barreling through the doorway. "Holy cow! You do look different! Come with me . . . food's on!" Steve grabbed Aaron by the arm and pulled him toward the dining room.

The food smelled amazing to Aaron, but he wasn't sure quite what it was. *What do dragon people eat? And what does Steve eat? He isn't a dragon, either.*

He paused in the hallway. "Hey, didn't you say you were adopted?"

"Yep, why?"

"Man, I'm sorry if I am being rude, but I was wondering where your birth parents went. How did you find the Dimeters? Or like, what happened?"

Steve's face tightened a bit, but he relaxed again quickly. "Umm, I don't know what happened to them.

All I know is Phil and Darla found me when I was four months old in a basket at the Mid-City Park. They said that they were out for a walk, and they heard me crying in a bush. There was a note with me that said, 'We're sorry, Steve.' "

Aaron felt awful for asking about what was clearly not a great memory, but Steve didn't seem that bothered.

"That's how we know my name is Steve!" He smiled big at that bit. "But that's really all we know. Well, the name and that I am giant!"

Aaron tried to focus on the positive. "Oh cool! How did y'all find that out?"

Steve cocked his head as he looked at his friend. "Umm, look at me. I'm eight feet tall at ten years old, my skin is impervious to everything except fire, and I am the strongest person in town!"

Aaron smiled at the pride on Steve's face. "That's awesome! So, are there other giants you have met? How big do adults get? Are there cool giant things you get to do when you're older?"

He was firing questions off so quickly that he didn't notice Steve's expression fall. "Wait, what did I say?"

"No, there are no other giants at The Table. We know I am of the giant race because the history books tell us giants were a huge part of the founding. They died out over time, and I am the only one left. We have books with descriptions and people who knew giants, but they are all old and don't have answers to my questions."

"You are not alone buddy, not anymore," Aaron assured him. "I am here, and we will figure some of this out together, somehow."

Steve looked over at Aaron with a few enormous tears in his eyes. "Thank you, dude."

They entered the dining room to see a giant table covered with food. *Pizza, wings, and tacos: My favorites!* Aaron practically leapt to the table, loading his plate with everything in sight. He hadn't eaten since the cheese sandwich at the river. After a few seconds of stuffing his face, he looked up to find the others staring at him in awe.

"I am so sorry," he said. "I didn't realize how hungry I was. I also didn't know what kind of food y'all eat, and I was happy to see it was this!"

Everyone at the table chuckled. "Yeah, duh," Vee said. "Kid, tacos are one of a dragon's fave meals!"

"I had no idea. That's cool," he said through a mouthful of food. "What do y'all drink? Is it like normal water, or like something else? Can you fly? Can you eat and fly? How strong are you? Can you breathe fire . . ."

Aaron paused, realizing he hadn't given them a chance to answer even the first question.

"Woah, woah, woah," Phil laughed. "We will answer all of your questions, but please try to get some of the food in your mouth first."

"And yes, we can breathe fire, and it's really cool," Vee added.

Aaron's eyes sparkled with excitement. *This place is so cool, and there much there is to learn. I need to take the chance to enjoy this time, a full day without yelling!* He peppered the Dimeters with questions on all the things dragons can or can't do until his voice began to get tired.

"Okay . . . I think it's bedtime," Darla interjected. "Let's get the dishes picked up, then brush teeth, then head to our rooms."

As he helped clear the table, Aaron remembered that he didn't have a toothbrush or anything else besides his hat. But when he entered the guest room, he saw a bag full of more clothes close to his size, a toothbrush on the nightstand, and a note. *Consider these things yours now. We are happy you are here. Darla.*

The note melted Aaron's heart. He laid on the bed and clutched the note to his chest. He had never felt this welcome anywhere. Even in his own home, he always felt like he was in the way. Right now, he felt wanted, and that feeling was the best. Aaron easily slipped off into a deep sleep.

8

THE FESTIVAL

"Wake up, Aaron! It's festival day!" Steve's voice reverberated in Aaron's ears. Terrified, he shot up in the bed before remembering where he was.

"Man, what an alarm clock," Aaron said as he opened his eyes to see Steve bouncing up and down in front of him with excitement.

"I am so pumped," Steve said, adjusting his bright orange "Tubular" T-shirt.

"Okay, okay, just let me get dressed."

Steve grimaced, leaving quickly and shutting the door. Aaron pulled a plain navy T-shirt and some khaki shorts from the bag of clothes, finishing the look with his green John Deere hat.

"This is real," he reminded himself. "Phil will be at work figuring out a solution today, so go enjoy this life while you still can."

An amazing smell from the kitchen caught his attention as he left the room. Coming around the corner, he spotted massive piles of bacon, waffles, and even biscuits and gravy. Aaron darted to the table, but managed to stop himself from attacking the food immediately. Everyone was already at the table, waiting for him.

"Good morning, pal!" Just the way Phil said hello directly to him warmed Aaron's heart. It felt good to be wanted.

Vee and Steve listed off the booths they wanted to visit at the festival and what foods they wanted to try. As they talked, Aaron grew depressed. He had no money and no idea what type of money they used here.

It was the same as being back home. Everyone else was doing something cool, but he was too broke. He also despised being the kid people pitied or felt obligated to give a handout. So, just like in the overworld, Aaron smiled and pretended everything was fine as the meal continued.

"Good news everyone," Phil announced after the table was cleared. "I chatted with Bob from work earlier this morning, and he is going to cover things for a bit so I can join y'all at the festival! I will only be able to stay for a little bit, but I wanted to get to see it with the people I love."

He patted Aaron on the shoulder as he finished talking. *So this is what it's like to have an actual dad. He is taking time off work for fun. This place really is wild.*

Aaron smiled up at Phil. "Awesome! I am excited to see it all!"

The dragon turned to his children. "Please stay out of trouble at the festival, y'all. I am okay with you going as long as you tell no one about him being a human. If you are asked for any reason, you say he's a shimmer."

The three children nodded. "Oh, and wear this shirt, Aaron. It will make you fit in more and give people less of a reason to question you." Phil handed him a light blue T-shirt that said "GO BULLDOGS!" in big white letters with "Southside Middle School" below it.

Darla turned to leave the dining room. "Okay, kids. The car is leaving for the festival in ten minutes. Be ready!"

The three remaining Dimeters scrambled through the house. Steve made sure he had his good fanny pack, which featured an all-leather belt and a red pouch that looked like it could withstand anything. Vee messaged her friends to check who would be there, and Darla gathered water and snacks. Aaron sat on the couch, watching in awe. *Yeah, they are dragons and giants, but they are just normal people getting ready for an event like humans do. They only look different.*

"All right, load up y'all," Darla shouted as she pointed toward the front door. In the elevator once they had all squeezed in, she pressed the B button for the basement.

9

TIME FOR A DRIVE

As the elevator descended, Aaron was so excited to see what dragons and these other creatures drove. He bolted out of the elevator into the . . . totally normal parking garage. There were no massive cool cars, and not even any different brands! They were mostly Fords and Chevys.

"So the cars are the same?"

"Yeah, the dealers don't care who is buying them," Phil said. "They just care that they get bought. We get the newer models, but about a year or two behind. There is an area in The Table where all the car-buying takes place. It's a massive operation that I don't even fully understand."

He stopped behind a 1989 blue Chevrolet Suburban with gray side panels. "Here we are!"

"I call first radio station!" Vee hollered.

"Aww, man," Steve whined.

They all piled into the Suburban: Steve in the far back, Vee and Aaron in the middle seats, and Darla and Phil up front.

They pulled out of the garage, and for the first time Aaron could admire the city in all its glory. He was glued to the passenger-side window, unable to look away. "These buildings are huge. This place is massive! This cave has to be the biggest ever."

"Hey, I want to show you something," Darla said. She whispered something to Phil, who began pulling onto an exit ramp. The road started rising higher and higher, like the side of a steep mountain. As they reach the summit, she pointed out the front window. The view took Aaron's breath away.

"This . . . is . . . awesome!" Beyond the city, he could see farms and rivers. This cave might be one hundred miles wide.

Darla smiled. "Yeah, it is awesome. Now let's get to that festival."

The fairgrounds were no less awe-inspiring. The Originals Festival felt like a renaissance festival mashed up with Disneyland. The colors, the costumes, the buildings, the food, the people—all of it was just spectacular. You could feel the happiness in the air. Phil parked the Suburban, and Aaron scrambled out, itching to get inside.

"Which way?"

Darla pointed toward a huge wooden gate held up by two giant towers. It looked like the front of a castle, only there was no castle.

"So, what is this festival for again?" Aaron asked as they walked to the entrance.

"This is to celebrate the creation of The Table," she replied. "Seven hundred and fifty years ago this week, the four originals broke ground on this safe haven."

"Oh, yeah, y'all mentioned something about those originals last night. Who are they?"

Darla smiled excitedly as they approach the ticket counter. "Let's show him the mural!"

Aaron was so lost in conversation and excitement that he had completely forgotten about needing a ticket. He took a step back and hung his head. *I am going to have to tell them I can't pay, then everyone will look at me with* that *expression.*

An elfish fellow's words derailed his train of thought. "Hello, ma'am. How many tickets would you like?"

"Five, please," Darla replied without hesitation, then she paid and walked forward. Aaron waited for his turn to speak to the ticket person.

While he was trying to think up a good reason he didn't have the money, Darla tapped him on the shoulder.

"Hey, what are you doing? Your ticket is right here. Who did you think the fifth ticket was for?"

Aaron hadn't heard how many tickets she bought; he just assumed he was on his own. He looked at Darla in disbelief and softly whispered his thanks. He wasn't sure how to feel about this situation.

The Dimeters were being so kind and risking a lot just to help a human, something that most people in their world despised. He was not sure how, but he would figure out a way to repay their kindness. He took the ticket and walked through the gates of the festival excited to see what new discoveries were on the inside.

As he entered the gates, the sights and sounds overwhelmed him. Aaron's eyes darted all over, trying to take everything in. He could hear music playing from the stage across the way, and the sounds of laughter and joy bloomed all around them. To his right was a line of carnival games with all kinds of prizes. The festival seemed to go on forever! *This place is awesome!*

Phil tapped Aaron on the shoulder. "Pretty cool, right? Do you want to try some of the games? I don't have a ton of time to hang out, but my favorite game is that one right over there." A giant smile spread across the boy's face. *He* wants *to hang out with me? Is this what it's supposed to be like? This is so nice!*

"Sure! What is the game?"

"It's so much fun," Steve bellowed and ran toward the booth.

Following Steve with his eyes, Aaron spotted a wooden booth with a red banner reading *FISHING WITH FRIENDS.*

"Hey, I know how to fish!" Aaron exclaimed.

"Well, that's a good start," Phil said with a grin, "but this game is not just fishing. It's fishing with friends."

"What does that mean?"

"We can show you. Let's go!"

Steve had already paid the booth attendant and picked out a fishing pole while he impatiently waited for them. As they walked up, Aaron spied someone at the top of a ladder against a large wooden wall holding a fis0hing pole.

The player was hanging it down the opposite side of the wall, where he couldn't see what he was fishing for. Aaron peeked around the other side, where he could hear someone yelling up to the person fishing.

"Left! Left! No, your other left! Okay, yes! Yes, yes, right there!" the partner shouted.

Closer to the wall, Aaron could see a giant rotating stage with several open wooden barrels. Each barrel was labeled with a different prize.

"Oh! Okay, so the friends part is they instruct you on where to drop the line and—"

"And whatever barrel you land in, you get that prize," Steve interjected as he waved the fishing pole. "Oh, it's our turn, Dad!"

"Let's do it!" Phil replied gleefully as he moved to the other side of the wall to give directions. Steve climbed to the top of the ladder.

It's so cool to see how Phil acts with Steve. He is so kind. I wish I was that lucky.

"Ahh, yes!" Steve's cries cut off the thought. "Yes! I got a ticket for the shop!"

Aaron looked up to see his friend holding up his catch. "Buddy, that means I can get one item from the festival store!"

Aaron smiled at Steve's excitement. *It's awesome to be around this much happiness. I love it here.*

"You're up, Aaron!" Darla said as she handed him the rod before he had time to object.

"You've got this, sweetheart," she whispered in his ear.

Aaron climbed up the ladder with the rod. From the top, he could see more of the festival . . . and how many people were watching him. He froze as reality set in. *I am in a new world, playing a new game, on a stage in front of tons of people. If I say or do the wrong thing, who knows how they would act. I have a few friends here, but not enough to fend off a mob.*

"Hey! You can do this," Phil shouted. "Now get that

line over the wall and let's win us a prize."

The sound of his voice and the confidence he had in Aaron was something completely new. His doubts subsided. *He is right! I can do this!*

"Look out below!" Aaron hollered as he tossed the line over.

"Okay, okay, left a little. A little more . . . okay, drop the line down!"

Aaron smashed the button to release the line and waited for what felt like forever. A few seconds later, he felt a tug on the pole and heard Phil again. "You did it on your first try!"

"I really caught something?!" Aaron reeled up his reward as fast as his arms would go. "One ticket to the shop, any item from shelf three and below," he read from the wooden block on his hook.

"Let's go shop," Steve pleaded as he pointed to a small stand to the left of the game piled high with items and knickknacks from the festival. "Mine is shelf three and below, too."

Aaron descended the ladder, still in shock from both winning a prize and feeling worthy. After the last rung, Phil walked up and hugged Aaron before he could say anything.

"Just . . . thank you," the boy said as he squeezed Phil as tightly as he could. "Thank you."

Darla looked at Phil and smiled. *This is why I married that man,* she thought. The two exchanged knowing glances—yeah, he's one of us now—and any worries about him being human or out of place faded from their minds. For a minute, they were just a family.

"All right then, let's go get that prize," Phil said as

he finally broke the hug.

Aaron snapped out of the daze he was in, clearing his throat and looking over to the stand and Steve. It featured five shelves. Shelf one was knickknacks, small plastic toys, and single pieces of candy. Shelf two was mostly coffee cups and pencils. Shelf three had stuffed animals and a few hats. Shelf four had larger stuffed animals and some T-shirts, and shelf five had those giant stuffed animals you typically see at human fairs.

"Dude, Aaron! Let's get matching hats," Steve said, pointing wildly at two hats side by side on shelf three. The simple blue and white trucker hats were designed with an Elfwater logo. Aaron wasn't sure what that was, and they weren't the coolest hats, but Steve wanting to match made his day.

"Totally!" Aaron said, and the boys handed the attendant their wooden tickets.

They happily grabbed the hats from the attendant and traded out the ones they were wearing for the new look. Darla smiled as she saw two boys, so different yet both somehow the same, smiling and posing. "Here, give me the other hats," she said. "I will put them in my bag."

Phil stepped in closer. "Hey, everyone . . . unfortunately, I have to get going to work now. Aaron and Steve, have a blast, but please be safe today. Okay?"

"You got it, sir!" Aaron smiled at Phil and gave him a quick hug. "Thank you so much again!"

After their goodbyes, Darla turned to the remaining three. "Okay, now who wants to see the mural?"

10

THE MURAL

"This way," Darla pointed. "I think it will help you understand this festival and this world a bit more."

"Ugh, I have seen The Mural," Vee grumbled. "Can I go hang with my friends?"

"Sure, go enjoy. Just be safe!"

"'Kay!"

"Funnel cakes!" Aaron spun around in the direction of the shouting to see Steve bounding toward the Fun Funnels booth.

"Would you like a funnel cake?" Darla asked her guest.

"Umm . . . no, thank you," he replied.

Darla was confused. "What? Do you know what a funnel cake is? They are delicious!"

"Yes, I know what they are," he said. "I am just not hungry right now. That's all."

She sensed something else was at play, but didn't want to press him too much. "Well, let me know if you do want something, okay?"

"Sure thing."

Darla bought funnel cakes for her and Steve before

they continued their walk to The Mural.

"So what's this mural thing look like?"

"Oh, you will know it when you see it," Darla said.

"Okaaay." Aaron was skeptical.

THE MURAL, read an oversized sign at the center of the fairgrounds. "So I am guessing it's that way?"

Darla smiled and nodded. A brilliant white marble temple adorned with golden accents came into view and stopped the human in his tracks.

"I see what you mean, Darla," Aaron said.

She chuckled and headed toward the front doors. The first room was covered in marble and featured just a spiral staircase. Darla, Aaron, and Steve trekked down at least five or six floors, from what Aaron could gather, to find a wall with a solitary iron door.

"Welcome to The Mural," Darla said cheerfully as she ushered the boys inside.

"Umm, okay," Aaron said, confused by the seemingly dark and dingy room.

"Sorry! Forgot the lights."

Aaron heard the click of a light switch, then *BAM*. Brain overload. "What is this? How did they? Look at all the . . . this is just crazy!"

The shine coming from the artwork was practically enough to require sunglasses, but taking in the rich, vibrant colors and the design itself left him reeling. The Table's sacred piece covered all four walls and appeared to form a timeline. A massive battle on the left side of the room transitioned to other scenes across the back and finished on the right wall with four individuals around a stone slab. Each had placed a hand at the center. *THE TABLE* was emblazoned in gold letters above the scenes.

After looking around slack-jawed for a few moments, Aaron turned to Darla.

"The history of The Table is one of my favorite topics," she said. "These images were painted here because this is where our society began. This cavern is the original site where the four came together."

Aaron was about to burst with all the questions he had, but he tried to hold them in so he didn't interrupt Darla's happiness in sharing with him.

"Long ago, there was a great battle with the humans and our kind, as you can see here," she said, pointing to the first portion. Mountains loomed over a large, open field of two distinct factions. On one side was a line of giants, elves, dragons, dwarves, wizards, witches, and other mythological beings. On the other was the human army: Knights on horseback, archers filling the sky with arrows, and men with shields and spears up front.

Aaron was about to explode. "I am so sorry, Darla, but is there a name for your kind, like how I am a human? Also, who are the four? I have so many questions!"

"No need to apologize. It's exciting to have someone to discuss this with . . . the kids have heard it all before. If you will let me give you a full tour, I promise it will answer most of the questions you have."

Aaron took a deep breath. "Okay, can do!"

"Yeah, and we are called Vendegeks," Steve piped up.

"The Vende-what?" asked Aaron.

"Ven-de-gek," replied Darla, drawing out the

sounds. "It is a Hungarian term for guests. One of the original four had ancestors from Hungary, and the word seemed fitting for a place where everyone is welcome. Most people just call us Vens, for short."

Aaron seemed to understand, so Darla continued. "As you can see here, the humans and Vendegeks fought a great battle, but the humans far outnumbered the Vens. The next scene here shows a group of Vens being chased from a village by angry humans. As you move toward the middle, that same group is finding and following a tunnel entrance to a cave below the surface. On the far right, you can see this very cave with the original four huddling in a circle and forming a plan."

Darla paused, knowing Aaron was ready to jump in.

"Who are the four? What makes them so special? Why does that fourth one look weird?"

"Let's skip over to the final piece here," she said, turning to face the wall behind them. That segment had four distinct painted columns, including one that looked especially ominous.

11

MEET THE VENS

"And these are the original four," Darla said loudly, almost as if she was looking for someone to cheer.

"Wow, these are big . . . and intense," Aaron said.

The first, labeled Penelope the Peaceful, depicted a beautiful blonde woman floating underwater, with her long, emerald dress cascading around her. She looked human, except for her shiny, pearly white skin.

"Penelope was a shimmer, the first we know of actually," Darla said as she looked lovingly at her favorite original. "She always pushed for peace and tranquility. It was her idea to call this place The Table. And remember when I said one of the four was Hungarian? That was Penelope, too!"

To her right was a section dubbed Darrell the Destroyer. An enormous black dragon, with its wings spread wide, glided through the sky as he billowed streams of fire and clouds of smoke. His head faced the viewer, making it feel like he was looking into your soul.

"This one is the coolest," Steve exclaimed. "He's my favorite."

"Ah, yes. Good ol' Darrell," Darla said. "Well, his name explains a lot about him. He was honestly a bit of an oaf and often resorted to violence. Penelope was not a big fan of him."

"Yeah, but he was an awesome black dragon who bravely fought in the great war for the Vens," Steve interrupted. "One time, he used his massive wings as a shield for others. They had to dig hundreds of arrows out of his hide after it was all over. No one knows how he could withstand that much pain, but he did, and he saved a ton of people. Just because his descendants are the Blackwings, you always—"

Darla cut him off. "Yeah, I always do because they are awful, and I can't stand them!"

"Who are the Blackwings?" Aaron asked.

Darla cleared her throat and found her even tone again. "We don't need to talk about that mess right now. Let's just have fun and enjoy the rest of the mural."

She looked at Steve and then back to Aaron before continuing. "Yes, Darrell was a great warrior for our kind and we all thank him for that. Now, let's move on to Brenda the Bold!"

Steve's smile faded a bit. "Fine," he mumbled.

The boisterous-looking woman with large square shoulders and a short stature sported shiny black armor. Her brilliant red hair flowed down her back next to a giant pickaxe slung over her shoulder. Her mischievous smile seemed to say, "We are about to do something super dangerous, but it will be fun!"

"Brenda was extremely rough around the edges, angry most of the time, and always up for a fight,"

Darla explained. "She once defeated a grizzly bear in hand-to-hand combat simply because someone said she couldn't. She was also a brilliant engineer and helped create the structures that support The Table's entire cavern system."

Aaron nodded, but his attention had already turned to the next piece. The final column was titled Unknown. A generic shadow was outlined on a black background.

"Okay, okay, let's talk about that one," Darla said.

"Yes!" Aaron yelped before realizing it. Darla smirked.

"So, the Unknown column is there because . . . it's unknown. We don't know who the fourth was, and it seems like they did not want us to know either, as they are the ones who made this mural."

"Is that, like, a bad thing?" Aaron wondered. "Or—"

"But why would they not just tell us," a flustered Darla exclaimed. "Why keep this a secret and give us no clues?"

Steve pulled Aaron aside. "I forgot to mention that Mom is a bit obsessed with figuring out the identity of the Unknown," he whispered. "Like, *obsessed*. It's not good."

Aaron walked over to Darla, who was still staring at the Unknown. "Well, the other three are pretty cool. This place is amazing!"

He jerked his head to the side while looking at Steve, signaling he was ready to leave. The giant nodded back, and they headed toward the exit.

"So, Darla, can you tell me a little more about Penelope?" Aaron asked. "She seems pretty awesome."

Darla knew what he was doing, but her love of the shimmer's story took over. She showered them in fun facts about her as they trudged back up the stairs.

12

AN EXCITING LUNCH

Back in the bustling festival, people in the distance crowded the food trucks for lunch. "Okay, who's hungry?" the mother asked.

"Me, me," Steve bellowed. Aaron was starving, but didn't want to impose.

The moment Aaron set his eyes on the food, his nose was filled with the mouth-watering scents of all sorts of dishes. He didn't know what he was smelling, but it must be delicious.

Aaron kept a steady pace behind Darla and Steve, still embarrassed about not having money. He hoped to create enough distance that they didn't notice he was going without. *This is silly. I fell down a hole, almost drowned, and landed in a whole new world. I don't even know what money they use here. But still, I don't want to be pitied any more than they probably already do. I'm fine.*

Darla paused to wait for him. "Just like the rest of The Table, all dishes and cultures are welcome."

The trucks' offerings varied from Indian food to dragon cuisine—surprisingly good, according to Darla, a dragon—and everything in between. All the cultures existing together in harmony was quite a sight to behold. And what an aroma!

Darla walked toward Dragons Dim Sum as Steve took off running for barbecue. "Yes! Fred's is open!"

Aaron stayed back, just looking around at everyone's dishes. Suddenly, he felt a hand grab his. "Stop worrying about it," Darla whispered. "This is yours. You owe us nothing . . . just enjoy, okay?"

In his hand was a wad of cash, five bills with a picture of the originals in the center. The words *EVERYONE IS WELCOME AT THE TABLE* were inscribed below the image.

"This is one hundred geks," she went on. "It's what we use for money. Just go get whatever you want to eat."

Aaron stared at Darla as a few tears escaped down his cheeks. No one had ever helped him like this. *She just wants me to be happy, and she doesn't want anything from me like my family. They only want me around when they need something. She* actually *cares about how I feel? So that's what that feels like . . .*

He squeezed her scaly form as tightly as he could as she patted him on the back. "There, there. Just please eat something. We will meet up over there by Steve," she said, pointing to where Steve was waving wildly at them.

Now that Aaron was fully taking in the options, he could make out at least 30 trucks. "The Table's largest corn dog" sounded like a delicious challenge. After about five minutes in line, a slender man with long silver hair greeted him.

"What will ya have, son?"

"Umm, I would like the largest corn dog listed on

the sign, please."

"Great choice," encouraged the man with pointed ears poking out around his ballcap.

"Would you like anything to drink with that? We have Coca-Cola and Elfwater products."

Still unsure of what Elfwater products were, Aaron settled on Dr Pepper. "You got it," the proprietor said. "That will be ten geks."

After handing Aaron his change, the man gestured for him to wait at the second window. *Wow, this place really is almost identical to home.* Everywhere he looked, people of all different races were together laughing and enjoying their meals. They seemed like one big family.

CRACK! BOOM! Lightning crashed into a tree in the middle of the food truck park. The branches exploded into fiery debris. Black dragons landed around tables, surrounding the diners. Smoke billowed throughout as people screamed and ran. Aaron was frozen in fear.

"Heed this warning, all," a deep, malicious voice called from the smoke. "Remove the Unknown, open the vault, and crown me king of this land! Or else!"

CRACK! Another lightning bolt hit the ground as fire spewed from above. The overwhelming smoke left Aaron gasping for air as he tried to crawl away.

WOOSH! Darla came flying in. With one big spin of her mighty wings, the smoke around Aaron swirled up and away into the sky. She grabbed him in her arms and flew him to safety.

His eyesight was hazy, but he could see Steve in his new blue and white trucker hat following his mother's path. *Okay, Steve is safe.* With that worry calmed, Aaron's body gave up and he passed out in Darla's arms.

13

THE PROPHECY

"Aaron, can you hear me?" Phil asked, though it sounded muffled to the human. "How are you feeling?"

The world slowly came into focus, and Aaron realized he was back in the guest bed at the Dimeters' home. *When did I fall asleep? How did we get back here?* He tried to sit up, but the pain of broken ribs and some new injury coursed through him. He felt woozy, but also warm inside to see the entire family concerned about him.

"Woah, woah, woah," Darla cautioned. "Take it easy. The poison from the gas makes you queasy. I don't want puke on my floor, if we can help it."

All Aaron heard was "poison from the gas," then came flashes of him waiting for his food and watching happy Vens. And with that came memories of the lightning, fire, and the smoke.

"What was all that back there?" Aaron blurted out, his voice a little hoarse.

"Remember the Blackwings that Steve brought up?" Darla asked. "Well, now you've met them and their leader. Bartholomew, or Bart, is a black dragon and a descendant of Darrell the Destroyer. He believes he should be king of The Table because of an old prophecy, so he and his gang of thugs terrorize everyone about removing the Unknown pillar from the mural."

"But why?" Aaron mumbled.

"There is a prophecy written around the inner walls of the mural that Bart thinks will get him what he wants" Phil said.

"I didn't mention it earlier because it's more of a political issue here in our world, and it didn't seem important at the time," Darla added.

Phil looked Aaron square in the face. "Bart is a nasty dragon who will do anything to get what he wants. He is not one to be messed with. Everyone around The Table knows that he will make you pay, somehow, if you get in his way. He is prone to violence and gets very angry when he doesn't win."

"And he throws tantrums like the narcissistic baby he is," snapped Darla.

"As I was saying," Phil said as he side-eyed his wife. "Bart is not one to be messed with. Stay clear of him—I mean it."

"I heard he burns down people homes if they don't do what he says," Steve interjected.

"That's enough, Steve. We don't need to keep talking about Bart. We are *all* going to stay clear of him. The end," Phil continued. "Now, about the prophecy. It has to do with the unknown identity of the fourth original. It states that sometime in the future, descendants of the originals will reveal themselves and unlock the vault door. Until then, the crown remains sealed inside."

"And that's why I want to solve this mystery so badly!" Darla said.

The poison and all the new information left Aaron's head swimming. He tried to focus, but eventually fell back to the bed and passed out again.

14

TIME FOR SOME ANSWERS

Bacon! Mmm, breakfast sounds good . . . wait, is it morning again already? Aaron's head was pounding as he tried to sit. Getting upright was not too bad this time, so he decided to follow his nose to the kitchen.

Walking was not nearly as difficult as he imagined it might be after his body gave out last night. He had never felt that depleted. As he reached the kitchen, he could see Phil at the stove frying bacon. Darla, Vee, and Steve were already digging in, with an empty chair and a plate near them for Aaron. They looked thrilled to see him.

"Well good morning," Darla said.

"Hey, buddy," shouted Steve.

"Good to see you're not dead," Vee added.

The Dimeters paused and laughed a bit after talking over each other. The noise and accompanying silence were wonderful for Aaron. *I don't know why they are so happy to have me here and show me all this love, but I will take it. I will never get tired of this.*

"Umm, is this seat taken?" he asked while grabbing onto the empty chair. A chorus of nopes answered him.

Aaron smiled and began to dig in. "Okay, now who is going to tell me more about this crown and vault and prophecy stuff?"

Phil took a deep breath. "I was wondering how much you might remember."

"That's about where it trails off for me, right around where you said there was a crown sealed in a vault."

"Ah yes, okay. When the vault is opened by the descendants, according to the prophecy, one of the four will be chosen to wear the crown and rule all of The Table," Phil said. "You see, when The Table was first established, kings ruled. It was the only system the founders had known. However, the originals could not settle on which of them should be the king. They met to decide who would be king or queen, and a great fight broke out. It is said that, during this fight, the unknown original was accidentally slain. The remaining three were so distraught that they locked the crown up where it is today, in the middle of the city."

"The vault has four locks, one for each descendent," Darla added. "Most people here are happy with how things have been, though, and think the idea is outdated."

"And how are things run now?" Aaron asked.

"We have a group of eleven leaders, with each one in charge of their region," Phil said.

"This place has eleven sections?" Aaron shouted. "How?"

Phil chuckled. "Yes, there is still a lot you haven't seen."

"So let me get this straight: There are four

descendants around here somewhere," Aaron said, "and one of the descendants—"

"Bart!" piped up Steve. "His name is Bart!"

"Yes, Bart. Bart is upset because the originals gave y'all no idea who or what the fourth original was. And he thinks that you should just crown him king or he'll take the throne by force?"

Phil and Darla exchanged glances and shrugged their shoulders. "Yeah, I mean . . . pretty much" the father said.

"So then why aren't these eleven leaders doing something about him? He is shooting lightning and poisonous gas into parks, almost killing people!"

"Aaron, as much as our world is similar to yours, you've got to remember that it is filled with people and creatures much more resilient than humans," Phil answered. "I mean, I can breathe fire, lift fifty times my own weight, and withstand just about any injury to my skin. So, to most of our kind, this was less of an attack and more of a minor inconvenience. There are so few that actually do get injured that it is unfortunately seen as a side effect of kingdom politics. Bart will get a slap on the wrist due to his lineage and the fact that most people are scared of the Blackwings."

Darla nodded. "They do things like this all the time in the shadows. They are not good people, at all. We have the eleven leaders who vote on decisions with majority rule, but there are heavy influences."

"How did they decide on eleven? Seems like a weird number," Aaron said.

"When the four originals became three, that odd number is what helped them make decisions,"

Darla answered. "There was never the possibility of a stalemate because they were forbidden from voting for their own proposals. From there, as The Table grew in size, they added more leaders, always keeping to an odd number."

"Down here, brute force is still the most effective way of making change," Phil said. "We know the human world has moved past this."

Aaron leaned back in his chair and chomped on a piece of bacon. "Well, not everyone. I'm sure some of that still goes on, too."

The others nodded and turned back to their plates. No one had been eating during the discussion, so the only sound for a while was chewing.

"So, Phil, now that you've been back to work since I got here," Aaron said, "when am I going home?"

Phil's eyes darkened, and he kept them glued to his plate. "Oh yeah, that . . . umm yes, well. I spoke to some friends, and they think they know a way to get you back up top."

Excitement overtook Aaron, but it felt clouded. *Is that sadness? I miss my mom and my room, but . . . I've never had a best friend before. No one treats me like this at home, either.*

"But it's extremely dangerous, and it might get all of us in trouble, or worse. Someone could get really hurt," Phil said. "Many of the people we talked about earlier who are so against humans happen to be the very same Blackwings you met yesterday."

"Is this about the crown? Or do they believe the stories about how dangerous we are?" Aaron was a bit exasperated.

Phil scrunched his face. "It's complicated. Bart believes that the Unknown may have been a human."

The words felt like an anvil. Aarons hadn't even thought of that possibility, though he hadn't spent a lot of time thinking about it. "Yeah, wow. I can see how that makes a lot of sense. A human could have definitely been helpful in the beginning, but then it's also awkward since y'all are hiding from them."

"So that's why you won't be able to leave until at least tomorrow evening," Phil said.

"Tomorrow evening? That's so long," Aaron whined.

"I was trying to say that the timing must be right for us to get a clear pipe up to the overworld."

"Umm, pipe?"

"Yes, that's how some of us can travel to the overworld," Phil said. "Remember the shallow pool and rope? Well, that is one of the spots where the water tubes meet an entrance to The Table. The ropes at each entrance are attached to a light source and a door leading into the streets or tunnels."

"Yes, like when I first got here," Aaron remembered. "Just take me back there, and I will swim out!"

"That is one of the issues. You shouldn't have been able to get here. Shimmers are the ones we use most for human research and interaction. Do you remember the other main fact about them?"

"Oh! They breathe underwater?" Aaron said excitedly.

"Exactly, and that means that it doesn't matter how long the water pipe is. The weird part is the pipe you came through is one of the longest we have. You should have drowned."

Aaron fell back into his chair. *I should have drowned.* "Then how do I get home if I can't go back up the pipe?"

Phil grimaced. "And now the other issue: Someone told Bart there is a human in The Table. It seems whoever it was saw Darla carrying you away from the incident. Thankfully, they must not have recognized her in all the chaos. But the Blackwings are on the hunt, with dragons stationed at each pipe for the next twenty-four hours."

"My mom will be so worried. It's going to be almost four days before I can leave. I know time is different here, but . . ." Aaron paused to do the math in his head. "That's like eight hours up there. That's not too bad after all. It's about how much time I spend on the river on a normal day, I guess."

He calmed down, realizing his family probably wasn't even looking for him yet. "So that gives us today to explore, and I want to see it all! The vault, the tunnels, the—"

Darla interrupted. "Woah there. Didn't you just hear Phil say the Blackwings are looking for a human? I think it's best if we just stay here at the house and play a board game . . ." Her voice trailed off as it became obvious the others didn't agree with her.

"Pleeease," Aaron and Steve begged. "At least the vault!"

Vee, who had been mostly silent all morning, looked up from her journal. "The vault could be cool."

Phil cleared his throat and gave them the dad stare

that meant business. "As long as Aaron wears that school T-shirt and you *all* pay close and don't wander, then I think it's pretty harmless to go."

Darla glared at him. "And you listen to Mom! She is right about the Blackwings being dangerous. They are all out at the pipe entrances harassing people, so I think y'all should be in the clear."

The look on her face made it obvious she was still not thrilled with the idea, but she gave in. "Fine . . . that is a good point about them being distracted. I do think it would be neat to get to share some more of our home's history with Aaron."

"Okay then, I am going to head off to work now that everyone is fed," Phil said. "Again, please be careful today. I will meet y'all down there later. We only work a half-day on Fridays, so I can come for lunch."

Everyone said their quick goodbyes to Phil, and he headed out the door. Steve and Aaron competed to see who could eat the most bacon, while Vee remained absorbed in her writing. Darla cleaned up the plates and prepared for the day. It was chaotic, yet harmonious. Aaron reveled in the "normal" for the first time in several days.

"Yep, this one is a keeper," he said, taking a mental picture.

15

HEADED TO THE VAULT

"All right, are we ready to go?" Darla hollered down the hallway.

"Oh yeah," Steve answered, with Aaron close behind him.

"Ugh, finally," Vee said.

Darla paused just before opening the front door. "Now remember, we *all* stay together."

Vee crossed her arms angrily.

"Aht, aht," Darla answered before she could speak. "No objections, Vee. Not right now. Once we get there and see what it is like, maybe we can explore the idea more. For now, we stay together as we walk *straight* to the vault, then *straight* back home like we told your father. Deal?"

"Deal!" the boys answered in unison. Vee rolled her eyes, but Darla didn't move until her daughter finally mumbled out a half-hearted agreement.

"Okay, then we're ready!" The boys barreled out the door, with Vee and Darla following close behind.

At the elevators, Aaron pressed the B button. "B for basement."

"Oh sorry, sweetheart," Darla corrected and pressed

another. "We need level one this time. It's just a few blocks away, since we are already downtown."

Aaron nodded. "Ah, gotcha. Glad to hear it's a short trip!"

He waited impatiently to see what adventure was waiting on the other side of the doors. The elevator doors opened back to . . . the same lobby they walked through the other day. Aaron couldn't help but chuckle to himself as they headed into the hustle and bustle of the neighborhood.

Now that each step of his journey wasn't some new surprise, the streets seemed almost normal. It reminded him of scenes of Time Square and the people hurrying from block to block, but instead of humans, there were elves, dragons, dwarves, centaurs, and many others. They were mostly dressed in clothing from the seventies or eighties, with all of them seemingly busy going *places* and doing *things*. It was a lot more action than his small community back home, and he couldn't look away.

"Umm, Aaron, your staring is not helping us blend in very well," Darla said out of the side of her mouth. "Could you stop that, please?"

Aaron snapped to attention. "Sorry! This is just so epic!"

"It's okay," Darla said with a hint of worry. "I know it's exciting. Let's just try to be careful."

Steve waved at his friend from a bit ahead, then pointed to a street sign. "Hey! It's this way!"

"The vault is four blocks up Main Street and then a left on First," Darla explained. "And don't wander away!"

"Yeah, yeah, Mom," Vee mumbled.

"You got it," Steve and Aaron said, finding themselves again speaking at the same time. They eyed each other and cracked up. Even with a bit of normal thrown in, the walk was still turning out to be fun.

Steve is just so great. I am so glad I fell into that cave. Wait, did I really just think that? Yes. Yes, I am happy, and it's about time that something made me feel that way. These people are amazing. I don't know how I am getting home, but I know I'll find a way to come back here, whatever it takes.

Aaron used the next couple blocks to ask all the fun questions that had been floating around in his mind. "So, like, you can fly and breathe fire, Darla? But then, Steve, you said fire is the only thing that can harm you. That's weird, right?"

He was finally allowing himself to loosen up and just be an excited ten-year-old, hopping from question to question without getting the last one answered. "And, Vee, how old are you? Like, you seem older than us, but also only sort of like an adult."

"That's because I *am* an adult," Vee reprimanded. "Well, almost. I am seventeen and a half."

"You are not an adult yet," her mother said. "Age doesn't make you an—"

Vee cut in. "I know. You say it all the time. Age doesn't make you an adult . . . maturity does. Blah, blah, blah."

"Well, it's the truth," Darla snapped back. She smiled at her stubborn daughter, who returned a half-hearted "love you, too" smile. *Better than nothing, I guess.*

Aaron stumbled as he listened to the women, looking down to see the sidewalk had changed to cobblestone. He stopped for a second to look around. The cobblestone had clearly been in use for a long time, maintained over the decades with newer stones filling in cracks and adding character. In the last block or so, the entire look of the area had changed. Ahead of them, a clearing sat in the midst of the city and all these buildings.

"That is the park that holds the vault," Darla said. "It is almost identical to Central Park in New York City in size and design. The vault has always been at the middle of the city, but it is not the prettiest site . . . just four stone platforms in front of a stone table. When Central Park was created in the overworld, the Vens thought something similar would be a great beautification project. Mid-City Park was born, and its creation was the last time this area was renovated. We do our best to keep this historic area as-is to remind us where we came from."

Darla's voice trailed off as she stared toward the monument. "Umm . . . and because of the prophecy, they had to build a fence around the lock mechanisms for the vault. Too many people kept trying to break into it. They never had any luck, mind you, but the amount of attempts put such wear and tear on the locks. After that, the leaders agreed to open the gates for one day each year at the end of the festival for those who want to try."

Aaron contemplated the process. "But why are they so obsessed with trying? Even if they find one of the descendants, don't they need all four, like Phil said? Not to mention, they still need to figure out the Unknown."

"Exactly! I don't get it all," Darla said, pausing a

she felt a rant coming on. She adjusted her outfit and continued walking. "I mean . . . yes, it does seem a bit silly. However, a dwarf by the name of Shamus walked up to Brenda the Bold's lock last year on Vault Day, and when he touched the wrist scanner—"

"The lock unlocked one of the four bolts," shouted Steve before looking over at his peeved mother. "Sorry, go on."

"Yes, like Steve said, it seems Shamus is one of the four descendants. That is the exact reason why Bart all of a sudden wants the Unknown removed."

"Woah. But they still only know one, right?"

"They know two," Darla said. "Remember, Bart is a descendant of Darrell the Destroyer."

"Oh, man," Aaron exclaimed. "Then they only need to figure out the shimmer one now and—"

"Yep, then they would have all three," Darla blurted out, finishing his sentence. "And if the kingdom agrees to remove the Unknown, then they have all they would need to make Bart king of The Table."

"Wait, how does he get the vault open with only three keys?"

Vee sighed as her mother explained. "Fortunately and unfortunately, the original four and our ancestors thought of everything. Being that there were only three left when the crown was created, they realized that there may come a day where something happens to one of the bloodlines. They wanted a back-up plan, if you will, to give us all a better chance at success. Oh, hold up here one second," Darla said, putting her hand in front of Aaron to stop him.

He was so enthralled in the story that he didn't even

realize they were standing at a crosswalk, waiting for the *MOVE* sign to change. *Huh, I guess not everyone here uses walking to move. Neat!*

"Turn left here." Darla pointed down First Street. "Okay, where were we? . . . Oh yeah, they wrote down a caveat to the plan."

"Cavvy-what?" Aaron asked.

"Caveat, a loophole, if you will."

"Ah, gotcha," Aaron said. "So what is the loophole here?"

"If three of the four are present, they will hold a vote. If the majority of the Table agrees to open the vault, then there is a special key that has been handed down from the original three to the leaders."

Aaron's eyes were wide as he put together the pieces.

"Bart has befriended Shamus by promising him power once Bart is made king, so now they both want to remove the Unknown and find the shimmer. They plan to round up every Shimmer this year and force them to touch the lock below Penelope. They are offering one thousand geks to anyone willing, and people need money. So, to them, it's a win-win. They don't realize that if one of them does turn out to be the descendant, they will instantly be under Bart's thumb. It will not be all sunshine and rainbows for them, I promise you. He isn't the kind of person that asks someone to do something, and he sure doesn't ask twice."

Aaron looked a little pale as Darla peered over at him. "Anyways, we don't need to worry about all that right now. Let's just enjoy the walk."

Aaron could tell Darla was worried about the vault and her community. *She's such a good person. That must be why she loves Penelope. I hope I am as smart as she is one day.*

16

ROOTWOODS

The buildings around the park were significantly smaller. All of a sudden, there were no more skyscrapers. Instead, this block was filled with small houses made from the red twisted wood he had seen in so many other places.

"Hey Darla, what kind of wood is that? I have never seen it."

"That's Rootwood," she said. "It's the most available and cost-effective material we have here. It comes from the Roottrees."

"Umm, Roottrees?"

"We can get wood from the overworld, but it can be very difficult and expensive. Some of the first citizens quickly realized they could not easily grow overworld trees here due to the lack of sunlight. But through researching how roots grow massively underground, they developed the Roottree, which is essentially just an all-root tree that grows in the dirt and along cliffs. The reason for the red hue is because our water source is connected to the Red River from the overworld. It has an underground tributary that fills a massive reservoir where we get all of our water supply."

Aaron's hands shot up over his mouth in shock. "Yuck, oh no! I'm so sorry, but I've peed in that water!"

Steve started giggling. "Haha, you said pee."

Darla laughed too. "Sweetheart, it goes through a filtration system, just like yours does in the overworld. Don't worry. We aren't drinking your pee water, or anyone else's for that matter."

Aaron blushed a little. "Oh yeah, that makes more sense."

They all laughed, except Vee. She cracked a small smile before remembering she was way too cool to laugh with little kids. "Ugh, why are you all so weird? Pee water? Gross!"

The others laughed even harder and keep walking as the landscape around them transitioned to greenery. Aaron sped up to the final crosswalk, thrilled to see the vault after hearing so much about it. "Penelope Parkway," he read on the street sign.

"The streets surrounding the park are named after the original four. This one we are crossing is Penelope Parkway, then there's Darrell Drive, Brenda Boulevard, then the final one down there . . . Unknown Street."

Aaron looked up and down the massive cobblestone streets and paths, with all the red, twisted rootwood houses, the massive trees, and the brilliant green leaves making a beautiful canopy over most of the park. *This is just so beautiful. Nature is my favorite, wherever I am.*

Once across the street, Vee stopped. "Okay, Mom. We made it to the park, and everything is just fine. Can I please go meet my friends at the food court on the other side of the park? It's the one on Brenda Boulevard. You know the one."

Darla pursed her lips as she debated Vee's request. "Who are you meeting?"

"Ugh . . . like, Stacy and Hailey."

"Anyone else?"

"Mo-om! I don't know everyone else's schedule. I mean, it's a public place. I can't control who shows up."

"Uh huh, sure you don't," Darla said knowingly. "But, yes, you can go as long as—"

"Yes! Bye, losers!" Vee took off running toward the boulevard.

"—you are careful," Darla sighed. "Teenagers! . . . All right, you two. Let's go see the vault!"

17

THE ANNOUNCEMENT

Shrubs and bushes lined the path leading to what looked like a cave of trees and leaves. As they entered the shade of the canopy, the scents of the park punched Aaron in the nose. *It can't be, can it?* He closed his eyes and took a deep breath. *Yep! This smells* just *like my woods back home!*

He heard birds chirping as he walked. "Hello," he shouted without even thinking about it, just like he would on the river. He opened his eyes to see Steve and Darla watching him and smiling. *Did I do something? Shoot, I said hello . . . to birds . . . out loud. They must think I'm such an idiot, or a weirdo.*

"Hello, birds!" Steve's voice turned Aaron's negative thoughts off like a light switch.

"Hello, birds!" This time, it was Darla's voice.

The Dimeters were admiring the birds, just as he was. They weren't making fun of him; they were joining him. *These are my people!*

"Hey, dude! Look." Steve grabbed him and turned his gaze toward the center of the park until Aaron could see steps descending into the earth. "It's the vault!"

Aaron's eyes darted back and forth across the landscape, not wanting to miss a detail. He ran up ahead of the group without realizing he left them behind. He found a semi-circle of amphitheater-style seating with a stone stage at the bottom. Around the top was a large iron gate and fence that encircled the historic space. On the stage were four stone pillars set evenly apart. Behind each was an immense painting, just like at the mural. The pillars sat at the feet of each painting and seemed to be where the genetic locks were installed.

Aaron wandered, lost in thought. *This place just gets cooler and cooler.*

"Aaron? Aaron! Hey, where are you?" Darla shouted.

SMACK! Darla basically flew into Aaron, wrapping him in a hug. "Oh, my gosh! You had us terrified! I am so glad you are okay! Don't run off like that again. . . . Hold that thought." Darla noticed the larger-than-normal number of people around them at the vault.

"Kids, there are so many more people here today than we thought. Vault Day isn't for two more days. It's almost like someone changed the date, but that can't—"

"Welcome to Vault Day," the PA system blasted. "Umm, Vault Weekend!"

"Seriously?" Darla exclaimed, the shock of the announcement freezing her in her tracks. Aaron and Steve followed her lead in staying still and listening in.

"As announced earlier, the leaders of The Table were . . . umm, asked by . . . public demand . . . to go ahead and open the vault early due to the increased interest this year," the PA voice stated. "We all like to be as accommodating as we can here at The Table

Historical Society, so we happily obliged. Everyone is welcome to come in—"

SCREECH went the mic. *THUD* went the person speaking. "Hey, okay! Here is the mic. Jeez, you could have just—"

The system was silent for a couple seconds, followed by some white noise and a deeper voice. "Uh, hello. . . . I mean, *HELLO*, people of the table," the dragon said. "It is I, Bartholomew the Destroyer, your soon-to-be king."

The familiar, thundering voice sent a chill down Aaron's spine. He went into fight-or-flight mode and took off running, with a confused Steve trailing him.

"Remember, I will pay one thousand geks to any shimmer who tries the lock, just for checking," Bart said. "And if you happen to be the right shiny person, well . . . Hey, Shamus, how is it being one of the descendants and working with Team Blackwing?"

"I love working with Bart, umm, Bartholomew I mean," came a boisterous voice with a thick Russian accent from the back. "Umm, yeah, it's amazing. I love it here, and the geks . . . let's just say there are plenty, it seems! It's like a dream, really."

"All right, that's enough" Bart said. "Well, remember that could be you too—just rolling in geks and power if your genetics match the code. So if you have shimmer in your family tree, what is there to lose? You are already here, so you might as well make a quick thousand geks."

The PA turned off, and shimmers from all over the park lined up in front of Penelope's pillar.

"This is not good," Darla said to herself. *It's going to*

be okay. Just grab the boys and get out of here. She turned to grab them, but they were no longer behind her. She spun around, frantically scanning the crowd until she finally eyed Steve's pink hat across the way. It looked like he was chasing Aaron.

No, no, no! Okay, just don't do anything out of the ordinary. She walked in the direction the boys went as "casually" as she could with her heart pounding out of her chest. She would figure this out and make sure the boys were safe.

"I'm coming, Aaron," Darla whispered. "You will be okay."

18

MEETING BART THE DESTROYER

Aaron did not realize he had run so far so quickly. He didn't even really realize he had moved at all until he had to stop to catch his breath. The terror that voice inspired in him took over.

"Aaron, wait for me!" Steve yelled as he gasped for air. "Are. You. Okay?"

Tears streamed down the human's face. "I just ran, Steve. When I heard that voice, his voice . . . I just ran."

WOOSH went wings flapping behind them. *Oh, thank goodness. Darla is here!*

The boys instead turned around to see an eight-foot behemoth. Bart was similar to Phil in stature and form, but his skin was made up of black scales and his face was more dragon than human. Steve yelped.

"Woah, woah, woah, you two okay?" the wannabe royal asked. "I thought I saw this shimmer running away from the lock without checking, so I wanted to make sure you all knew about the one thousand geks just for trying it out."

Steve and Aaron are too petrified to speak. *WOOSH*. Darla landed directly between Bart and the boys. "Hello, Bart!"

He stepped back a bit, surprised that a random dragon lady would dare interrupt them. "Wait, is that you, Darla?" Bart asked as he looked a little closer. "Darla Stoneson? It's been a long time . . . like twelve years or so?"

Darla looked a bit ashamed. "Something like that. And it's Dimeter, but that doesn't matter right now. Uh, what I mean is, these are my boys, and we are headed home. Have a good day, Bart."

"One of your boys is a shimmer?" Bart asked with obvious suspicious.

Darla just smiled. "Yep, we adopted both boys at the same time when they were babies."

"How nice of you. And what is his name again? That guy you left me for."

Aaron and Steve snapped their heads to inspect Darla's expression. "Wait! Mom, you dated this guy?" Steve asked loud enough that everyone nearby stopped to look.

Darla turned several shades of red. "We will talk about it *later*, Steve. Hush it now."

Steve got the hint and stepped back as Bart let out a deep breath. "Oh, you didn't tell them, Darla? I'd think you be proud to be connected to a descendant."

She wanted to roll her eyes, but she knew Bart was capable of terrible things when he was upset. "No, umm, I guess it didn't come up. Anyway, have a good day."

She attempted to shepherd the boys away, but Bart blocked their exit. "But I didn't see your boy check himself on the lock. It's a free one thousand geks, why wouldn't he want to do it?"

Darla racked her brain for a way to get out of the situation. "Well, I think he already did it. Right, sweetheart? Didn't you try last year? It was a no-go, unfortunately."

She waited for Aaron to agree, but he wasn't yet able to form words. "Right, sweetie?" she asked as she grabbed his hand. "It was last year?"

"Uh-huh," Aaron said softly.

"Yeah, see? It's too bad, though," Darla faked disappointment. "One thousand geks would be nice. Oh well. Let's go, boys."

"Well, the boy doesn't seem sure," Bart said as he again stepped in their path. "And if you could use the geks, I don't mind paying for my own peace of mind as well as yours. So go ahead, boy. Head on up to the line, and I will chat with your mom."

Aaron's eyes pleaded with Darla for an escape as she sought to reassure him to go along with it. "It's not like it's a human detector," she leaned down and whispered to him. "They will just think you're another dud shimmer. No big deal."

Darla was filled with a fiery anger, but she forced a smile when she turned back to Bart. "Only if you are sure it's okay. Aaron, go over to that line there and see if it's you. We will take the free money if he wants to give it."

Aaron stared at her, terrified. While Bart looked the other way, Darla mouthed a message. "You can do this."

With his Table mother certain, he calmed his nerves a bit. "Hey, Mom, can Steve keep me company in line?" he asked.

Darla smiled widely. "Of course, honey. Go on."

19

THE GENETICS TEST

Aaron and Steve headed toward the shimmers assembled across the front of the stage, waiting to scan their wrists in the lock scanner on the other end. The line was long, but moved pretty quickly.

"This is crazy, Steve. Like, what is happening? What if they find out I'm hum—"

Steve grabbed Aaron in a bear hug, stopping his words mid-sentence. "You can do this, I promise," he whispered.

"Thanks, bud. I am just terrified to put my wrist in there. Does it hurt?"

Steve hadn't ever been scanned. He had no reason to try it, so he never thought much about the process. "I don't know, but I will be here with you through it. Don't worry."

Aaron took a deep breath. "I will just go up there, scan my wrist and walk away. Easy peasy."

Steve nodded and patted him on the back. "And you've got your lucky hat! What could go wrong?"

They were only a few people away from the front. Normally on Vault Day, pillars for Penelope and the Unknown would have people checking to see if they were "lucky." Today, it was just Penelope, since the importance of the Unknown descendant was in question.

The pillars were lined up evenly across the stage, so visitors walked past each one as the line moved. Penelope's was the last one they walked past, just after the pillar of the Unknown with its huge shadowy painting.

What if . . . what if the Blackwings are right? What if the Unknown was a human?

Steve could tell Aaron was getting worried again. "It's almost over," he said. "You are up next."

Before Aaron knew it, a vault guard was at his side and pointing to the scanner. "You're up. Please scan your wrist in the device."

His feet felt cemented to the ground. *Is this going to hurt? It looks like it will. Are they gonna kill me if they find out I am human?*

"Hey, buddy!" Steve's voice rang in his ears. "I will do it with you!"

Aaron looked to his right to see Steve standing at the Unknown scanner. The giant looked to the guard. "It won't hurt for me to scan myself on the Unknown one, and it will help him feel comfortable. So, we good?"

The guard shrugged, then nodded at Steve. It wasn't going to mess with Bart's plans, and it would get another shimmer scanned.

Steve moved his arm closer to the scanner. "Okay, Aaron, your turn. Get over by the scanner, and we can do it at the same time."

Aaron was still terrified, but locking eyes with Steve gave him enough courage to get it done. "Okay, let's do this."

They closed their eyes and stuck their wrists out. One, two, three, *SCAN.*

"Aaron's a shimmer!" a shocked Steve shouted.

Aaron opened his eyes again to find the pillar clamped down his arm and lighting up. He tried to yank his arm out, but had no luck. *What is it doing? How can I be a shimmer?* Thoughts raced through his head and smashed together like overloaded freight trains.

"Wait, what? I'm an Unknown?" Steve's voice again barreled toward Aaron. The giant's wrist was also trapped by a glowing device.

Aaron could barely stand up between the new discoveries and the roar of the crowd.

"The descendants have been found!" people throughout the park shouted excitedly. "Spread the word! The descendants have been—"

KABOOM! The earth shook from the impact of a huge ball of fire smashing into the stone stage, covering the area in front of Darrell's pillar with smoke and ash. With one *WOOSH* and a huge *THUD*, Bart was standing there smiling the biggest smile anyone had ever seen. He was even showing off the huge dragon teeth that he normally liked to hide.

"Well, well, well. Hello, everyone!" Bart shouted excitedly to the crowd forming around the base of the stage. "The trials are over. Leave *now*! I want this stage cleared of everyone but those two, myself and the dwarf . . . umm, Shamus."

He stared down at the crowd, but no one moved

much "Do it now!" he roared before causing a full-on panic by spewing fire above the crowd.

"Hey! How dare you try to leave me over there in the corner of the park," Darla bellowed as she landed on the stage. "Bart, you get away from my boys. They go nowhere without me. I'm not afraid to fight you!"

"Stop," Bart ordered Darla. She stopped for a brief moment, but her eyes darkened as she contemplated strangling him. "I'm happy you are here, Darla. I am sorry I flew off like that. You can understand my excitement to not only see that the shimmer has been found, but the Unknown, too! It's just . . . I've been waiting for this for such a long time. We can finally open the vault."

"Hold on for a minute there," called out a voice from the audience. "I, too, will be here with *my* sons!" Phil flew up from the almost-empty seating area and landed on the stage next to his wife. "Hey, sweetheart. What did I miss? I was on my way to meet you for lunch, and all of a sudden there were lights and people cheering. What is—"

"Hey, y'all. Can you stop talking and try to get us loose?" Aaron asked as he wrestled with the scanner.

"Yeah, please help us already," Steve screamed.

Darla ran to Aaron, and Phil ran to Steve. "It opens after a few minutes," Phil told the boys.

"Just try to breathe," Darla added. "We will keep you two safe."

She held Aaron in an embrace as he cried. "We will figure this out together," she lifted his chin and told him. "You are not on your own."

Aaron wiped his eyes and shifted his focus to his

friend. "You okay, pal?"

Steve lifted his head from his father's shoulder. "I think so."

"Okay now," Phil said, "a few more seconds and—" *CLICK*. The scanners released their wrists.

Aaron leapt with excitement, almost knocking over Darla. Phil was out of breath, trapped in the grip of an excited and happy giant. The boys ran to each other, grabbing the other's hands.

"Dude! You are a . . . no, *the* shimmer!"

"And you are the Unknown. What does that mean for you?"

"This is crazy! Who knew giants were so cool? I mean, I had an idea, but dang!"

"Ahh, this is so much, dude!"

Bart saw his opportunity and moved toward the center of the stage to address the group. "So," he mumbled, but no one paid him any attention. The two boys kept excitedly chatting, and Darla and Phil were just happy to know the boys were okay.

"It's about time!" Bart sneered as he saw Shamus finally appear onstage. He tilted his head toward the sky and let out a deafening roar that caused everyone to go silent.

"That's better," he said. "So here's the deal: Once we open the vault, no one will touch *anything*. Do you hear me?"

"We don't have to listen to you," Darla snarled.

Phil stepped in front of her before she could continue. "Hey, this is Bart you're talking to. He will hurt whoever he needs to to get what he wants."

Darla stomped her foot in frustration, but then

noticed Bart seemed worried about letting her out of his sight. That was enough to cheer her up inside. "I understand, honey."

"However," she said, turning to face the bully, "please understand that if you hurt a single hair on either boy's head, I will be your only nightmare and I will haunt your drea—"

Phil grabbed her arm and pulled her to the side of the stage. "Okay, that's enough. He gets it." *Please don't get us all killed,* his expression said.

"Fine," she said. "Bart, what is next in your little plan?"

Aaron was thrilled by Darla's bravery. *She is just incredible. Bart is such a jerk. I don't want to help him with anything. But what about this whole shimmer thing? What does it even mean?! Wait, get it together. He doesn't know you came from the surface, and it won't go well if he finds out.*

He took a deep breath and let it out slowly. "I guess I didn't check it before, Mom. Whoops."

Darla looked confused, but then caught up to him. "Oh yeah, we must have been mistaken."

She was so proud of Aaron. Despite his entire world changing in an instant, he was still strong enough to continue the ruse and give them a chance to see another day.

20

WORKING TOGETHER

"How can this be real? I have always been told giants don't belong in politics because they are not smart enough," Steve said to himself as he rubbed his wrist and looked at the Unknown pillar. "Well, haha. Seems like y'all were wrong."

He looked at the painting. "Umm, what in the world? Are y'all seeing this, too?"

Bart, Shamus, Aaron, and the Dimeters turned to see him pointing up. "It's changed!"

Sure enough, instead of a generic black shadow, there was an entire mural.

"This is incredible," Darla shrieked. "We will finally know the identity!"

"What does the sign at the top say?" Phil asked. "I can't see it from this angle."

"Richard the Righteous," Steve read in a tone that encompassed all the emotions at once. "They were my ancestors! Wait, what does righteous mean?"

"It means a good person, or someone who is always fighting for good," Darla replied with a beaming smile. "What a way to explain Steve. Righteous nails it."

"So, if Bart became Bart the Destroyer, do I get to be Steve the Righteous?" he asked, almost out of breath with excitement.

"Sure, I guess" Phil said. "I am not really sure how it works."

"Will you all please shut up and pay attention?" Bart grumbled. "My patience is wearing thin."

"Finally," Bart said as the others looked to him with a mixture of fear and hatred. "Shamus, go to Brenda's lock and scan your wrist. And you two . . . what are your names?"

"Umm, my name is Aaron."

"And I'm Steve!"

"Well, Aaron and Steve, would you be kind enough to take your places at your scanners?"

Darla, Phil and the boys exchanged glances. Without a better idea, Steve and Phil stepped toward Richard's scanner. As Steve placed his hand on the scanner this time, one of the four lock mechanisms above the door slid open.

Darla grabbed Aaron's hand, looked him in the eyes and nodded. Her presence calmed him enough that he could place his hand on Penelope's scanner again. The second lock mechanism slid back.

Bart motioned to Shamus, who placed his hand on Brenda's scanner and unlocked the third segment.

Bart's eyes were wild with hunger for the power that rested behind the door. "This is my destiny!" As he put his hand on Darrell's scanner, the fourth and final lock opened. The door to the vault shook violently, knocking off all the dust and dirt that had built up in the cracks over the years.

"Stay back, all of you!" Bart screeched as it began to slowly slide out of the way. He leapt in front of the vault and raised his head. *ROAR!*

Darla, Phil, and the children huddled away from the vault.

"Stay there!" Bart ordered. Turning toward the front of the stage for the first time, he noticed that all the people ordered to leave the area had now gathered around the fence at the top of the bowl.

"Umm, I just mean that I would like to go first," he said with more composure in an effort to protect his public image.

As the door opened, the old air that had been trapped inside escaped.

"Grody," Steve hollered, holding his nose and flapping his hands in front of his face. "What is that smell?"

The others chuckled, except for Darla. She was determined to keep a close eye on Bart and his efforts. *What would make him need to be first so badly? There's still a decision to be made, unless . . .*

She looked up at the vault door in time to see a black tail slither inside, with Shamus running right behind it. "He is trying to get to the crown first and keep it for himself," Darla shouted to her family. "Phil, we *have* to stop him! The prophecy only states that the four needed to be together to open the vault, and whoever wears the crown is king. What is keeping Bart from crowning himself?"

Phil, Darla, and the boys bolted into the vault as fast as they could, hoping they were not already too late. Inside, they found a small stone room with a staircase at the center spiraling into the ground. The staircase was only passible in single file, so Darla took the lead. Aaron went next, then Steve, with Phil bringing up the rear.

They could hear Bart complaining to Shamus. "Why isn't there an elevator?"

"That's them," Phil said excitedly. "Go, go, go, go!"

"Hurry up, dwarf!" Bart and Shamus disappeared from the bottom of the staircase and continued deeper into the vault.

At the bottom of the stairs, the Dimeters found another small stone room. This one had a stone doorway that opened into what looked to be a long hallway. Darla ran toward the door in time to see a giant boulder moving to close them in.

"No, no," she yelled. "They are blocking the door!"

But it was too late. The doorway was completely covered.

"Dang!" Darla shouted, trying not to cry as she pounded on the boulder.

"I got this, Mom," Steve said. He puffed out his chest and moved her to the side. It was his time to shine, and he was ready.

GRRR. Steve shoved the boulder back at least six feet.

"Great job, sweetie!" His mother was so proud. They rushed into the next room with renewed vigor, although they had no idea what they were about to witness.

21

INSIDE THE VAULT

Aaron stumbled as he walked past the boulder and into this new room, in awe of the beauty before him. Watching where he was going was an afterthought.

An ancient wooden table with four chairs sat in the center of a sprawling black stone cave. Bookshelves lining the back walls held several titles, some trinkets, and other knickknacks. Four doors took up space in the back as well. Like the start of his adventure, the room included one of those unusual "glowing moss" chandeliers and a small pond.

Bart and Shamus didn't notice the family's arrival. They stood next to the table, arguing and pointing to an oversized glass bubble on top.

"The crown!" Darla shouted.

"Oh good . . . you made it," Bart said sarcastically through his teeth.

Darla darted between him and the crown. "Yes, we did, no thanks to your boulder," she hissed as she pressed him away from the table.

Aaron kept his distance with the rest of the family. *Man, Darla is scary! Well, to anyone she is mad at. I'm happy she is on my side.*

Bart had been caught off-guard by her aggression, but he regained his composure quickly. "Remember, Darla, we are now out of the sight—no witnesses," he said, pushing her back and spreading his wings. "Do you know what I do to people who stand in my way? You *will* do as I say, or else!"

With a powerful roar, he sent her sprawling back toward the family. Phil caught her, and small streams of smoke billowed from his nostrils. "That's it! I am gonna kick Bart's—"

"Hey, look at me," Darla turned his face toward hers. "It's not worth it. We need to take care of the boys. We need to play his game long enough to get us all away safely."

Phil begrudgingly agreed. "Boys, we all need to calm down. She is okay. I love that you are angry, too, but now is not the right time to act."

Aaron and Steve shook with rage, but they knew Dad was right and took a step back.

"That's better," Bart gloated. "As long as everyone does what I say and follows my instructions, no one needs to get hurt. Sound good, everyone?"

He reveled in the dark, defeated looks on their faces, finding new vigor. "Good. Now, the crown seems to be sealed in the bubble. I thought it was glass, so I tried to break it. Obviously, that did not work. . . . It must need to be unlocked somehow."

"Are we *allowed* to take a look?" Darla asked.

Bart's eyes flashed with anger, but he knew he couldn't get the reward alone. "Sure."

"It doesn't look like we are getting out of here until

that crown is out, so let's get to looking, okay?" she said to her family, hoping to pull out their confidence and critical thinking. "We can do this." *I hope they have some ideas because I have no clue, and I'd really like to be gone before Bart loses his mind and considers killing all of us. Okay . . . that was not a helpful thought. Shoving that down and moving on!*

Taking a closer look around the cave led to more discoveries. The four bookshelves and four doors on the back wall each had a letter emblem above them.

"P, B, D, R!" Aaron yelled, ending the awkward silence. "It's the initials of the original four."

"What?" Bart said.

"The letters here represent the four: P is for Penelope, B is for Brenda, D is for Darrell, and R is for—"

"Richard," Steve boomed with pride.

Bart glanced around the room, and it clicked. Everything in the room was present and labeled in groups of four: The shelves and doors, the chairs at the table, and the books and cup atop the table.

"Hmmm," Darla said, scrutinizing all the details around her. She noticed an envelope on the table that was labeled in ancient script Darla translated as *READ FIRST*. The others were still preoccupied with getting the crown out, so they didn't see her find. *Okay, let's see what this says.*

She stepped away from the table, checking on the others again quickly before opening the envelope. Inside was a yellow piece of paper, folded into fourths. She held it up to try to read the faded writing. "Welcome to the Great Halls of the Four," she translated. "If you are reading this, then the descendants have been found and the crown can be bestowed upon its rightful owner. In order to pass the trial to free the crown from this table, you must be very wise and pure of heart. For once crowned, you will rule all of The Table and its lands."

"What are you looking at, Darla?" Bart snarled. "Give it to me! I'm tired of all this waiting!"

"Okay, fine," she relented. "It looks like instructions on removing the crown."

Bart's eyes transformed from anger to excitement. He snatched the letter out of her hand. "What does this even say? I have never seen this language!"

Darla smirked. "Oh, you can't read it? Well, that is just too bad."

Bart reared back his head and spewed fire into the air. "Darla, you would be wise to stop with the sarcasm and tell me how to get the crown before I hurt someone . . . or two someones."

"Please don't hurt anyone, okay? I will read you the letter. Just give it back to me."

An evil smile crept across his face. "That's better. Now read it, *word for word*, and if you even *try* to trick me—"

"I get it," she cut in. "No funny business."

"Good, then you finally understand your situation." Bart handed her the document.

"The trial is a simple one, but needs to be taken seriously as the consequences could be dire if the trial is failed," she read. She took a quick glance at Steve and Aaron, sighed, and continued. "For the trial to commence, at least three of the original descendants must be seated at the table. Press the button next to the crown, and the trial will commence. The winner of the trial will be the rightful owner of the crown."

What could this trial even be? Are the boys safe, now or even in the future? Should we even do this? Her panicked thoughts were interrupted by the bully's booming voice.

"Let's get this trial going, you two," he motioned to Aaron and Steve. "Sit down!"

Aaron and Steve looked at each other and then to Darla and Phil, who were now tightly holding hands.

"Bart, we don't even know what the trial is," Darla pleaded with him.

"We don't want our boys to get hurt," Phil added.

"I do not care about your wants!" Bart roared, with small flames escaping the sides of his mouth. "The crown is mine. They will sit at the table now!"

Darla and Phil nodded at the boys, who walked to their ancestors' chairs.

"That's better," snarled Bart, "Shamus, I have no idea what this trial will entail, so I need you there with me. Take your seat already!"

Shamus immediately took his position.

"Ok, where is this button?" asked Bart.

"Umm, is that it?" Aaron pointed to a small button that had popped up next to the bubble.

"Looks like it!" Bart jeered as he smashed the button.

22

THE TRIAL

S*LAM!* Holes appeared in the floor under the descendants' chairs, swallowed them up, and immediately closed again. *SLAM!*

"No!" the parents screamed.

"Where did they go?" Phil asked desperately.

"I don't know," Darla answered. "It doesn't say anything else in the letter! Steve? Aaron? Can you hear me?"

No response. The dragons paced the room, looking for any other buttons, cracks, or clues. "Where did they take my boys?" she yelled to Phil.

He wrapped her in a warm, winged hug. "I don't know, but we will figure this out together. We don't know for sure that anything bad has happened yet, so all we can do is stay calm and try to help. Here, let's check some of the books."

Darla sniffled, knowing Phil was right. "Okay, yeah. Let's try that."

"Ahh!" Aaron screamed as he fell. *THUD!* Aaron

smacked into the cold stone floor of another cave.

"Hello?" he heard to his left. It startled him, but he knew that voice.

"Steve!" he hollered into the darkness.

"Aaron!" he heard back. "I'm over here!"

As he moved toward the voice, a blinding light surprised them. One of the mossy chandeliers had lit up the cave like it was midday.

"Argh," Bart grumbled.

When Aaron's eyesight adjusted, he could see Bart standing across from him, Shamus to his left, and Steve to his right. *Just like how the chairs were set up.*

The new cave was about the size of the one above them, but it had nothing but slick, flat walls and a ceiling of stalactites. No exit to be seen. Instructions, which Shamus could thankfully read, were etched into the wall: *FIND A WAY OUT.*

Aaron and Steve stared at each other, then at Shamus and Bart. Each looked more confused than the next as they searched for any sign of an exit.

"Hey, look," Aaron said excitedly as he pointed to the ceiling. There, in one corner, was a small ladder coming down the wall. Only a few rungs were visible, making it nearly impossible to reach.

Bart pushed past them all, attempting to fly to the ladder. Every time he tried, though, his wings got caught on the stalactites. "Why? Dang it!" he yelled, frustrated. "Giant, get over here!"

"Yeah, okay," Steve said as he walked over to Bart.

"Stand under the ladder, and I will stand on your shoulders," the dragon ordered. "I should be able to reach the ladder and get myself . . . umm, get us out."

"No, Steve," Aaron pleaded. "He is just going to leave us here."

Bart grabbed Aaron by the shirt and held him out in front of his snout. "I have had enough of you all. You know why we are here." He looked Steve dead in the eyes. "Do as I say or he dies."

"Okay, jeez! Whatever you want, Bart!" Steve said. "Please just put him down!" Steve was seething as he envisioned bashing Bart into the ground, but he didn't want to get Aaron hurt.

Bart smiled that wicked, awful smile. He dropped Aaron with a *THUD*. Steve rushed to help him, but the dragon wouldn't allow it. "Aht, aht. No. Get in position and stand still."

Aaron groaned. "Hey, buddy, I'm okay."

Steve grimaced, knowing there were no other options. Bart climbed up Steve and balanced on his head. He was just short of gripping the ladder as it swayed with each swipe. "Shamus, be useful and come grab this thing!"

Shamus scrambled up Steve, then climbed up Bart until he was standing on his scaly head. He stretched out his hand and grabbed the ladder, steadying it just enough for Bart to grab it and pull himself up to the ledge leading in the wall. But as he grabbed the ladder, it clicked slightly, followed by a constant hissing down below.

Bart raced up the ladder with Shamus holding on to him for dear life. Looking back down at Steve and Aaron, he spotted gas coming from the bottom of the chamber walls. "Haha! I win, and the crown is mine," Bart said, ripping the ladder from the wall with one giant tug before disappearing inside. "You can't leave now!"

The cloud of yellow gas seeping into the room continued to get thicker. Aaron, still in quite a bit of pain, sat on the floor. "What are we supposed to do now?" the exhausted human whined.

Steve scoured the room, unsuccessfully, for another exit. He turned back to his friend. "You need to climb up on me and get out *now*!"

Aaron refused. "I won't leave you!"

"Oh, yes you will," Steve replied between coughs. In one smooth motion, he snatched Aaron by the shoulders, hugged him, and tossed him up to the ledge. "It's the only way!"

Aaron smacked the higher ground with another huge *THUD* on the ledge. He peered over the side as he tried to catch his breath. He hoped to see Steve on his way up, but couldn't make anything out. The chandelier went out, and it was pitch black again.

"Steve!" *What do I do now? I am just a kid.* He began to cry. The cave started rumbling wildly, causing him to look over the ledge again. The cavern floor was rising.

Steve thought it was all over for him. He sat on the ground, choking on the gas and choking back tears. He could feel the floor rumbling beneath him, too. Air rushed into the room and pushed out the poison.

In the middle of the room, a stone column descended from the ceiling. A chamber inside opened up. Steve was still woozy from the gas, and rubbed his eyes to make sure he was seeing what he thought he was seeing. "Is that the crown?"

Sure enough, the ancient treasure was nestled

right there in the center of the column. As he stared, words appeared on the wall across from him: *THOSE WILLING TO DIE FOR OTHERS ARE WORTHY OF WEARING THIS CROWN.*

He picked it up and turned it around in his hands. "Wow," he whispered.

Before he could continue that thought, the chamber closed, and the floor shook and moved up around the center column. He locked eyes with Aaron. The floor came to a halt when it leveled off with the ledge. From the ceiling appeared a spiral staircase, step by step around the column.

A very worried Darla paced the Great Hall of the Four. In the block of time that had passed since the trial began, she frantically flipped through the originals' books looking for any sort of information about the trial. As she slammed down another unhelpful title, a mechanical whir caught her attention.

"Phil, look!" she said as one of the doors on the back wall opened. "Maybe it's the boys . . ."

Her voice trailed off as Bart and Shamus came running into the chamber.

"Yes, I am the winner!" Bart rejoiced. "I am king! Give me my crown!"

He ran over to the bubble where the crown was, staring as he waited for it to pop open. "Umm, I was the first one up! Why isn't this working?"

He angrily clawed at the bubble until it started vibrating and disappeared into the table. Bart smiled as he waited for his reward, but it didn't return. His mood quickly changed as the floor underneath the table and chairs shook like an earthquake.

Stairs appeared one at a time, spiraling into the floor as the ground continued to shake. As the dust settled, Bart ran for the stairs, confident his crown was waiting for him at the bottom.

When the adults reached the bottom, dust from the changing landscape surrounded them. Darla flapped her wings to clear the air, looking up just in time to see Steve walking toward them with Aaron leaning on him for support. "Oh goodness! They are okay!"

Darla and Phil ran to the boys. She squeezed them in a powerful hug.

"Okay, okay, Mom. I am a little sore," Steve said softly.

Aaron chimed in. "Yeah, I'm a mess, too."

"How *dare* you hold my crown," Bart roared with anger and jealousy.

Darla looked up from the hug confused. "What? . . . oh, Steve! You got it!"

Bart slammed into Steve, knocking him to the ground and sending the crown flying out of his hand. "This is mine," he snapped and grabbed the crown from its resting place. "I shall finally have what I rightfully deserve!"

He placed the crown on his head. "Bow down to me!"

Steve winced in pain on the ground as Darla ran to him. "Are you okay?" she asked worriedly.

"Yeah, I think so," he replied.

She smiled down at her son, then turned to Bart

with a fiery snarl. "You! What do you think you are doing? Don't *ever* touch my children. Clearly, Steve won the trial. The letter says the crown belongs to him!"

Fire flashed in Bart's eyes. "Fine. I will take the crown from him the old-fashioned way . . . by killing him!" He spun to face Steve, lying helpless on the ground, and unleashed a massive fireball.

THWACK. "Ahh!" Bart crumpled to the ground, and the crown rolled off his head to Aaron's feet. Without realizing it, the human had jumped in front of his friend and deflected the fireball by crossing his arms in front of his chest. It hit the dragon directly in the face.

Did that just happen? Aaron was momentarily too stunned to speak. *Whoa. Yeah, it did.*

He picked up the crown and handed it to Steve. "Hey, I think you dropped this."

Once he gave the crown to his friend, he could feel himself fading. As he lost consciousness, he heard Steve shouting. "That was so cool," the giant said.

23

SHIMMERS RULE

Aaron's eyes fluttered open. "Umm, where am I? Where is Bart?" he asked as he tried to sit up, still groggy. Once upright, he knew he was back in "his room" at the Dimeters'. Darla was sitting next to his bed, asleep with a book on her face. "Wait. I can remember—"

"Hey, buddy!" Steve came barreling in, startling his mother.

"What? Oh good. Aaron is awake," Darla said. "We were so worried about you!"

"Yep, but what happened? All I remember is Bart trying to kill Steve and then—"

"And then you saved me with your cool shimmer powers," Steve finished the thought.

"My what? I did what? How?"

Darla smiled at the boys. "Yeah, we didn't know about that one either. No shimmer has ever had to face a fireball, as far as we know. But when you did, it just bounced off of you and hit Bart, knocking him out cold!"

Shimmer powers? And I took out the head of the Blackwings? "Okay, but how did we get home?"

"Well, once Bart was knocked out, Shamus made a run for it. He knew he was outnumbered," she said. "Steve carried you. Once we were out, I called the authorities and explained what took place in the vault to them and to the leaders. They found and arrested those two, who will have a trial in the near future. But rest assured that Bart and Shamus will no longer bother us."

Aaron could finally breathe easy. "So now what?"

Phil had joined them in the bedroom during his wife's retelling. "Well, now that we know you are a shimmer, you can use the pipes to go home."

Aaron wasn't sure how to feel, but his mind was flooded with plenty of options. *Nice, I can get back to my home. But wait, I don't want to leave my new family here. Does my regular family miss me? Would the Dimeters even let me move in for good?*

Phil could tell Aaron was struggling. "Remember, that means you can travel both ways: Up the pipes and back down."

"I can come back!" Aaron screamed with joy. "I can come whenever I want, and with the time difference, I can spend a couple days here before anyone would notice!"

But then his eyes darkened as he reflected on his time in the park. "What about the crown and the fact that I am a descendant?"

"Don't worry about that right now," Phil said. "The leaders are still trying to figure out the best course of action. I promised them you would return by next weekend to discuss things further, but I also let them know the importance of you getting home. . . . Now let's get you to the pipes."

Aaron grabbed his hat from the nightstand and made his way to the living room for quick goodbyes with the family.

"All right, it's time to go, before it gets too late," Phil said as he walked into the hallway.

Darla wrapped Aaron in a big hug. "Remember, you always have a home here, and you better not be a stranger."

"I won't, I promise you," he said. "I couldn't imagine not seeing you all again. Thank you for everything, Darla. I so appreciate it!"

Tears welled up in his eyes as a pouting Steve walked up to him. "Hey buddy, cheer up," Aaron said. "I will be back soon, I promise."

Steve smiled slightly and grabbed Aaron in a huge bear hug.

"Ouch! Okay, okay, I love you too."

"Sorry," the giant said as he let him loose.

Aaron smiled at his best friend. "No big deal, big guy."

He started to follow Phil into the hallway, but quickly turned back. "Bye to you too, Vee," he added with a wave to where she was sitting on the couch with her journal. She looked up, gave a small wave, and returned to her writing.

"Okay then," he said as he joined her father. They walked to the elevator, and Phil pressed B for basement. When the doors opened to the parking lot, they walked quickly toward the car.

"So the pipes are not as straightforward as you might think," Phil told him. "You will have to get used to them first, and you can get lost."

"Yup, I will pay attention," Aaron said as they reached the car. "Man, I hope I never stop finding cool new things in this place."

"Oh, I wouldn't worry about that," Phil said. "There's still plenty for you to discover."

After just a few minutes of driving, Phil slowed the car down. "Okay, this is our exit."

The road wound around into a tunnel until Aaron bolted up straight in his seat. "This is the place where I met Steve!"

"Yep, the pool entrance is right over there." Phil pointed toward the mossy door Aaron had originally come through.

After parking, they walked over to the moss and pushed their way into the cave where Aaron had woken up confused and alone a few days prior. A tall, pale man stood in the corner.

"Hello, Horace," Phil said. "Aaron, meet Horace, one of our eleven leaders. He is the oldest shimmer at The Table, and he is in charge of all pipe transportation. He is going to give you a quick lesson on how these work."

"Howdy, Aaron," the shimmer said, extending his hand.

Aaron smiled and shook hands. "Yes, sir. Nice to meet you."

"I also heard you just found out that you are a shimmer. That's great! Welcome to the family!" Horace said as he patted the boy on the back.

"Thank you, I think."

"You think?" his guide asked sarcastically. "I promise

you we are way better than most people even know! Let me tell you—"

"But right now, we are focused on getting Aaron home . . . right, Horace?" Phil interrupted.

"Oh, right, yeah. So you need to know how to use the lava links? The best way to start—"

"The lava what?" Aaron shouted.

"Oh, yeah, that's what the pipes are called," Phil said. "Sorry, son. I know some of this hasn't been well-explained yet. Basically, between the overworld and The Table are old lava tubes that formed many years ago. They have since filled with water and become impassable by anyone who can't breathe underwater."

"Exactly," Horace chimed in. "These tubes connect to places all over the world, and we have several entrances and exits mapped throughout each tube. As fast as a shimmer can swim, it only takes a few minutes to get to places once you get the hang of it!"

Horace was thrilled to show someone new all about the tubes he and his crew worked so hard to maintain. "Here, take a look at this," he said as he pulled out a large leathery map.

The document, which had to be four feet wide and two feet long, showed all of The Table similarly to an ant farm. In the middle was a cavern with a city depicted. Above that were several lines heading to different spots on the surface of the cavern. Each line was a different color, and the bottom-right side included a key.

"As you can see, the lava links are color-coded inside so we know which ones go where. We are mapping new ones all the time," Horace said. "The link you used is a new one for us. We knew about this cavern entrance to The Table, but the spot you came through from the overworld was unknown. We have since scouted it and added it to the map. That yellow line is your path home."

Aaron lit up with excitement. "So I am good to go? Wait . . . how do I go?"

Horace and Phil chuckled. "Well, first we need to go over a couple things," the older man said. "First, the tubes are pretty dark once you are inside, so it can be overwhelming trying to navigate them. You need to pay attention to the glow sticks. Follow the yellow ones any time there is a turn or change.

"Second, there is a current, but it's not so strong that you can't turn around if you get lost. The tubes are about five feet in diameter, so it's a snug fit, but not too bad. It will only take one or two minutes from when you leave here to arrive back in the Red River.

"Third, take note of where you are once you exit the tube so you can return there. We weren't sure what kind of marking would not be too obvious to other overworld people. Just outside the tube opening, though, we set up a return rope pull that will open the cave door. And lastly, following the red glow sticks will lead you to the main entrance for The Table when you are ready to return here."

Aaron was listening intently, but his eyes glossed over as his mind wandered to the shimmer adventure ahead. Phil put his hand on the boy's shoulder.

"Okay, Aaron, I think you have all the information you need to go. Feeling okay and ready to head out?"

"Thank you so much. So much. I can't even . . ."

Aaron grabbed Phil and hugged him as tightly as he could. "Yep, I think I am ready. Just one question: How do we get out of this cave and into the tube? I don't remember another way out."

"We are a bit sneaky with our tube entrances," Horace said. "Did you check the small pool over there?"

"Yeah, I did, but there wasn't anything there, I don't think."

"Well, let's look again." Horace pulled on a vine hanging alone in a corner. A swirling vortex appeared in the water, like a drain going down into the earth. The sound of rushing water filled the cave.

"Now just hop in the vortex and follow the yellow glow sticks," Horace shouted. "If you get lost, just follow the red ones back to the main entrance."

Phil noticed that Aaron still seemed a little skeptical. "You are a shimmer, Aaron. Your genetics said so, and you can do this."

Aaron, looking a little more confident, moved toward the pool and tucked his lucky hat and his new Elfwater hat firmly into his pocket.

"Remember where you come out so you can get back to us," Phil called to him.

"Okay!" Aaron paused to admire the dragon man. Phil nodded for him to make the leap.

Aaron gave him a thumbs up, closed his eyes tight, and hopped into the vortex.

24

BACK TO REALITY

WOOSH! Aaron practically flew through the water, moving so fast through the tunnel that things were a blur until he could steady himself. He began to calm down and realized he was now just floating in place.

I am a shimmer! He snapped back to the directions he had heard. *Yellow, I need to follow yellow.* As he swam forward and his eyes adjusted, he could make out a faint yellow light in the distance. *Oh, man. I* am *swimming very fast.*

All of a sudden, water was crashing all around him, and he sped past another yellow glow stick. *PHOOMP!* He opened his eyes, a bit bewildered and shaken now that he'd stopped moving. The sunlight burned his eyes. *The sun?!*

"I made it!" Aaron took in his surroundings, figuring out he was floating in the river just down from his favorite tree. He spent a few more seconds right there, enjoying the warmth of the sun—something he never thought he would miss after ten scorching Texas summers.

He heard a car in the distance crossing the highway

bridge. "Shoot! I need to get home!"

As he made his way out of the river, he remembered Horace's advice. Aaron stacked a pile of stones on the shore next to the entrance to a small, dry cave with a small stone door that was now closed. Once he was confident he could find it again, he sprinted toward home.

Out of the corner of his eye, he saw Chuck and his crew walking down the road across the field. The bully locked eyes with him, and Aaron could see the insults already brewing.

"I am a shimmer and royalty!" Aaron shouted as he sprinted past them. "So suck it, Chuck!"

"Hey! Don't . . . you fat . . . whatever!" Chuck, confused by what Aaron said, fought unsuccessfully to find his words.

Yeah, you really got me there, Aaron thought playfully. *Be mean . . . that's fine. I get to go back to The Table tomorrow and you will be stuck here.*

He sped up the path through the backwoods and up the hill until he could finally see the old parsonage. After running his hardest, he burst through the back door.

"Hey, everyone! I'm home!" *Silence.*

His sister stirred in the next room. "Umm, okay," the troll said, annoyed. "Tell the newspaper. No one cares that you went fishing, Aaron!"

Yikes. That's the response I get? Ouch. Aaron was shocked and hurt that his family didn't even miss him. *Oh yeah! It's been only hours to them . . . just another day on the river.*

"Whatever, sis," he responded. "I love you, too."

The rest of the house sounded empty, so he headed to his room. Completely exhausted, physically and emotionally, he collapsed in bed and buried his face in his pillow. "How did I get so lucky to get a second family and a best friend all at once? This is amazing. I can go back whenever I want . . . whenever things are too much here . . . and no one will question it."

Aaron already missed Steve, Darla, Phil, and even Vee. "So, like, I might even be a Table leader now. Things are going to get wild when I get back. Either way, being welcome is the best reward."

He took out the hat from the festival and smiled while reveling in his adventures. *Man, I can't wait to see them all again.*

He drifted off to sleep with the Elfwater hat on, dreaming of the next time he would use the lava links to return "home."

BOOK TWO

AARON'S JOURNEY

1

TIME TO HEAD BACK

"Ahh—ouch!" Aaron winced as he let out a yawn. His eyes shot open. As he rolled over, he felt a huge bruise on his side.

Where did I get—The Table! he thought to himself. The ten-year-old sat bolt upright in his bed, and his head swirled with memories of the adventure he been on the day before.

I must have fallen asleep. The last thing I remember was getting home and no one really noticing I had been gone. I still can't believe The Table is real. For a few seconds, he just sat there smiling.

He shook his head and scanned the room for some idea of the time. His eyes landed on the brown and black digital clock radio on the other side of the room. 6:00 AM, its digital faceplate read.

Phew! I can still get out of here and down to the river before Rick shows up and ruins everything.

Aaron's tyrant of a stepfather was a horrid man who would brutally punish him for even the smallest infraction. Aaron's biological father passed away when he was a baby, so he had no memory of him. The only thing Aaron really knew about his real dad was that everyone said he was "a very kind man" and what he looked like; no one would or could tell him more.

Aaron looked identical to his father in pictures his mother had given him, so much that it was almost weird. It was like looking at a picture of himself that he never took.

Aaron's mother married Rick four years after his father's "tragic accident." They had lived with Rick for five years already, and it had been the most miserable five years imaginable for Aaron. Rick had no desire to be a father figure. He saw children as free labor and was not shy about it when Aaron's mom wasn't home. When she was around, Rick would pretend to be a nice, normal father. The minute she left, the anger would boil up with Aaron as its target.

Don't worry about him. He is still asleep. You just need to grab your bag for some clothes and get down to the river. You are a shimmer! You are a descendant! His recent discoveries gave him comfort as he scrambled around his room to gather his things.

I am going to be there for the day, so that's . . . four nights on Table time. What should I bring? he thought as he eyed the room. *It doesn't matter, dude. You are going back to the Dimeters!*

The excitement rattled his brain for a moment, then he eventually grabbed a couple pairs of gym shorts, a few crumpled plain white T-shirts, some clean underwear—his mother haunted him with stories of something bad happening while he was wearing dirty drawers—and some socks. He shoved all of it into his backpack along with some old sneakers and zipped it up tight.

Even though it had only been an evening for Aaron, it felt like months since he last saw his new underground family. He excitedly tossed on his blue swim trunks, a black T-shirt, and his lucky hat. He eyed the blue and white Elfwater hat he had gotten from The Originals Festival sitting on the end table next to his bed.

Hmm, maybe it's time for a new lucky hat. He smiled, picked up Elfwater hat, and plopped it onto his head. He looked into the mirror on the wall in front of him and, for the first time, saw how the hat looked on him. His heart warmed as he thought of seeing his giant pal, Steve, in his matching "best friends" hat. That thought fueled him even more to get out the door and on his way.

I can do this. Same as yesterday: Just cross the living room and go through the kitchen to the back door. Okay, go!

He walked out his bedroom door into the living room where Stacey the Troll—his teenage sister did look like one, at least in his opinion—was again sleeping soundly on the couch. Only this time, she had pulled the couch over in front of the kitchen doorway.

No, no, no! Aaron screamed internally. He knew that meant he would have to pass through the loud, creaking screen door on the front of the parsonage, and it would wake up Rick. His stepfather did not like to be woken up; if he caught Aaron, he would make sure he remembered to be quiet as a mouse the next time.

Dude, you got this. You literally deflected a dragon's fireball yesterday. Aaron took a deep breath and then let it out slowly. His shoulders lowered slightly, and he calmed a little.

Okay, go!

Aaron crept toward the front door. His first obstacle was the old wooden floorboards. If he stepped on the wrong one, he might as well give up. The sound was practically like an alarm going off. Aaron liked to pretend the living room was a minefield and that he was a soldier escaping a POW camp. He slowly stepped forward onto the first board that he knew was safe and hopped his way from safe board to safe board.

Almost . . . there. . . . Made it! Aaron rejoiced silently. *Now I just need to get outside.*

Aaron knew the door would creak loudly no matter what, so the best thing he could do was make it quick. He took one more deep breath and slowly let it out.

One. Two. Three! In one effortless move, he tossed open the screen door, rolled out onto the porch, then reached back just in time to stop the screen from slamming.

Yes! Now let's get to The Table. An elated Aaron turned around to walk down the steps and off to the river.

"Whoa, whoa, whoa! Hold up there, Aaron," Rick snarled from the bottom of the steps.

Aaron froze in fear.

"You didn't expect me to be up so early, did you?" Rick said as he got into Aaron's face and grabbed him by the front of his shirt. "You planning to just up and leave me with all this yard work to do?"

Rick's face turned red, almost purple, like he was about to explode. He spoke just loud enough to be terrifying, but quiet enough not to bother Aaron's mother in the house. "And this is after you woke me up yesterday and then left before I could get my hands on you!"

"Umm, yes, sir. I mean . . . no, sir. I mean . . ." Aaron tried to respond, but couldn't get the words out fast enough in his terrified, trapped state.

"Well, which is it?" Rick snapped as he let Aaron loose.

Aaron, frozen with fear, stared at the ground and shrugged his shoulders.

Rick let out a quiet, evil laugh. "Oh, it's that way, huh? Fine. It's time for your chores, and you cannot leave this house until every single one is completed and I say you can leave."

Aaron looked up at Rick with a small, sly smile. "I've already finished them."

Aaron knew his stepfather well enough that he was always a few days ahead on his chore list so Rick couldn't use that against him.

Rick's eyes glinted in the sun. "Oh, really? Well, this is a new chore that your mother and I talked about last night. We need you to move the entire wood pile to a new spot over there across the yard."

He smiled as he pointed to a space about one hundred feet away from the pile's current location. Aaron's heart sank.

With the time change, I will be late getting back if I don't leave soon, and I don't want to worry the Dimeters. Maybe I can reason with Rick. Aaron knew better than to think it would work, but he was desperate.

"But why do we need to move the wood? It looks good where it is."

Rick grinned menacingly. "I *said* we need to move it."

"Well, could I maybe do it to—"

Before the word could escape Aaron's mouth, Rick snatched him by the shoulders and looked him square in the eye.

"You aren't sassing me, are you, son? You know what happens to kids that sass too much." Rick tilted his head toward the wooden paddle on the porch next to his chair.

Aaron looked at the paddle and winced. "I'm sorry, sir. I didn't mean to sass at all, I promise. I just had some friends that I wanted to meet up with."

"Ha! Friends? No one cares about your friends! Get to work or get the paddle—your choice."

Aaron winced again. "Yes, sir. I will get on it now."

He walked toward the massive wood pile and looked it over. *This is going to take at least an hour to move! With Table time, I am going to be almost half a day late! Well, the only way forward is to move this stupid pile.*

He grabbed two logs and got to work.

Rick watched for a few minutes as he drank some sweet iced tea. He eventually wandered off somewhere on the other side of the house.

After almost exactly an hour of moving logs, Aaron finally dropped the last two logs onto the new pile. He took a big gulp of water from the hose in the garden and then flopped to the ground to catch his breath.

Finally done. Ugh! That was awful, but at least now I can get going.

At that moment, Rick walked back out into the yard.

"All done, Rick! I am going to get going!"

"One minute, Aaron. I think we made a mistake. . . . Yeah, we did. The wood actually needs to go back to the original spot." Rick, unable to hold back, and let out a chuckle.

"What? Why? But I just?!" Aaron's voice rose quickly. His face was red from anger and heat.

Rick snatched Aaron by the shirt again and pulled him up to his face.

"You woke me up, then left and ran away. Maybe next time you will remember to be respectful and quiet while others are sleeping!"

Aaron's eyes flashed with anger, and Rick saw it. He laughed again. "Don't make me get the paddle, son."

With those words, Aaron's temper came down. Dejected, he let out a defeated sigh. "Okay."

He began to move the massive pile of wood, piece by piece, back to its original spot.

I am going to be over twenty-four hours late in Table time! I hope they aren't mad at me. I can't lose their friendship! The thoughts rolled around in Aaron's head for the next hour.

"Done!" Aaron said triumphantly as he dropped the last piece into place.

After he got another drink from the hose and caught his breath, he made his way back up to the house, where he found Rick on the porch with his mother.

"Rick, I am all done!" He gave his mother a big hug. "Morning, Mom."

He looked back at Rick. "Can I go now?"

Rick wanted to say no, but he did not have anything

to hold over Aaron, especially while his mother was around. "Sure, but next time, remember to keep quiet in the mornings," he grumbled.

"Yes!" Aaron blurted out with a quick fist pump. He hugged his mom again, then grabbed his backpack and fishing gear. "Headed to the river. I will be back later tonight. Love you, Mom!"

He darted out of the yard and across the field before anyone could try to stop him.

Finally! Here I come, y'all! Aaron smiled as he sprinted toward his underground home.

2

THE RIVER

"Hi, birds!" Aaron hollered at the wildlife as he passed, but he didn't have time to stop. He had to get to The Table.

He raced straight down the side of the river, right past his tree and on toward the entrance for the lava links. As he got closer, he spotted the large pile of rocks he had made on the riverbank right next to the underwater cave. *There it is!*

He dove into the river and swam toward the cave's mouth. He stopped and floated for a second above the entrance, a little hesitant for some reason.

You can do this, he reminded himself. With a deep breath, he dove down to the former lava paths now filled with water that the shimmers use for transportation.

WOOSH! The tube sucked him in, and he was practically flying through it.

Okay, remember: Your exit was a yellow glow stick, so look for yellow. You are a shimmer, and you got this.

Aaron slowed his swimming to where he was a little more in control of his direction, and he began to see the glow sticks.

Green—nope. Orange—nope. Blue—nope. Yellow—no. Wait! Yes! Aaron panicked as he swam right past his exit, then started losing control of his speed.

Out of nowhere, Aaron felt a hand on his shoulder.

"There you are!"

He turned around to see Horace, the elder shimmer who helped him leave through the tubes the day before.

"Hi, Horace!" Aaron blurted out before he remembered he was underwater. He expected to choke, but nothing happened. *Oh yeah, I can breathe underwater!*

"Hello, Aaron! I am so happy we found you! We started searching the tubes for you after you were late thinking maybe you got lost. And, well, looks like you did! I am glad we found you. Now, just follow me and we will go to the main downtown tube exit. It's the closest one!"

Without waiting for a response or giving Aaron a chance to explain the delay, Horace swam away.

Before he got far, though, he paused and looked back. "Just focus and follow the red glow sticks. The more you focus your eyes, the clearer it will become. Oh, and pull on your left earlobe really hard!"

"What? Pull on my left earlobe? Why?" Aaron replied.

"Just trust me. It's a shimmer trick," Horace hollered through the rushing water.

Aaron nodded, calmed himself, and searched for any sign of red in the water. Everything was so blurry that he could barely make out any colors at all. He focused as hard as he could, but it was still blurry.

"Pull your left earlobe," Horace shouted again.

Aaron eyed him with doubt, as this seemed like

a curious request. He also had a hard time trusting people after dealing with his lying stepfather so often.

Horace, a little frustrated now, gestured for him to just do it.

Fine, whatever. Aaron pulled on his left earlobe.

Nothing happened.

Aaron looked at Horace questioningly.

"Harder!" Horace mouthed and gestured again.

Aaron grabbed onto his left ear and gave it a yank.

POP! The noise inside Aaron's head was like when you pop your ears due to a pressure change, but this one was three times louder than any he had ever experienced.

Aaron looked around him. *I can see everything!*

All of a sudden, it was like he had the world's best swim googles on. It was even better than goggles, though, because everything around him was crystal-clear despite the water surrounding him. *This is amazing! I love being a shimmer!*

He looked to Horace.

"Finally! It's so much easier now, right?" Horace asked with a smile.

"Wait, I can hear better, too?" Aaron squealed when he realized that it sounded like he and Horace were just chatting like normal on land, but they were underwater!

"Why didn't you tell me this last time?" Aaron asked. "This would have helped a lot on the trip home."

"I am sorry, boy. Yes, it probably would have. It just slipped my mind in all the commotion to get you home. I told you, son, there are a ton of cool things about being a shimmer. This is just the beginning,"

Horace said. "But enough of that for now. We need to get you back to town so the others will know you are safe and so we can start the celebration!"

He darted off in the direction of the red glowsticks, which were now easy for Aaron to spot.

Not wanting to be left behind, Aaron rushed after him, in shock at how clearly he could see underwater. The tubes—how they worked, the glowsticks, and the other details he'd received—made even more sense now.

I really am a shimmer, Aaron thought. *Man, I can't wait to tell Steve about this!*

3

RETURNING TO THE TABLE

Following the glowsticks was so easy now that he didn't even really need Horace's help. Before Aaron knew it, they were speeding along through the tubes.

"Exit is up on the left," Horace told him. They took the tube marked with a red glowstick that read *MAIN EXIT* in big red letters. As they swim through the exit tube, it turned upward and ended in another body of water.

Aaron was a bit confused when they came out. This was much bigger than the pool he remembered from last time. This looked like a large lake; he almost couldn't even see the edge.

Horace raced to the surface and headed off across the top of the water. Aaron headed up behind him. As Aaron cracked the water's glossy surface, he could not believe what he was seeing. They were downtown all right. He recognized all the tall buildings they had driven past on the way to The Originals Festival. Along the shore, a huge crowd had gathered on what looked like a sandy beach of sorts, and music was playing. Horace was halfway to them already, waving for Aaron to hurry. In the distance, Aaron heard a familiar voice.

"I think I see Aaron!" came from a shape that undeniably was his best friend, Steve.

"It is me, Steve!" Aaron shouted in the giant's direction. He began swimming as fast as he could toward them. As he got closer to the dock, he could start to make out faces. There were Darla, Phil, Steve, and even Vee!

They were all smiling and waving at him. That melted Aaron's heart and made him swim even faster to his new adoptive family. Horace had just reached the dock, with Aaron not far behind him. Once he was within about a hundred feet of the dock, he started to take in just how many people were there. It looked like the entire Table had shown up. The closer he got, the more he could hear cheering and music.

Is this all for me? Aaron's thoughts ran wild with excitement, fear, nervousness, worry, and doubt.

"I am so happy you are okay!" Darla's voice pulled Aaron out of his thoughts enough to see that he had made it to the dock. She attacked him with a tight hug.

As she wrapped her dragon wings around him, he felt the love in her heart. For him, it had only been overnight. For her, it had been almost seven days. She had clearly been distraught for the last twenty-four hours of not knowing where he was.

"I am so sorry I am late," he said into her shoulder. "Rick, my stepdad, was being awful and wouldn't let me leave. I didn't mean to worry you, Darla." He looked up to find her giant, warm smile beaming down at him.

"Oh, I don't care about being late! I just care that

you are okay now."

"Hey, buddy!" Steve bellowed as he picked up his friend in a huge bear hug.

"Eep," Aaron squeaked as the air left his lungs. "Okay, okay, big guy. Ease it back."

Steve grinned widely and put Aaron back down.

Phil stepped up next and stuck out his hand to shake Aaron's. Aaron pushed it aside and went in for his own version of Steve's bear hug on Phil. He squeezed tight, and Phil returned the hug with a huge smile.

"It's good to see you, too!" Phil said. "Thank Penelope, you are safe!"

"My horrid stepfather, Rick, was upset with me for waking him up yesterday, so he made me do extra pointless chores this morning. I am sorry for worrying everyone!"

Vee, who had been standing in the back, moved closer. "Hey. Good to know you are not dead or whatever," she said and patted Aaron on the head.

Aaron looked up at her and smiled, She quickly flashed one back, but then immediately erased it. "Ugh, whatever. This is lame," she said and stepped back.

"Thank you, sweetheart, but it wasn't just us that were looking for you," Darla said as she pointed to the crowd that flowed all the way from the shoreline and down the dock to the end where they were standing.

Aaron hadn't noticed, but the crowd had gotten much closer to the family while they were greeting each other.

"The people are very excited to get know you as *the descendant that you are*!" Darla yelled and lifted Aaron's arm up. The crowd ignited into cheers, and a band made up of a flute, a drummer, and a guitarist played a lively melody. The crowd pulsed with roars of Aaron's name and chants of "De-scen-dant."

All of these people are here to see me? I don't know what I'm supposed to do with that.

"Excuse me, sir!" a small voice cut in.

Aaron looked down toward the sound to see a young boy standing there with a pad of paper and a pen in hand.

"Yes?" Aaron replied.

"Umm, could I have your autograph?" the boy nervously spouted out.

Aaron was a bit taken back. "Sure, but why do you want my autograph?"

"You're a shimmer, and so am I! You also took a fireball to the face and beat a dragon! And you are one of the descendants of the original four! I want to be just like you one day!"

Aaron could only smile. "Okay!"

Not sure how to even sign an autograph, Aaron took the pen from the kid and wrote, *Have a gr8t summer! Signed, Aaron,* and handed it back. The child took it and ran away, giddy with excitement.

Upon seeing this, others in the crowd started to push forward toward Aaron. Some began to run to try to get there first. Others began pushing their way through. Aaron was mortified and didn't know what to do.

WOOSH! "I've got you, sweetheart!" Darla's voice cut through the increasingly loud crowd as she swooped down and scooped Aaron into her arms.

"Thank you, Darla!" Aaron said, exasperated, as

they flew away. "That was crazy!"

They landed a few blocks away, and Darla turned her attention back to him. "You okay?"

"Yeah, I think so," Aaron replied.

"Good. Sorry about that. I was worried that might go haywire. The people of The Table have been waiting for over a week to find out more about this human who is actually a shimmer and a descendant who just showed up by coincidence. They have *a lot* of questions and are just really excited to learn as much about you as they can. . . . Okay, we are just a few blocks from home. Let's hoof it from here to avoid attracting attention. The rest of the family will meet us there. That was our Plan B if things got out of hand."

Aaron nodded and followed Darla down the street. As they walked, Darla filled him in on what had happened since Aaron went back to the overland.

"So, we have done a lot of research on the originals and why they sealed the vault in the first place. There were so many books down there! It was amazing, getting to read all the history. Oh! We found a letter inside the bubble that originally held the crown!"

"It's this way," Darla said and pointed for them to take a left onto Boulder Avenue. "Just a couple blocks straight down now."

Aaron nodded and turned to walk down the road. "So, you found a letter? Who was it from? What does it say?"

"Well, the letter states that there are four rooms in the back of the vault," Darla began.

"Oh yeah, I remember seeing those!" Aaron interjected.

"Yes, those four. Well, the letter states that each door leads to a room that is dedicated to an original."

"That's awesome!" exclaimed Aaron.

"There is more. The letter goes on to say that each descendant has a task that has been put before them by their ancestor, and they must accomplish it to prove themselves as true leaders. The originals had intended that, of the four descendants, one would be named king, and whoever that was would need to take on this quest that tests all the qualities of a king. They did not know which it would be, though, so they made one for each. . . . All right, home is right over there," Darla said as they stopped at a crosswalk.

She pointed across the street to the old but familiar apartment building. Aaron looked up at the structure and smiled, knowing he had a room up there.

While they waited for the *MOVE* sign to change, Darla continued. "Being that Steve was the 'real' winner of the crown and he decided he wanted The Table to continue as a majority-rule society, the elders have agreed with Steve that if the four descendants each complete their respective tasks as set aside by their ancestors, then The Table will accept their leadership and will add them as a part of the Elder Council."

Darla paused as they reached the front steps.

"So, umm, am I supposed to go on some sort of quest or something? Whoa," Aaron said.

Darla smiled. "Yes, but we have plenty of time to discuss that. Right now, we need to get you inside, dried off, and dressed for the celebration!"

She turned to walk inside. Aaron quickly grabbed the door for her, then followed her through.

"Umm, celebration?" Aaron asked as Darla pressed the button for the elevator.

"Yes," she replied as the elevator door opened and they walked inside. "It's an event where everyone gets to know you and the other descendants."

The door closed as Aaron processed all of the new information.

"The celebration will also be where the historians will put on a show to explain all of this a little more," Darla continued. "They have been practicing and are quite excited. . . . "

She trailed off as she could see the look of overwhelm on Aaron's face. "Hey, Aaron, look at me."

"Yes?"

"I know this is so much to take in right now, but please know the entire Dimeter family is here to support you. If you ever need anything, don't hesitate to ask, okay? We love you."

Tears began to well up in his eyes. "Thank you, Darla. Just thank you. I don't know what words to say to—"

DING! The elevator chime cut off Aaron. Darla gave him a quick side hug. "Not a worry, Aaron. We are happy you are back here with us."

The maroon carpet and white halls of the seventh floor felt like home to Aaron. It was only his second time there, but there was something about the Dimeters that made him feel so at ease. He loved it there. They headed past the doors for the other apartments until they came to a stop in front of 7C. Darla pulled her keys from her pocket with a small jingle.

SLAM! The door flew open, and Steve came barreling out, ready to smother Aaron in another giant bear hug. "They are home!" Steve shouted back into the apartment as he squeezed.

"Steve, *inside* voice," Darla reminded the giddy giant.

"Sorry, Mom," Steve said as he finally put Aaron down.

"Oof," Aaron sputtered. "Hello to you, too, Steve."

The apartment's front hallway was one of Aaron's favorite places in the entire community. He could see the happiness on the faces in all of the family photos covering the walls. They were photos filled with love. As he scanned the walls after closing the front door, he saw a new frame right smack in the middle. Above the frame it read *RESERVED FOR A NEW FAMILY PHOTO WITH AARON.*

Aaron's eyes immediately filled with tears, and he almost sobbed on the floor. He was overcome with emotion. *No one has ever wanted* me *in their photo. I normally get forgotten, but they put up a frame before they even have a photo. How did I find these amazing people?* Aaron's thoughts collided as he tried to hold back the tears.

"You okay, sweetheart?" Darla asked Aaron as he stared at the empty frame.

"Yeah. Umm, yep," Aaron said, wiping away the tears quickly so no one would notice.

Darla smiled a warm, knowing smile and patted him on the shoulder. "Let's go see the others."

They headed into the living room, where Vee was sitting on the couch writing in her journal.

"Hi, darling. Hey, Aaron," Phil's voice came from a room farther away. "I'm just in the back. Be right there!"

"Hi, Phil," Aaron replied. "Hello, Vee," he said with a more sarcastic tone.

Vee looked up from her journal, gave him a simple head nod, and then returned to writing.

"Aaron, you can take your backpack to your room and change into the clothes we laid out for you," Darla said. "We need to get to the celebration. Everyone is waiting for us."

Aaron nodded and headed down the hall. *My room. My own room that they want me to have. I love this place.*

"Dimeters, be ready to roll in fifteen minutes," Darla said with love, but also with the authority of a mother you don't want to cross.

4

GETTING READY FOR THE PARTY

Aaron opened the door to his room, and what he saw inside touched him. The entire space had been redecorated. The walls were a beautiful, brilliant blue, with white crown molding around the ceiling and floor. The bed even had a Dallas Cowboys bedspread!

How did they know my favorite team and my favorite colors?!

He scanned the rest of the room and spotted a small leatherbound journal with a neat-looking pen attached. He walked over to the side table it sat on and picked it up. Upon further inspection, the journal was a dark brownish-purple, and something like leather made up the cover. It was bound together in the middle with rope or twine. On the front, it had the word *ÚTIKÖNYV* carved into the cover. *What is this?*

As he pondered the book, Phil's voice broke the silence. "Hey there! Looks like you found Penelope's guidebook!"

"Ahh! . . . Sorry, Phil. You snuck up on me. What's that about Penelope's . . . guidebook, did you say?"

"Didn't mean to startle you, but yep. You are

holding what we have been referring to as Penelope's Guidebook. Remember how there were several books down there in the vault? Well, the historians found a book from each original intended for their descendant. Each looks similar to the one you are holding, but the name on the front is in that original's native tongue. The word on the front of that book translates from Hungarian directly to "guidebook" in English.

"Oh yeah, Penelope was Hungarian!" Aaron said, excited to finally understand a few things around there. "So, what's in it?"

"We think it's a guide or journal from the original to their descendant," Phil said. "However, once it is opened by a descendant, it can only be opened by that person from then on. We learned that bit after Steve opened his."

Aaron eyed the journal with even more curiosity.

"That's why we left Penelope's here for you—so that when you arrived, you could open it and it would be attached to you," Phil continued.

Aaron smiled. *Is this what it feels like to be important? What is in this thing, and how does it work? How does it know it's me and not someone else?*

"I have so many questions—" Aaron began.

"Ten minutes left, Dimeters!" Darla interrupted from the living room.

"I know you do, son. I promise the coronation and the presentation the historians have will explain all of this. But right now, you need to get changed and we need to get going. Most of The Table is waiting for us," Phil said with a smile. "I know it's a lot, but please just go ahead and open the book so we know it will be attached to you. Trying to keep the historians' grubby hands off it while we waited for you was a pain—don't want to mess it up now. I have to go change my shirt, so I'll see you in the living room in ten!"

Aaron sat down on the bed, took a deep breath, and looked down at the book in his lap.

Okay, Penelope, what did you want me to see?

He picked up the book and examined the mechanism that kept it closed. It seemed to be just a plain leathery strap across the top with a push-button clasp. He gripped the small piece of strap on the other side of the button and pulled it up. *POP!* The button clasp came apart, and he began to open the front cover.

FLASH! A brilliant light exploded off the first pages and temporarily blinded Aaron.

"Ahh, my eyes!" he screamed.

"You okay, buddy?" Steve yelled from down the hall.

"What? Umm, yeah, I think so. I'm not sure what just happened," Aaron was a little wobbly and confused.

"Five minutes, Dimeters!" Darla's voice burned through the fog in Aaron's brain like a lighthouse beacon on the shoreline.

Oh no! I haven't changed! Aaron closed the journal and set it down. *I will have to look at that more later.*

On the back of a chair in the corner, he saw a nice navy polo with a small white insignia in the top left corner. It looked like some white wavy lines. Also on the chair were a pair of khaki slacks and some shiny dress shoes. *These clothes are too nice for me. I can't. . . . You don't have time for this. Just put them on!*

Aaron quickly got dressed so he didn't disappoint

Darla. As he was putting on his new favorite hat, he turned and looked at himself in the mirror.

Umm, not exactly me, but these clothes are so fancy. I have to *be careful.*

"Aaron, honey, we are leaving!" Darla said from the living room.

"Sorry! I am coming!" He tossed on the shoes, grabbed his guidebook, and headed to the door.

"Do the clothes and shoes fit?" Darla asked as he walked into the living room. Before he could answer, she stopped him in his tracks and spun him in a circle to inspect his look. "Oh, they do! That is great! I wasn't sure on the sizes, but they look great!"

Aaron turned a bit red, as people don't normally compliment him. "Umm, yes they do. Thank you," he said sheepishly.

"Looking good, bro!" Steve added from the couch.

"Thanks, dude! You don't look too shabby yourself!"

Steve's outfit was similar to Aaron's; his polo was purple, though, and his white insignia looked like a large sledgehammer. Everything else matched, right down to the best friends Elfwater hats. Aaron smiled, seeing that Steve had his on as well.

"So, what is the meaning of these polos, and why is Steve's different than mine?" Aaron's curiosity couldn't be contained.

"We will talk about it in the car," Darla said. "We are really late, and we need to get going. I promise I will answer all the questions I can."

Aaron smiled, nodded understandingly.

"Okay, everyone to the elevator!" Darla commanded.

5

DRIVING AND ANSWERING

Once the elevator doors opened at the basement floor, they all rushed over to the Suburban and piled in. Phil was driving this time, with Darla in the passenger seat, Aaron and Vee in the middle row, and Steve taking up the entire rear seat. Once they were all buckled, Phil maneuvered their way out of the parking garage.

"Okay, the park is not too far from here," Phil said. "It recently opened up on the other side of the city. The elders wanted to use this as an opportunity to show it off and get people interested in using the new facilities. Should be a quick fifteen-minute drive."

"Now that we are on the road," Darlan began, "you asked about the polos, Aaron?"

"Yeah. Why do they look similar but have different colors and insignias?" Aaron asked.

"The colors are representative of the originals' race and home origin. Purple represents the giant race, and their sledgehammer symbol signifies their unmatched strength. Green is the dwarven race, and their anvil symbol represents how naturally gifted they are with creating armor and weapons. Red is the dragon race, and their fire symbol represents the passion that burns inside of them for the fight. Blue is your race, and its seaweed symbol is to represent nature, but also their love of water."

"Oh, it's seaweed!" Aaron exclaimed. "Sorry."

"I promise you I understand. It's exciting, but also overwhelming. The insignias are the official branding for each race. Anything you see that symbol on," Darla said as she gestured toward his left lapel, "belongs to or was built by the shimmers. Same with the giants and so on."

"So, they are like a royal crest?" Aaron asked.

"Yes, you got it!" Darla replied.

"Okay, here is our exit. Only about five minutes now," Phil announced to his passengers.

Aaron, knowing his time was growing short to ask all the questions he had been holding onto, started blurting out as many as he could.

"So, you said when I left that Bart and Shamus had been taken into custody. What are they going to do with those two positions? Is someone going to take their place? Who are the historians? What is this journal thing? Have the others read their journals? Where did these crests come from?"

"Take a deep breath. The historians' presentation will explain most all of those things. I can answer the question of whether they are replacing those two morons, though, and the simple answer is yes. They are being replaced, but with whom, we don't know yet. That's part of what is being announced today at the celebration." Darla winked at Aaron, and he nodded.

"We're here!" Phil said as they pulled into a parking

lot filled to the brim with vehicles. "Glad they saved us a spot."

Aaron looked out the window for the first time on this drive. As he peered out, the beautiful green landscape seemed to go on forever. Right outside the car was an enormous park, much like the one downtown that held the vault, but twice as large. This one also wasn't surrounded by apartments and high-rises; it was instead open air up to the top of the giant domed cavern.

"Let's head up to the main stage," Phil said, pointing past the oversized rootwood sign that read *PENELOPE PARK* in giant blue letters and had the seaweed symbol on either side.

"Last one there is a rotten dragon egg!" Steve yelled to Aaron as he took off.

"Hey, no fair!" Aaron shouted as he gave chase. "You got a head start!"

Darla and Phil watched the boys run off, then looked at each other with contentment before leaning in to kiss.

"Eww, gross, Mom and Dad! Save it for later, please!" lamented a disgusted Vee.

Darla and Phil chuckled and gave a sarcastic apology as they tried to catch up to the boys.

6

THE CELEBRATION

"I'm going to get you, Steve!" Aaron yelled as best friend sprinted down the path ahead of him.

Steve was doing his best to keep it close. He was known for his ability to run long distances, but he also wasn't going to lose to Aaron. "Oh no, you won't! I am going to win—"

SMACK! Steve ran directly into one of the historians, who was walking around a blind corner. Books and papers flew everywhere, as did the historian.

"Oof! Ouch!" the historian garbled as he tumbled to the grass.

"Oh no! I am so sorry!" cried Steve, who tried frantically to pick up all the books and give them back to the man still was too disoriented to stand up.

"It's okay. It's okay. Ugh . . . you hit like a freight train, son," the historian said.

"Well, hello there, Barry. I am so sorry," Phil said to the historian as he and Darla walked up. "Hopefully, they didn't hurt you. You know how kids can be."

"Not a worry, Phil. I remember when you and I would race to see who could get to the playground the quickest at recess. We ran into plenty of people in our time."

Both men chuckled at the thought, then came back to reality.

"Boys, this is Barry, our head historian and one of the eleven elders. He also happens to be one of my best friends from the old days. We grew up together and were inseparable. But one day, Barry was selected to go to the historians' academy, which is a huge honor for anyone from The Table, and one that not many get. I moved on to a job as a sanitation specialist, and we kind of just drifted apart since our professions didn't really have our paths crossing until—"

"Until you, Aaron!" exclaimed Barry. "So, you are the great Aaron who defeated the Blackwings?"

Aaron looked the historian up and down. He was a man of average height with skin that was darker than Aaron's, closer to a golden brown. Barry had short black hair that was freshly cut in a military style and a jet-black goatee on his chin. His square, black-framed glasses matched his suit, which was complemented by a simple white shirt and a beautiful orange tie. On the left lapel of the suit jacket, embroidered in orange, was what looked like a small book .

"Umm, yep. I am Aaron," squeaked out the bashful shimmer.

"Oh, son, it is so nice to finally meet you! We were so excited to learn about you," spouted the excited historian. "We have an entire presentation set up for you that we are anxious to get to perform!"

Barry must have realized he was gushing by the blank stare on Aaron's face. "I mean . . . we are very excited you are here. If you all would head directly on up this path, you can be seated and our program can begin."

"You got it, Barry! It was great to see you. I am excited for those drinks next week!" Phil replied as he motioned for the family to continue on.

"Wow!" Aaron whispered as they crested the top of the path. Before them was a semicircle amphitheater with stone benches that went down five levels to a small pit in front of a beautiful black stone stage. It reminded him of the park with the vault. A giant sign hung above the stage, with what looked like a cloth covering it. Aaron looked around the place, and it was *packed* with every type of creature he could imagine. As he looked at all of the different species and races that filled the crowd, a revelation came to him. *Umm, I know all of them.*

That is a dragonkin; their home is in the volcanoes of what the overworld refers to as Italy. His mind raced. *Wait, how did I know that last part?*

He looked into the crowd again, this time landing on a tiny family of what he could only have previously described as "winged people." But now, his mind flipped like a rolodex and the thoughts came before he could stop them. *Those are centurions; they are known for their loyalty and their strong fighting spirit. They are known to get violent when someone mentions their small size.*

"Tickets, please!" barked a small gargoyle in a maroon and gold attendant's uniform. The name *SUNNY* was written in gold pen on his name badge.

Aaron snapped out of his daydream, shaking his head. "Umm, what? Sorry."

The gargoyle doubled down. "Tickets, please!"

Darla stepped forward and addressed the gargoyle directly. "Royals don't need tickets."

She then cleared her throat and spoke loud enough for the entire amphitheater to hear. "Presenting your royal descendant, Sir Steve of the giants!" When she pointed to Steve, the crowd cheered in approval.

"Presenting your royal descendant, Sir Aaron of the shimmers!" The crowd cheered again, but they seemed a little quieter, like they weren't sure what to make of Aaron just yet.

The Dimeter family made their way down the stairs through the middle of the amphitheater and directly to the stage. It had four empty chairs at center stage with a podium off to one side. Standing at the podium, beaming with pride, was Barry.

Phil and Darla turned to the boys. "Okay, you two head on up there, and we will be right here in the front row," Phil said. Darla pointed to their reserved seats in the family area.

Aaron looked at Steve and nodded. No one needed to tell either boy whose seat was whose. Each seat had the color of the original and their crest on its back. As soon as the boys stepped onto the stage, Barry spoke into the microphone.

"Ladies and gentlemen, two of your four original descendants! Let's hear it for them!" The crowd replied with thunderous applause. "Okay, let's get this show on the road!"

As soon as he said those words, the stage lights dimmed, and vapors from fog machines on the sides began to fill the air.

"Welcome to the celebration of the descendants!" Barry exclaimed.

With a flash, all the lights went out. It was completely dark.

KABOOM! Fireworks exploded in the sky above the park—red, blue, green, and purple balls of light just below the beautiful cavern roof.

"This place never stops amazing me!" Aaron shouted as he stared into the sky.

"Just wait! The magicians are about to perform," Steve whisper-yelled to Aaron as he leaned closer.

"Magicians? Like real magicians?" Aaron asked. His mind filled with images of Merlin, magic wands, and everything else he could remember from the fairy tales he'd read when he was younger.

"Yep! They are amazing at magic!" Steve whisper-yelled back. "Look!"

He pointed to the front of the stage, where five people dressed like Barry had joined the announcer onstage. The fireworks subsided, and the lights came up slightly, thought it was still pretty dim on the stage.

"The Society of History and Magic would like to thank you all for coming to our performance this evening!" Barry's voice rang out through the speakers. He gestured to the other five people on the stage, and they all bowed to a great cheer.

"As you can see in your programs, we have a lot to get to this evening. So, let's kick it off with a bit of . . . *magic*!" As he said that, he threw something on the ground and a puff of white smoke covered the stage for a few seconds.

Everything went silent.

Aaron's anticipation was at an all-time high. *Real magic. I get to see real magic!* His eyes strained to see through the smoke, and he began to hear music.

The rest of the lights burst on, and the music grew even louder, and the crowd started clapping along. He could barely make out a few figures in the smoke.

SWOOSH! Barry came sprinting through the smoke and slid right down the middle of the stage to the very front, impressively in time with the music. He was sporting a shiny orange sequined vest with a white handkerchief in the front pocket. On the back of the vest was the same book symbol from his jacket lapel. He also had on some sort of microphone headset.

"Here we go!" Steve hollered excitedly as he clapped along with the beat.

"Are y'all ready? I can't *hear* you!" Barry amped up the audience even more.

Aaron smiled. *Wow . . . even real magicians like to make an entrance!*

"For this first illusion, I will need a volunteer from the audience," Barry said as he scanned the crowd.

People all over the stands raised their hands. Cries of "Pick me!" could be heard through the entire park.

"I wonder if the newest member of our society would like to give it a try." Barry turned to look at Aaron. "Sir, would you like to help me with this one?"

He gestured for the boy to join him at the front of the stage. The crowd went wild for that idea.

Aaron smiled. "Okay! That sounds fun!" He got up from his seat and walked to meet Barry at the front.

"Stand here for me, please." Barry moved Aaron over a bit.

"For this, I am going to need you to memorize something for me," Barry said with a smile. "Can you do that?"

Aaron was a little confused, but not terribly so. "Sure."

"Here we go!" Barry reached into his pocket and pulled out a deck of cards.

Aaron was taken aback. *I was expecting something more . . . magical.*

"Now, I want you to pick any card in this deck. Don't show me, but show the audience and then put it back, okay? Remember, don't show me anything," Barry instructed as he fanned out the cards.

"Okay," said Aaron. *Jack of Hearts. That's easy to remember.*

He looked at Barry, who then looked away from the audience in a magnanimous way. He showed the card to the crowd, which rang out with oohs and ahhs for a few seconds. He turned the card back face-down in his palm.

"All done? Now, could you please put it back into the stack?" Barry said as he fanned the cards back out and looked away.

Aaron slid the card into the middle of the deck.

"There is no way I could know what card he selected, right?" Barry asked into his headset while he flamboyantly shuffled the cards.

He then held the deck in front of him, toward Aaron.

"Aaron, I need you to gently tap the cards in my hand, but be careful not to knock them out because that could ruin the trick. I'm trusting you here, okay?"

Barry said, unable to hold back a slight smile.

Aaron looked at Barry curiously, but agreed. He reached out gently and tapped the side of the cards in Barry's outstretched hand.

"Oh no!" Barry yelled dramatically as the cards went flying as if Aaron had hit them with a gust of wind. Barry ran in circles, pretending to be in a panic.

"Aaron, what did you do? It's ruined." He was unable to fully hide his grin.

"Umm, I am sorry. I guess?" Aaron mumbled.

Barry stumbled over to Aaron, looking like he was crying. Barry pulled Aaron in for a hug while sobbing and mumbling. After a few seconds of that, he pulled back.

"Oh wait!" Barry yelled in his dramatic fashion. "I think . . . there is something . . . in Aaron's pocket!"

He leapt back and pointed to the boy's front right slacks pocket.

The crowd let out a collective gasp.

Aaron glanced around and smiled, then reached into his pocket and pulled out the item inside. As he revealed it to the crowd, the card was in fact the Jack of Hearts.

The crowd went crazy at the sight. Everyone hooted and hollered like they had seen a miracle. Barry bowed to Aaron and gestured for him to return to his seat.

That was just a simple card trick, Aaron thought as he walked back.

"How awesome was that?" Steve asked as Aaron returned.

"Yeah, it was pretty cool," Aaron replied, a bit

dejected over the lack of real magic. They had these tricks in the overworld.

Barry and the rest of the historians performed a few more feats of "magic." They sawed a "volunteer" from the audience in half, did more card tricks, and then finished with Barry making his assistant "disappear" inside a box after saying the magic words.

Steve had been at the edge of his seat the entire time. "This is my favorite part," he hollered when Barry waved his magic wand over the front of the box that held the assistant. Smoke puffed from the bottom in a small explosion that almost covered the noise of the trap door opening in the stage.

Aaron looked at Steve and smiled. *Eh, look how happy he is. It's okay that magic isn't real here either. I was just excited that it might be.*

"Thank you! Thank you! You are too kind!" Barry's words cut into Aaron's thoughts, and the descendant looked back to the front of the stage.

7

HISTORY

"That concludes the entertainment portion of the evening," Barry announced, breathing a bit heavy from his performance. The lights went black for a few seconds, and music rumbled from beneath the stage. A spotlight turned on, lighting up the left front corner of the stage. There stood a beautiful reddish rootwood podium with a microphone and a small light, fancier than the first one of the night. Barry was standing behind it, dressed in what looked to be traditional robes of some sort.

"Now, onto the history portion of the celebration!" Barry shared in a grand way while waving his hands in front of him. As he did, he began chanting something that Aaron could not understand in a low tone. Then, the other five historians appeared behind him, dressed in the same robes, and began chanting as well. The air above center stage swirled.

What is happening? Aaron looked to Steve for answers, but he seemed bored by the swirling vortex in front of them.

"Holy cow! What is that?" Aaron asked with a hint of terror in his voice.

"Oh, that? That's just the memory reel the historians are conjuring up," Steve answered nonchalantly, but with a smile nonetheless.

The chanting got louder, and the vortex swirling out even bigger.

Aaron leaned back over. "They are doing a what with a what?"

"They are conjuring up a—"

CRACK! What looked like a giant movie screen appeared from the air directly above center stage.

"A memory reel? Yeah, that," Steve said, pointing.

Aaron was lost, staring at this mystical screen.

"A memory reel is something that pieces together memories of our ancestors from books and journals we have, and it plays them like a movie," the giant explained. "It's one of the coolest powers the historians have."

"So, they really *are* magicians?" Aaron blurted out.

Steve smirked. "Of course, dude!"

"Umm, is this thing on?" A female voice came across the microphone.

Aaron snapped out of his daze and looked across the stage at the podium.

There stood a dragon lady that looked almost identical to Darla, with green scaly skin, long brown hair, and bright blue eyes. This dragon lady looked to be a few years younger, though, and was wearing blue slacks and a rainbow tie dye T-shirt that said *I'M HERE TO LEARN* on the front. She had square brown-rimmed glasses and wore an orange kerchief around her neck.

"Umm," the new dragon lady continued. "Hello! I am Liz the Learned, and I will be commentating along with this memory reel. You see, from what the historians have gathered . . ."

She swiped her hand in front of her face. The large screen thing came to life and focused in in on a picture until everyone could clearly see the four originals discussing something in the vault. "They have been able to compile a few short memory reels that, when pieced together, explain what took place so many years ago and what the original intent was for The Table. This first memory reel is from the day they closed the vault."

She reached out in front of her and pressed an invisible button, causing the screen to play the reel.

"Then it's agreed!" A soft, but firm, feminine voice came across the speakers.

Aaron stared at the screen in shock. There, right in front of them on the screen, was his ancestor Penelope the Peaceful! He knew her immediately because he recognized her from The Mural!

The memory reel felt like a home movie that one of them had shot on a handheld camcorder, except there was no one filming.

"How are they doing this?" Aaron whispered to Steve.

"The historians have some way of making it with magic. They lay the items out around them and then chant the same—"

"Yes, I agree, too!" A loud, booming voice from the speakers stopped Steve mid-sentence. Both boys looked up to see the face of Richard the Righteous filling up the screen. He was twice the size of any of the other originals, but had the most welcoming face. He was more than twelve feet tall and at least six feet wide. He wore a simple purple T-shirt with the hammer emblem on the left chest, a massive pair of blue jeans, and the biggest pair of work boots Aaron had ever seen!

"Yeah! It's Richard!" Steve couldn't take his eyes off the screen. They filled with tears as his ancestor continued.

"All of those in favor of The Trial of the King, say aye."

All four of the originals raised their hands and resounded "aye" collectively.

"Then it's agreed," confirmed Daryl the Destroyer. "We will each leave a task for our descendant to do once he has become king to prove his worth—"

"Or she," cut in Brenda the Bold. "He or she."

"Ah yes, sorry. He or she," continued Daryl. "To prove their worth as king or queen, we agree that we each must create a task for our descendants as we do not know which will become the ruler."

"And that task must include a trip to the original's homeland to first be tested by their own people," chimed in Penelope. "A leader must know about their people before they can lead."

"Yes, that!" added Richard. "That is very important to me. The giant race is proud, and I want anyone who is leading them and The Table to know where we all come from."

"Well, let's hope this entire idea works out the least bit. This is all in hopes that our descendants one day make it back here, don't die in The Trial of the King, and then can work this out better than we could!" Penelope had out some frustration in her voice.

"Well, if Richard would just listen to me and take

responsibility for what he did!" Daryl snarled.

"What *I* did? It was an accident!" Richard angrily hollered back.

"Was it, though?" Daryl replied with fire escaping his lips.

"What about you, Daryl? I did nothing, compared to the torture you do to people day in and day out."

SPLASH! A stream of water smashed into both angry originals' faces. The streams came from Penelope's hands as she yelled at them. "Enough, you two!"

The screen paused, and Liz's voice came back across the speakers.

"Unfortunately, that is all we could gather from that day's events, but as you can see, there were a lot of tension and trust issues within the original four. So, each original has created a 'rite of passage' for their descendant. From what we can tell, the originals never intended there to be an Unknown.

The crowd that had been mostly silent let out a series of shocked gasps at the new information.

Steve and Aaron had been staring at the screen, captivated by their royal ancestors.

"This next reel is one that we discussed leaving out, but felt it was important as it tells a huge part of The Table's history," Liz said. "We apologize to anyone who is bothered by its graphic nature."

Steve and Aaron exchanged confused looks, and Aaron mouthed, "Graphic?" to Steve. He shrugged, and they both looked back to the screen.

Liz swiped her hand in front of her again, and the screen changed somewhat. The new reel was still in the vault. Liz pressed the invisible play button again, and the screen came to life.

This time, the vault was empty and darker. They saw a giant outline come walking into the frame. The screen paused, and Liz's voice came back across the microphone.

"This next part is a bit fuzzy, as we can't find anyone who witnessed it. It's just what people wrote happened in their journals that day." She then pressed the play button again.

The outline became clear. They could see Richard the Righteous, but his face and body were charred to a crisp. Penelope ran from the room, sobbing. Brenda and Daryl came into focus in the background. They were talking, but could not be heard. Neither look distraught, but instead panicked, like they broke a window playing ball inside the house.

The screen flickered and changed to the room where The Mural is. Daryl, Penelope, and Brenda stood in front of the painting of Richard the Righteous.

The speakers blared with the sound of Penelope's voice. "So, we are in agreement?" she said. "No one ever needs to know what actually took place that day. None of us will write it in our journals or ever tell a soul. Richard's death would cause too many issues, and we could never explain it to the rest of the giants if they knew the truth."

"Agreed," the other two said in unison.

The screen flickered and changed once more. It showed a large stage with a pulpit bearing a giant picture of Richard's face on the front, just above a huge rootwood box. Behind the pulpit was Penelope, but this time she was dressed in a somber black outfit. Behind her on the stage where four chairs equal distance apart from the middle. The one on the far left had the emblem of the sledgehammer on it; in its seat lay a beautiful bouquet of purple flowers. Next to that chair was an empty one that had the shimmer symbol of seaweed, and Brenda and Daryl were seated in the other two.

"We are here today to mourn the loss of one the greatest people to ever live, Richard the Righteous," Penelope said.

The screen flickered, and Penelope was seen talking to what looked like a female version of Richard. The woman was ten feet tall and had the same rough skin Steve did.

"Please reconsider, Whitney. We love the giant race, and The Table is safe for everyone." Penelope seemed to be pleading with the giant woman. "We will protect you all!"

"Like you protected Richard?" Whitney asked with steel in her eyes. "Penelope, it is not safe here for giants. We are going back to the homelands. The Table is being overrun by dragons who hate giants. With fire being our biggest weakness and the suspicious nature of Richard's death . . . no one really knows what happened, but we know he was alive when you four went into the vault. Now, he's not! That was the last straw. We have been oppressed by the dragonkin long enough. As the new leader of the giants, I declare that we will no longer be part of The Table."

Whitney turned away from Penelope sharply and walked away.

Aaron noticed tears streaming down Steve's face. *This must be so much for Steve to take in. So, what did happen to Richard, and what does all of this mean?*

The screen flickered and changed again. "We should just remove Richard's line from the succession plan completely," Daryl snarled as the screen showed them all standing in front of Richard's mural again. "There are too many questions already! Let's just remove him so they will eventually stop asking!"

Brenda came into view. "I've been thinking about this, too. How can we keep order and keep everything we have already planned in place for the succession?"

She waved to someone off-screen. "Azooz, come here! Everyone, this is Abdulaziz, or Azooz for short. He is a historian that can help us with the Richard issue."

A man that looked almost identical to Barry approached. Daryl and Penelope looked him over skeptically.

"What can *he* do for *us*?" Daryl asked sarcastically.

Brenda smiled. "Watch," she said as she turned to Azooz. "Go ahead."

Azooz stepped in front of Richard's mural, put his hands into the air, and chanted.

The picture on the mural slowly began to swirl counterclockwise. The color faded until all that was left swirling was a black circle. The name *RICHARD THE RIGHTEOUS* had been replaced with *THE UNKNOWN*.

Penelope read the words and looked at Brenda. "The Unknown? What does that mean? How does this help with our problem?"

Brenda looked up at them. "Well, now we don't

have to change anything in the future plans we already have set. We have already done all this work to set up the future, so let's not completely remove Richard. That would cause too many questions, right? People would want to know what happened to him for the rest of time in The Table. But if we use this incantation to seal away the original mural, then the only way for this to be revealed is if the descendant of Richard was found in the future. However, the giants have sworn to never come back. We can keep all plans in place and not have to worry about anyone ever finding out."

As she finished speaking, she had a bright smile, full of pride in her idea.

Penelope and Daryl looked both intrigued and also very skeptical.

"But umm, what about the king trial? We set the vault to only work if all four are there," Penelope pointed out.

"Yeah, but that's an easy change to make. We can give the elders an extra key to the vault and let them know that as a backup plan, in case not all the lines survive, they can use the fourth key to open the vault . . . or something along those lines."

The screen paused, and Liz spoke up. "A lot to unpack in that! We don't have all the information by any means, and we still don't really know what happened to Richard the Righteous. We do now know a little more about why there was The Unknown and what the original four had intended with the succession plan."

She paused for a quick minute to let everyone take in what they saw and heard. "We know that Steve—"

Cheers erupted from the crowd when she said Steve's name, so she waited for it to calm down. "We know that Steve won the trial of the king, but made the decision with the elders to continue The Table as a majority-rule society and to give the other descendants equal say to his."

Another round of cheers came through, and Liz smiled.

"Because of this, though, the elders did not think it fair for Steve alone to have to prove himself a worthy leader. They have agreed that each descendant must go on the journey set aside by their ancestor, and not only that, but they also all have to go together to learn from each other's cultures and embrace the differences therein!" Liz said that last bit with way more enthusiasm than the crowd or anyone would have thought to use.

The crowd cheered softly, then went silent. Liz's face turned a bit red.

Barry came up to the podium from offstage and jumped in. "Okay, well thank you so much, Liz! We appreciate you doing that."

Liz looked up out of her slight panic and mouthed a thank you to Barry as she exited the stage.

8

THE SELECTIONS

"Okay, folks! It's time for the part of the evening you all have been waiting for! That's right: The selection of the two new descendants!"

The crowd whooped and celebrated louder than they had for anything else that evening.

Aaron looked at Steve, shaking his head. "This is crazy!"

Steve just smiled and nodded.

The lights on the stage strobed. With a large puff of smoke, the podium was gone and Barry had changed back into his suit and tie.

"Ladies and gentlemen, are you ready for the selections? I can't *hear* you!" He paced the stage as he shouted. "For the selection of Brenda the Bold's descendant, the elders have spoken, and with ninety-one percent of the vote, they selected . . ."

Barry pulled an envelope from his pocket and slowly opened it. He looks at the crowd one last time before pulling out the piece of paper concealed inside. He read it and smiled. "You know her. You love her. It's Emily the Elite!"

When those words left his lips, the crowd rose to its feet. They went berserk with chants of "Emily! Emily! Emily!"

Aaron looked over at Steve with question in his eyes and spoke over the sounds of the cheers.

"Who is Emily the Elite?"

Steve tried to explain, but the lights dimmed again and a spotlight burned through the darkness, scanning the crowd until it finally found its target. Bathed in the light was a woman about four feet tall with broad shoulders and muscles bulging from all directions out of her hot pink tank top. She had massive biceps that she flexed for her fans. The words on her tank—*STRONG IS NOT WRONG*—waved in the slight breeze. She wore black and teal biker shorts and white Nike high tops to complete her ensemble. Her long, brown hair was pulled back in a messy ponytail.

Steve leaned over to Aaron. "There is Emily. She is great at everything . . . like, everything. She is awesome! She is the current champion of The Table!"

Aaron looked even more confused.

"Oh, yeah! We have a yearly compctition that tests a person's physical and mental strength, and she won last year! It's called The Contest of Champions. Wow, here she comes!"

He pointed to Emily, who was walking through the crowd toward the stage. Steve waved to Emily as she went up the stage steps, but she didn't seem to notice.

Barry was waiting there to meet her. "Emily, tell us how it feels to be selected for this great honor!" He shoved the microphone into the champion's face.

"Well, it feels good to be able to make my family

and my kind proud. Shamus was a turd, and it feels good to be able to have a chance to clear our name and show The Table what the dwarven race is made of!" Emily flexed her muscles. "Huzzah!"

Barry pulled the microphone back before Emily busted the sound system with her shockingly impressive volume.

"Okay . . . well, thank you, Emily. Go get comfortable, and we'll get to the next pick."

Emily turned and waved to the crowd once more, then headed to her seat.

"Hi, Emily!" Steve blurted out as he waved wildly at her. "Huge fan!"

Aaron blushed with embarrassment for his best friend when Emily looked his way. He smiled a sheepish smile and waved a small wave. Emily waved back to both and whispered, "This is gonna be awesome!" She smiled and took her seat.

"And now, the second of the two selections. Are you ready?" Barry played to the crowd, and again the crowd roared in response. "All right! Here . . . we . . . go!"

He reached into his coat pocket and pulled out another small envelope. "With a little lower but still impressive seventy-three percent of the votes, the elders have selected . . . "

He looked at the piece of paper from inside the envelope. "Well, well, well, if isn't our very own Liz the Learned!"

The stage lights went out again, and the spotlight started its path through the audience to locate its next target. It darted all over the place until someone from the audience yelled. "She is over here!" The spotlight rushed to the voice, and Liz was there, holding her hand up to the blinding light.

"Umm, there must have been a mistake. I, umm, didn't put in for this. Yeah, sorry. I don't—"

The crowd's chants of "Liz! Liz! Liz!" were too loud for anyone to hear Liz's protests. They weren't taking no for an answer, and those around her started collectively pushing her toward the stage.

"Liz, get on up here!" Barry insisted. "You are the next dragonkin royal!"

She finally gave in and walked to meet Barry.

"Tell us, Liz: How does it feel to be selected?" Barry inquired as he put the microphone to her face.

"Umm, I don't really know why I am here. I didn't even sign up for this. I think there may been a mistake of some sort." Liz looked shaken up.

Barry seemed just as puzzled as Liz, but he knew the show must continue. "What a jokester! You know that everyone in the bloodline for the originals was an option."

"No, I did not."

Barry forced a smile, but Aaron could tell he was frustrated. "What a kidder, this lady! All right, head on up to your chair so we can get the first picture of the new royal four of The Table."

She nervously eyed the others onstage as she walked toward the seat with the fire emblem. Aaron, Steve, and Emily all waved hello to her and smiled. She looked around the audience again, as if pleading for someone to stop her from taking the role.

"Please go ahead and have a seat, Liz. We need to take the photo," Barry said with a hint of irritation in his voice as he pointed to the photographer who had joined them onstage.

Liz looked up at the camera man to mouth a silent apology, then took her seat.

All four of them looked at the camera and smiled. Each face told a different story: Excitement, anticipation, or fear for what lay ahead of them. The crowd cheered as the picture was immediately posted up on the screen for all to see. Fireworks went off above them again in the originals' colors—purple, red, blue, and green explosions of light flashed against the black rock ceiling of The Table's great cavern.

"Fellow Vendegeks, welcome your four royals!" Barry exclaimed. He pointed up the stage, then joined the applause of the audience, now on its feet.

As the crowd quieted down, Barry brought the microphone to his mouth again. "Well, that concludes our program for this evening, folks. You don't have to go home, but you can't stay here," he said with a chuckle. "But seriously, if you would like a picture of the four together, we will keep the front of the stage available for the next five minutes for pictures."

He looked back at the four and covered the mic. "I promise I will get them out of here after five minutes. Just smile and wave."

Vendegeks of all shapes and sizes mobbed the front of the stage, with camera flashes going off rapidly. Aaron couldn't see much of anything. He just tried to smile and wave, like Barry had instructed.

They sat there for what felt like forever, but Barry spoke up exactly as the five minutes eclipsed. "All right! That's it! The stage area and the park will be closing for royals, their family, and personnel only. We want to say thank you again for coming out to this new park, and we hope to see you at the next city event!"

Most of the audience slowly dissipated, but several people lingered at the front of the stage requesting photos with their favorite descendant. It was mostly Emily that people wanted photos with, but there were some for Steve, too. Many seemed intrigued by the giant and the drama that had just unfolded onscreen.

Aaron smiled at the attention Steve was getting. *Yes! Show them how awesome you and the giants are!*

He looked over to Steve, excited to see his giant, dopey smile. Except he wasn't smiling at all.

"Steve, you okay?" Aaron asked, since his best friend looked like someone had punched him right in the gut.

"Hey! Buddy! You okay?" This time, it was a little more direct and louder to get the attention of the giant staring off into the cavern sky.

Steve looked down at Aaron and blinked his eyes a few times. "Umm, yeah. Yeah. We can talk about it later."

Aaron could tell his best friend was in fact not okay, but he also knew this was not the best place to dig into it. "All right."

"I'm so proud of you boys!" Darla boomed as she leapt up the steps. She grabbed Aaron and Steve and pulled them to her for a hug, wrapping each in a wing. "Great job! You both did so well! I bet you have a million questions, Aaron. . . . And you too, Steve. We had not seen the memory reels before tonight, either. That was a lot to take in."

She sighed as she looked to her son. Her eyes said

she knew he had to be reeling inside.

Steve nodded and struggled to smile. This confirmed her suspicion.

"Are you sure you're okay, sweetheart?" She didn't want to make it worse by pushing too much.

'Yeah, just thinking about some stuff," Steve mumbled.

"There are my guys!" Phil came bounding over from where he was talking to Barry. He gave both the boys a quick hug. "I am so proud of y'all! I am blown away by everything that just happened. What do you two think?"

Aaron looked over to Steve, who had plastered on a fake-but-convincing smile.

"It's definitely a lot to take in," Steve said and flashed his fake smile again.

Aaron, worried about hurting Steve, went along with the ruse.

"Yeah, what Steve said. There is just so much to process from this."

Darla and Phil's faces had turned to worried, so he kept talking. "But man, am I excited! And yeah, Darla, I have at least two million questions."

Both parents seemed calmed by that, and their smiles returned. "Well, let's get home and get some rest," Darla said.

9

EXPLANATION

"Hello, descendants!" Barry shouted after turning off his microphone.

Aaron looked around and realized the amphitheater was almost empty, and the other families had joined them onstage. Emily had at least ten people there with her—an entire entourage! On the other side, Liz only had a few people. It was maybe a brother or friend and her parents.

"Thank you all for being here! We are excited for each of you to begin your journeys as soon as you can," Barry continued. "Now, to cover a few things we did not discuss in the presentation."

Darla raised her hand to ask a question.

"Please hold all questions until the end," Barry said quickly. "As we said, each descendant is now responsible for completing their journey as set before them by their original. We also agreed that they should take these journeys as a group to learn from each other's cultures, but also to ensure their safety with numbers. On that topic, we do have another announcement to make. Seeing as each descendant is under the age of eighteen—"

"Hey! I will be eighteen in three months!" Liz bellowed from the side of the stage.

Barry smiled, but his eyes showed that he was not happy about being cut off.

"Yes, as I was saying . . . because each descendant is a minor, we wanted to make sure they had adult chaperones on their journey. Everyone, meet your chaperones." Barry pointed to Phil and Darla, who smiled and waved.

"Awesome!" the Dimeter boys said in unison.

Darla and Phil smiled again, even wider this time after seeing how excited the boys were about the news.

"Mom! Dad! Why didn't you tell us?" Steve demanded.

"We couldn't, sweetheart. They asked us not to," Darla answered.

Barry tapped his foot while waiting for them to finish. "Yes, yes, we are excited for the Dimeter family. The two of them volunteered to supervise these expeditions, and the elders could not think of anyone more protective or responsible. Now, there is also a matter of the contents of the originals' vault rooms. Because each room is potentially filled with historic items and valuables, the elders have decided that each descendant must complete their journey to fully claim the contents. If you do not finish or return, the funds and contents of the vaults will go to the community with their use to be voted on by the elders."

There were a few grumbles from some parents, but not enough to address, so Barry moved on.

"Here are your guidebooks, Emily and Liz." Barry handed them both books that looked identical to the one Aaron got earlier, other than color and insignia.

"About the journals: How do they work? I think mine worked, but it's like I know everything about every creature in The Table now! My head is swimming . . ." Aaron slowed to a stop, realizing that he was rambling a little and everyone was staring at him.

"Exactly, Aaron. Each journal has a deep genetic connection. Once it is opened by its owner, basically all the information is absorbed into the owner's brain," Barry explained. "Essentially, everything that is written in it is now written in your brain."

"Any data that you add will then be passed along to whomever you deem worthy to inherit the book from you, and then it will do the same with them. There is a spell to set that up, but it's something we can go over in the future. For now, just know that the journal will only respond to its owner."

A few heads nodded.

"Now, last but not least, no one else will be allowed to go on these journeys with them. The originals had intended these trials to really test the descendants and help them become better leaders. Having extra people there will only cause distraction. Other than that, you should be good to go."

As Barry finished, he looked around at everyone assembled. "Any questions?"

Before he could call on someone, he was peppered with questions from every direction. "Woah, woah, woah! One at time. Darla, you first."

"So how do we decide which journey to take first?"

"Ah, yes. The elders did not specify an order in which they needed to take place, only that in one year's time they need to be completed or at least have the last one started. They also stipulated that at least three of the four descendants must be present on the journey. We understand one not being able to make it, but the importance of these trips can't be overstated."

A sea of hands still awaited him. "You know what, y'all, I am sure you all have a ton of questions. For time's sake and for my own, let's take the night to think about it and talk about it with your loved ones. Then, I will answer whatever questions you might have left after that. Just swing by my office downtown, and we will be happy to help!" Barry then quickly turned and exited the stage to the left.

Everyone looked around at each other and mumbled some mixture of "Nice to meet you" and "Guess we should go" before making their way out to the parking lot.

As the Dimeters walked back down the path they had originally come in on, the questions began building again in Aaron's head.

Wow, what a crazy night. Finally, it's my turn. I get to be the special one! I can't believe what took place with Richard the Righteous. . . . Wait! Steve might still have family out there.

Aaron couldn't stay silent. "Holy crap, Steve! Your giant family might be out there."

Steve glanced over with giant tears welled up in his eyes. "Yeah, but like, what if they aren't there? Why was Richard killed? What happened? Where did the giants go? How did I get left here? Did no one want me?"

The questions tumbled out so quickly that they turned into blubbering, and Aaron couldn't even understand his overwhelmed friend after that.

Darla stopped and wrapped Steve in her amazing wing hug. "Hey. Hey. *We* want you, and *we* love you. No matter what, we are your family, and we *will* figure this out. It's going to be okay, honey."

Steve gripped Darla tighter as he cried.

"It will be okay, I promise you. We love you," she whispered gently in his ear while she lovingly patted his head.

Aaron and Phil joined in the hug, and for a moment, they just held each other in silence.

"My loves," Phil said, clearing his throat. "Let's not talk about all of this right now. These boys need some rest."

He pointed up toward the parking lot, and they continued on.

Once buckled in the Suburban, Aaron very much wanted to ask all the questions he had. There were so many!

Where does Penelope's journey take me? What all is in the vault room? They said it was valuable, but I don't own anything! What could it be? How long is the journey? Who is going first?

The thoughts fluttered past one by one as he leaned his head on the cold glass of the passenger-side window. He closed his eyes, imagining what the shimmers' homeland would look like.

10

BREAKFAST

Aaron opened his eyes and stretched out his arms. *Man, I slept hard, that was a good . . . wait! What happened? Where am I?*

He scanned his surroundings and immediately calmed down. *Oh yeah, I'm in my room at the Dimeters, in my bed. But how did I get here?*

He could hear someone cooking in the kitchen. *And that smell . . . is it? Yes, bacon!* He hopped out of bed and noticed he was still wearing the fancy clothes from the celebration. He grabbed his duffel bag off the floor and headed toward the bathroom.

"Hey there, sleepyhead," Phil said as he passed Aaron in the hall.

"Umm, hey. How did I get into my bed? Last thing I remember was thinking about the shimmer home world on the car ride home."

"Yeah, you and Steve both passed out hard in the car on the drive," Phil said with a chuckle. "We tried to carry you both inside, but Steve has gotten way too heavy for us. We had to wake him up, but then he carried you inside so that you didn't have to wake up. I think he might still be sleeping."

"Okay, that makes sense. Guess I was more tired than I realized," Aaron replied and continued on. He headed to the bathroom to take a quick shower.

Huh? His brain swirled as he opened the door. The bathroom floor looked normal enough, with its shiny white tiles. The walls were similar, with a red-and-blue checked pattern ringing the room at the middle.

The toilet dominating the middle of the room was twice the size of what he was used to, and there was not a back to it. *I guess dragons and giants use the toilet a little differently,* he thought as he approached what looked like a "normal" clawfoot bathtub with a blue shower curtain near the far wall.

He pulled the curtain aside on the giant tub, excited to see how crazy the fixtures would look. Instead of some wild Table contraption, Aaron found a removable showerhead on a hose, like he'd seen in the overworld. *Okay, so not everything is different. That at least makes it easier to figure this stuff out.*

He quickly showered and changed into the gym shorts and plain white T-shirt he had brought from home. He took out his Elfwater hat from the side table where he had left it and placed it on his head. *All right, now that you look ready for adventure, let's go get some bacon!*

He found Phil, Vee, and Darla in the kitchen. Phil was standing at the stove, wearing a brightly colored apron that read *KISS THE COOK.*

"Howdy, y'all!" Aaron said as he walked into the kitchen.

"There he is! All cleaned up," Phil said, turning toward Aaron. "Would you like some eggs?"

"That sounds great!"

"How do you like them?"

"Over hard, please!"

"Coming right up!" Phil cracked more eggs into the pan while Aaron took his seat at the table. Aaron started filling his plate with the bacon piled high on a serving dish in the middle. He then grabbed a couple biscuits from a tray on the left side of the table.

"How did you sleep, Aaron?" Darla asked.

"Like a rock! I don't even remember falling asleep."

"Morning, family!" an excited voice bellowed from the hallway.

Steve strolled into the kitchen, smiling and happy as could be—the complete opposite of the night before.

"Morning, buddy! How are you feeling?" Aaron asked. Even though he was the one who asked, all the others looked to Steve for the response. They appeared a little worried, too.

"All good! I am excited to see what these journeys hold for us. I am going to find the giants and bring them back to The Table!" Steve announced with certainty.

"Oh. Well . . . okay," Darla began. "I like the positive change in attitude. Now please remember that, unfortunately, we don't really know what all is in The Unknown's —I mean Richard's—vault room, so please don't get your hopes too high. There is still a lot of murkiness around the reason the giants left, and I just don't want you to get hurt."

"Don't worry, Mom. I know it won't be easy, but I also know I have my best bud Aaron to go with me. And you two will be there as well! We can figure this out as a family." Steve took his seat and began dismantling the remaining pile of bacon.

"Sounds good to me. Steve, would you like any eggs?" Phil asked.

"Of course, Dad! You know my order—five eggs, over hard, with—"

"With a little sriracha and cheese on them. Yep, I got it coming up next." Phil scooped out the eggs for Aaron and tossed them onto a plate. "Would you like any cheese or sriracha?"

"Yes please to the cheese and no thank you to the sauce. I don't like spicy food *at all*," Aaron answered.

"You don't like spicy stuff?" Steve said in disbelief.

"I like the flavor, just not the heat," Aaron replied as Phil handed him the plate full of eggs. "These look delicious. Thank you!"

"You're most welcome."

"Now that we all have some food, are we ready to talk about last night and the next steps with the journeys?" Darla asked excitedly.

"Yes!" the boys hollered.

"Wow. Can we bring the levels down *just a little*?" Vee grumbled from the other side of the table. She glared at the boys, then went back to writing in her journal. "Geez!"

"Don't worry about her," Darla said. "She is just grumpy that her crush Jimmy didn't say hi to her this morning when he walked by the house."

"Ugh, whatever! Stop it, Mom!"

"Fine. So, whose journey are we going on first?" Darla was back to excited.

"Well, I think we should start with going to the

vault so the boys can open the rooms and see what is inside," Phil suggested. "The rooms have not been touched, as the genetic locks use a magic similar to the journals. Once a descendant has opened the door to the room, it will be linked to their biology until that link is removed. The doors in the room will only open for that descendant from that point on."

"Yes!" Again, both boys were in unison. Vee snarled quietly.

"Then eat up, grab your journals, and we can head to the car in thirty minutes. Now that all the eggs are cooked," Phil said as he handed Steve his plate, "I am going to go take a shower and get ready myself."

"All right, y'all, you heard him," Darla said.

There was no argument from the boys, who immediately started scarfing down their food. Both finished quickly, rinsed off their plates, and put them in the sink.

Steve looked to Darla. "Can we be excused, Mom?"

"Of course."

The boys raced down the hall toward their rooms.

"Man, I can't wait," Aaron said.

"Same, dude! Same."

"I wonder what all is in Penelope's room. Is there, like, cool underwater tech? Or maybe I get a cool trident!" Aaron said, dreaming out loud.

"I don't know. I just hope there is something in there that can point us to where the giants went when they left." Steve sounded a little worried.

"Don't worry. We will figure it out together! We won't stop until we do!" Aaron said with the utmost confidence.

That seemed to helped Steve relax a little, and his smile returned. "I am really pumped to see where this adventure takes us."

"Me too, bud. Me too."

11

HEADED TO THE VAULT

"All right, let's go!" Darla called out from the end of the apartment hallway. Phil, Vee, Steve, and Aaron entered the living room.

"You boys got your journals? You need to keep them on you at all times, and make sure you are using them!"

Oh yeah! The journal!

"Thank you, Darla! I almost forgot it," Aaron replied and took off to grab it.

So now I know everything that Penelope wrote in this, he reminded himself, then pondered on that for a moment. *So, what all do I know?*

"Aaron, sweetheart, you good?" an impatient Darla called from the living room, breaking into his thoughts.

"Yeah, sorry! I'm coming!" Aaron hurried back to the living room with his journal.

"It's okay," Phil assured him. "Someone is just really excited for her boys and really excited to see inside these rooms."

Darla gave Phil a look that shut him up, then she turned to Aaron with a smile. "Yes, I am quite excited to see where all of this goes, not only for all of us, but the entire Table. Let's get going, y'all!"

They took the elevator down to street level. It was only a short walk to the downtown park that held the vault. As they walked, Aaron tried to take in all the sights and sounds. The last time he had made this trek, he was still trying to make sure he wasn't dreaming. He noticed that some of the shops were very similar to the ones he knew, but with slight differences. They passed a RadioShed that looked a lot like RadioShack electronics store they had in the overworld. Another example was the Abercrombie and Stitch Co.

"Does it all seem a bit familiar, Aaron?" Phil asked.

Aarons snapped out of his daze. "Yeah, I just wasn't sure how to explain it."

"Remember how we told you that the vehicles here are the same as the ones from the overworld? Well, it's pretty much the same with all products. There is a distribution area of The Table that one day I would love to show you more of, but basically, they import most things here from the overworld. We don't have the materials to make many of these things. They then make small changes to the products to make them more 'our own,' " he said.

"I get it. . . . Wait, is that a McDonalds?" Aaron pointed wildly at the golden arches he could see in the distance.

"Yep!" Steve said.

"But why isn't it a little different, like the others?" Aaron inquired.

"That's because it's really McDonalds. It's a secret, but the founder of the real McDonalds is from The Table," Phil said with a smile.

Aaron's brain went into information overload, and it was obvious on his face. Darla noticed.

"All right, that's enough of that chat for now," she said. "Yes, there a lot of things about The Table you will learn because our worlds are more intertwined than you might think. But not right now. It's time for the vault rooms!"

They had made it there quicker than Aaron had remembered. He had been so lost in thought that he hadn't noticed they were already standing at the entrance. He looked up at it, recalling the last time he had been here. He smiled as the thought of what could be in Penelope's room overtook his brain.

It was like both boys felt the same drive and excitement at the same time. Steve looked at Aaron. "I'll race ya!"

"You're on. Go!" Aaron hollered out, and both boys took off running.

"Be careful!" Darla called after them.

"Hey, can I go to the mall? I don't really care what's in the vault rooms, and no one cares what I think about it anyway," Vee said, somehow already annoyed. "It's just down the street."

Darla looked to Phil, and they both shrugged. Vee smiled a tiny smile and jogged away.

"We do care, by the way," Darla said. "Just meet us back here in one hour!"

Vee waved her hand at her mother in agreement as she headed for the mall.

"Welp, let's go see what those boys have gotten into," Phil said with a smile.

12

THE PRIVATE ROOMS

Steve was not the fastest runner, but neither was Aaron. As they closed in on the gates to the vault entrance, the boys were neck and neck. Steve knew he could easily beat Aaron but loved the idea of them racing.

"I'm gonna win!" Steve shouted.

"Nope, I am!" Aaron yelled back.

SMACK! Aaron ran directly into Liz the Learned, who was leaving her vault room.

"Oww!" Liz let out a painful cry as her books and papers went flying. The dragon and shimmer crumbled to the ground in a heap.

Aaron stood back up and immediately started apologizing as he picked up her things in a panic. "Sorry. I am so sorry. Sorry," he said like a broken record.

Steve reached over and gave Liz a hand to stand up. "I'm sorry about that," he said to her.

She dusted herself off and adjusted her clothes. She was wearing capri-cut blue jeans, black Converse and a red polo with the dragonkin fire emblem on the top left side of the shirt. She also was wearing the same orange kerchief around her neck from the night before.

"I'm fine. It's okay, but y'all need to look where you are going," Liz replied after a few seconds.

Aaron was still stuck in his apologetic whirlwind, trying to fix everything as quickly as he could. Liz walked over to him and put her hand on his shoulder.

"It's really okay," she told him. "I know it was an accident."

Aaron smiled. "Thank you," he said and continued to clean up, though it was calmer and more controlled.

Once they had all the papers and books back in a neat stack, Aaron held out his hand to Liz. "Hi. Liz, right? I am Aaron. Sorry again for running you over. It's nice to meet you!"

"Hi, I am Steve!" the giant said and shook her hand a bit too vigorously.

"Woah, friend!" Liz said as she pulled her hand back from his steel grip.

"Sorry about that, too," Steve said sheepishly.

"It's no big deal. Let's just try not to break my hand going forward. Cool?" Liz said with a playful smile.

Steve smiled back. "Deal!"

Phil and Darla finally caught up to the boys. As they approached, Aaron gestured to them. "And this is Phil and Darla! They are the Dimeters and just the best people. They are coming on the trip with us!"

"Hello, Liz! I was good friends with your mother back when we were in the academy, but that's a story for another day. It's so nice to finally meet you!" She gave Liz a big hug.

"Nice to meet you, Liz," Phil added.

"Likewise, Mr. and Mrs. Dimeter. When my mother

found out who the chaperones were, she was so excited and *much* calmer about it, knowing you were going with us. She is back in Daryl's room. There is so much stuff down there. These are just some of the books I want to take back home and study, so I'm placing them in our car."

"You have been in the room already?!" exclaimed Darla. "Tell us everything! What was in there? Was it cool? Historical? Is there treasure?"

"Okay, honey," Phil said as he pulled her toward him. "Let her enjoy this. We will go check out the boys' rooms."

"Oh, I don't mind," piped up Liz. "Besides, the only thing in Daryl's vault room was gold and a list of his accomplishments."

Darla froze. "So there were no artifacts or journals? Or more books? Then what is all this?" She pointed to Liz's stack of stuff.

"These are from the main room and the dwarven room. Emily opened it up earlier and didn't care for any of the books. She just wanted the armor, weapons, and gold that was in there."

"Both have been opened?" Darla interrupted.

"Yep, she is down there now with her entourage looking through it all."

Darla stared at the books and papers in Liz's arms like they were the only things that mattered in the world. Liz noticed her interest and spoke up.

"Mrs. Dimeter, would you like to look at these books when I am all done?"

"Yes, please!" an excited Darla said.

"Sounds good," Phil chimed in. "Let's go check out

the boys' rooms now. These two are chomping at the bit to see what their ancestors left them."

"Yep, good point," Darla said as she shook her head to focus her thoughts. "It was so nice to talk to you, Liz. And yes, let's definitely discuss all these things in the near future."

Both boys took off through the gate and headed directly to the now wide-open vault door in the middle of the stage, disappearing inside. Aaron could hear others as they descended.

Once they got into the main vault room, he could see two of the four giant rootwood doors in the back were open. Through one door, Emily and her family were talking and laughing. The other door had a few people inside, but they were not nearly as boisterous.

Aaron looked to the door with the P on it for Penelope. His heart beat against his chest, and he felt lightheaded with the rush of anticipation.

What is back there? Will this tell me how I became a shimmer? What did Penelope want me to see? The thought hurricane continued for what felt like forever, but it was only a few seconds.

"Buddy, we got this!" Steve's voice cut through the swirling questions like a knife.

Aaron looked at his giant friend, took a deep breath, and slowly let it out. "Yep, we got this!" He walked over to the door and looked down at the genetic scanner, which was similar to the one used to open the main vault door.

Steve moved in front of his door, too.

"Hang on, boys!" Darla yelled from the room entrance. "One of us wants to go with each of you at the same time. It's not fair to make one of you wait."

Phil made his way over to Steve, and Darla went over to Aaron.

"Okay, go ahead," she said to them. The descendants placed their hands in the scanners.

CLICK! The lock disengaged, and a large blast of musty air spilled out from behind the door as it opened inward.

Huh. I thought there might be more to it than that, Aaron thought as the door opened fully.

"Holy crap!" Aaron yelled out as he peered inside.

The scene before him was nothing short of spectacular. His eyes darted wildly around the room, trying to take it all in. The room itself was a medium-sized square. On the center of the back wall was a giant portrait of Penelope, like the ones at the vault entrance and The Mural. In this picture, however, Penelope was wearing what looked to be some sort of armor made of blue material. It had the shimmers' seaweed insignia on the left chest, and the armor glistened in the light of the moss chandelier that hung from the ceiling. It was magnificent, almost as if the portrait was alive. A massive bookshelf took up the entirety of the left wall from floor to ceiling, containing what had to be hundreds of books. Its red rootwood had faded with time and was now a beautiful pink hue.

Entering the room, he walked over to a rootwood desk with several notes and photos on top. The desk was pinker now than the usual dark red rootwood. He looked at the wall above the desk, taking in the framed photos there of all kinds of different people.

I wonder if they are related to me, he thought to

himself with a smile. To his left was a rootwood door marked with the shimmer symbol. To his right was a giant cupboard made out of what looked like coral reef. He walked over to run his hand across one of the cupboard doors.

They seem to be made of wood, but it's not rootwood like everything else. He smiled again as tried to take in the entire room. He noticed a a hole in the floor in the middle of the room with a ladder sticking up from inside.

What is that? His thoughts conflicted over where to explore at first.

"This is amazing!" Darla's voice from behind him broke the silence.

"Yeah, it is," Aaron said, still a bit dazed. He looked over at the desk and saw one letter that stood out. "Hey, that says to read it first."

"Well, let's go read it!" Darla replied.

Aaron walked over, picked up the envelope, and tore into it. A silver chain with a brilliant blue pebble attached to it fell out into his palm. The second the stone touched his skin, it glowed slightly. "Cool! I wonder what this is!"

He held up the chain in the light to get a better look, then put it around his neck to investigate later. He returned to the letter in his hand, unfolded its brittle edges, and began to read.

Hello my dearest,

I am so happy to know that my descendant won the Trial of the Kings and is now ruler of The Table. I am proud to know my lineage was strong enough to do so. We have been a powerful family of shimmers, and I am happy to know that has not stopped. Now, this letter will help you understand this room. It was set up to help you on your journey to our homeland. You see, the coordinates for the shimmer home are a secret to outsiders. That is why I wrote them down in my journal. If you are reading this letter, that means you have the journal and the coordinates are now already in your head.

Aaron looked up from the letter at Darla with a hint of bewilderment in his eyes. Then, they shifted wide open in shock.

"I do know them! All I did was think, 'What are the coordinates?' and they popped into my head!" Aaron shook with excitement.

"That's amazing, sweetheart! What else does the letter say?" Darla asked.

Aaron smiled again, thinking about how cool it was that all of this was happening to him. He had always felt like he was meant for something important, and now he knew that was true.

He continued reading aloud.

Now that you know where to go, here are a few things to know about this room and the journey that lies ahead of you. The necklace in this envelope is now your personal shimmer stone necklace. Please always keep it on your person and never let anyone else have it. That stone will help guide you on your journey if you will let it. The pictures above the desk are of my family line. All the pictures there are ancestors of yours, and the other letters on the desk are correspondence I had with them when I left the homelands to help create The Table. They are now all yours and may help you on the journey. In the middle of the room, there is a ladder that goes down to our family vault. It is filled with everything you might need to help with your travels. Please read the instructions on all the devices before using them. Last, but not least, here are five things to remember on the trip.

Don't eat the red seaweed. It looks edible and delicious, but it will make you sick.

Look for the shimmer symbol everywhere you go. There are more of us out there than you know, and the symbol means you can trust them.

Dolphins are not to be trusted, especially the ones from the Atlantic. They are smart, but crooked.

Sea turtles are a shimmer's best friend; they will always lead you the right way.

And most importantly, don't ever trust a dragonkin.

Aaron looked up at his adopted dragonkin mother. "Definitely didn't expect that," Aaron blurted out.

"Yeah, me either." Darla seemed rattled. "Does it say why? Or anything else?"

"Nope, just *Yours truly, Penelope the Peaceful* at the bottom."

Aaron, still a little shaken up by the warning, looked at Darla. He could read the fear on her face, as if Aaron might take his ancestor's advice.

"Well, Penelope obviously didn't know the Dimeters!" He folded the letter up and put it into the front cover of the journal. Darla smiled at him and gave him a huge hug.

"So, what did we find over here?" Phil asked from the door. His voice was a little more somber than fit the occasion.

"It's amazing! Look at all of this! There is even more down that ladder over there, from what my letter said. What is it like over in Steve's? I bet there are so many cool things!" Aaron said as he broke from Darla's hug and ran over to Phil.

Phil hugged him back for a few seconds while giving Darla a pained look. She nodded and joined them at the door.

Phil stepped back from Aaron, trying to hold back tears. "I am so happy for you, buddy. But just a quick heads up: Steve's room wasn't really the same as yours . . ."

"What?" Aaron looked over to the open door with the giant R on it and ran over.

"Steve! What's going on?" Aaron shouted as he ran into the room, where he found Steve sitting on the black stone floor holding a piece of paper. The entire space was empty—nothing but stone walls and floors. Steve was in the middle, staring at the document.

"Oh, dude. I am so sorry, man," Aaron said as he sat next to his friend.

"I just don't understand," Steve said. "Where is everything? Everyone's room had tons of stuff about their family, or cool armor and books. I got *this*!"

He smashed the piece of paper down in front of Aaron so hard that the room shook, and the boom it made echoed throughout. The paper had some numbers on it, but that was it. Just a blank piece of paper with some random numbers.

Aaron's heart sank. *That's the only thing in here? Poor Steve. This has to be awful for him. Richard couldn't come up with anything else?*

Phil and Darla ran into the room after hearing the boom.

"Big guy, it's going to be okay. I promise," Darla said as she wrapped him in a dragon hug. He cried into her shoulder for a few minutes.

When the embrace finally ended, Darla picked up the piece of paper.

"Steve, I think these are coordinates!" she said. "In Penelope's letter to Aaron, she said they used coordinates to locate the home of the shimmers. It could be the same for the giants!"

Steve's face lit up. "How do we use coordinates? Can we go now?" He paced the room with renewed excitement. "I'm gonna find the giants and bring them back to The Table!"

"What's going on in here?" Emily asked from the doorway. "We heard a boom. Wow! Empty room much? Haha. Umm, I mean . . . what's the commotion about?"

Behind her, Aaron heard Liz. "Yeah, what is happening over here?"

She slid past Emily and into the room. Her face went pale. Liz smiled awkwardly and adjusted her glasses. "These walls are beautiful in here," she said and slowly tried to back out of the space.

"No, stop! It's good you are both here," Darla said. "We all need to chat about a few things, but it's a members-only kind of conversation. So, unless you are a descendent or a chaperone, could you please exit the room?"

She snapped a quick look toward Emily's relatives trying to make their way in and listen. They left, and Phil closed the door behind them.

"Okay, now it's just the six of us, did either of you find coordinates or some random numbers in your rooms?" Darla asked.

"Umm, there were some numbers on the wall by the map in mine." Emily said.

"Yes, there are in mine, too!" said an excited Liz. "I was actually on my way over here to talk to Darla about them when I heard that noise."

"That's awesome! That means each one of you holds the coordinates to your ancestors' homeland. Now, these coordinates are extremely valuable, and many people will want them. You see, before The Table began, each race had a home that was hidden completely from the other races and the overworld. They were each built in caverns just like The Table and operated on the same time as The Table. Each holds the creation story for its race, and the cities themselves are protected landmarks. Now, some coordinates have been leaked over the years, so locations for Emily and Liz are more well-known. The reason is the dwarven people kept being sought out for armor and weapon crafting, so much it was almost impossible to keep their homes a secret. So, they instead announced it to the world, and now anyone can visit—"

"Anvil City!" Emily blurted out joyfully. "I can't wait to go!"

"Yes, exactly. It is known as Anvil City, and it's somewhere off the coast of what the overworld calls Greenland. The city does allow visitors, but only dwarves are allowed to live there. From what I have heard, it can be difficult to get visitor passes."

"I have heard they have a gladiator ring in the middle of the city, and anyone can fight! Whoever wins there is the champion of the city, and I would love to be double champion!" Emily gazed off into the distance, lost in her fantasy.

"That sounds lovely, Emily, and hopefully we will get there soon," continued Darla. "However, the other homes may not be as easily found. Of course, the dragonkin home world is a slightly different story."

"Yeah, I know," Liz said with shame in her voice. "We all know where the dragonkin home world is."

Everyone in the room nodded in awkward agreement, except Aaron.

"Umm, not all of us."

"Oh, that's right. Sorry, Aaron," Darla said. "The dragonkin home world is under a mountain in Italy called Mount Vesuvius."

"Isn't that a volcano or something? Why do I know that name? I feel like I learned about that place in school at some point."

"Yep, that's the right place," replied Liz.

"What you are probably referring to is the city of Pompeii," Darla added.

"Yeah! I remember now. Didn't the city get destroyed by the volcano, like it erupted so fast that no one could leave or something? I remember seeing people that looked like statues," Aaron said.

Liz's face had turned a shade of bright red, and she stared down at the floor. Darla stepped over to her and patted her shoulder. "It's okay, sweetheart. It wasn't us. They made choices we couldn't control."

That left Aaron even more confused. "What's going on?" he asked.

Darla looked over to him while comforting Liz. "You see, the volcano was not a complete accident. It was intentional, set off by the dragonkin who lived below. They were furious with the humans for the way they had been treated. History says it was supposed to have only scared the humans away and given them plenty of time to leave. However, someone inside the city wanted to harm the humans and set it off with no warning. The dragonkin's immunity to fire protected them, but the humans were completely obliterated. To this day, they don't know who specifically set it off, but it has been something held against all dragonkin ever since. Once the disaster took place, it was pretty easy to know where their home was."

Is this why Penelope told me not to trust them? Aaron wondered. *How could they have done that? How do Liz and other dragonkin feel about this?*

"It's a bit of a sensitive subject," Phil added.

"Yeah, I can see that," Aaron said.

"Now back to you two boys," Darla said. "No one knows anything about the shimmers' home. There are some here at The Table who say they have visited it, but they seem to have been sworn to secrecy. So, either they are lying or it's a really well-kept secret. And Steve, we obviously only have the coordinates at this time. No one has spoken to the giant race since Whitney the Wise led them away. You are the first and only known giant to be in The Table since then."

13

WHO WINS?

"Now the big question: Who goes first?" Emily asked.

Aaron and the others looked around in silence for a few seconds as they contemplated the possibilities.

"I know!" hollered out Steve. "What if we use the oldest tradition at The Table to help us decide? Rock, Paper, Scissors!"

Everyone except Aaron nodded in agreement immediately.

"Rock, Paper, Scissors? That's a thing here, too?" Aaron asked, elated.

"Yes, it is, and it's a great way to choose!" replied Darla.

"But we have four people. How do we choose who battles who first?" Liz spoke up.

"What if we put all your names in Aaron's hat, then we will draw two names, and those two have to go first. Then the other two who weren't picked will battle, and the winners of the two battles will face off to see who goes first!" Phil's eyes lit up as he explained his idea.

"Sounds fair to me!" Emily said, and the rest of the

room agreed.

Darla pulled a pen and paper out of her purse to write down all four names. She then tore the paper into pieces and asked Aaron for his Elfwater hat. She shuffled the pieces around inside it and then asked Phil to draw two names.

"First up, we have Aaron," Phil said, unfolding the next piece of paper, "and Emily!"

"Let's go! First pick!" Emily exclaimed. "You ready to go down, son?"

Aaron smiled. "Oh, it's on!"

They lined up across from each other as Darla explained the rules.

"Remember: It's one, two, three, then shoot. We are using the normal rules—no extra things, just rock, paper, and scissors. Rock beats scissors. Scissors beats paper. Paper beats rock."

"Yeah, yeah, we know. Let's start this thing!" Emily said.

"Are you both ready?" Darla looked at them, and they nodded.

"All right. One, two, three, shoot!"

What do I throw? Will she use rock? Probably. I bet she doesn't think paper is strong enough.

Aaron threw out his hand flat to show paper, just in time to see Emily did the exact same thing.

"it's a tie! Go again," Darla said.

"Okay, shimmer boy, get ready to rumble!" Emily jeered.

"All right, ready? One, two, three, shoot!" Darla called it out a little faster than Aaron expected, so he didn't have time to overthink.

He tossed his hand out flat again. Emily's balled-up fist thrust out right next to his hand.

"Yes!" Aaron yelled out.

"Aww, come on!" Emily said as she stomped off.

"So that's Aaron with the win. Aaron, you will play against whoever wins between Steve and Liz. Liz, Steve, are y'all ready?" Darla asked, then began her countdown after they nodded. "One, two, three, shoot!"

Steve's hand came out flat in paper, following Aaron's lead. When he saw Liz's hand come down with scissors showing, his heart sank. He looked up and smiled anyway. "Good game, Liz."

"Umm, I forfeit," Liz said quickly.

"Are you sure?" Darla replied.

"Yeah, well . . . it's kind of unfair for me or Emily to want to go first. Both of you have some big questions you could get answered on this journey," Liz said with a kind smile. "For me and Emily, it's not as big. You two should battle it out."

"Yeah, I guess that makes sense. I forfeit, too," Emily added.

"Thank you for the gesture, Emily, but Aaron already . . . You know what? Just thank you. Boys, what do you think?" Darla asked as she turned back to them.

"I want Aaron to go first," Steve said. "He has so much he can find out about where he came from. It's only fair."

"Well, I can say the exact same for you, buddy. I want you to go first!"

"Boys, the best way to decide this might just be the way we already were. Whoever wins goes first, then we can do the other journey right after this one. We have to do all of them in this first year anyway."

The boys looked at each other, shrugged in unison, then laughed in unison, both of which were unintentional.

"Works for me. You in?" Aaron asked Steve as he reached out his hand.

"Deal!" Steve said and shook Aaron's hand heartily.

"Then are you boys ready for the final round?" Darla asked.

They agreed, and she began. "One, two, three . . . shoot!"

Aaron shoved out his hand, balled in a fist. Steve's hand game jutting out like scissors.

Oh geez! I won?!

"And the winner is Aaron!" Darla called out to everyone.

Steve picked up Aaron in a hug immediately. "I am so happy for you, dude! I can't wait to see where the shimmers come from!"

"Oof. Okay, you can put me down now," Aaron squeaked out in between breaths.

Steve set him down and Aaron continued in his normal voice. "Thank you, but are you sure? I feel bad."

"Don't! I am excited to go with you, just as much as you are excited to go with me next. All we can do now is get going!"

"All right, that settles it. We are going on a shimmer journey!" piped up a thrilled Darla. The boys ran over and hugged their parents.

"I think everyone should take the rest of the day to get packed and prepared," Phil said with a mix of duty and excitement. "We will be leaving first thing in the morning!"

Everyone in the room cheered, except Aaron. Emily and Liz headed back to their rooms. Once they were gone, he spoke up.

"Umm, how long do we think this journey will take? We have already used up a day of my time here. If I don't get home by dinner tonight in the overworld, my mom will be furious and looking for me," Aaron said, looking stressed. "We probably only have three more days on Table time before I need to go back."

Darla and Phil looked at each other and grimaced. "You're right. We're going to have to figure that out. This journey could take a couple weeks. I don't know why we didn't think of that!"

"I've got an idea," Aaron said. "It's the weekend before school starts. I have to be home by Saturday evening for sure because Sunday is 'chore day,' and Rick won't let me miss that. But I wonder if I could call my mom and ask if I can stay at my friend Steve's house tonight. I am sure if she talked to his mom, she would let me!"

Darla began to object, then paused to let the thought train run its course. "I mean . . . that could work. Twenty-four hours in the overworld is almost twelve days here, so that should be plenty!"

"Yes!" Aaron said as he pumped his arm in excitement. "I get to go on a journey!"

"Let's just keep it in perspective for now," Darla reminded him. "Your mother still needs to agree, and we still need to pack. Oh, and we almost forgot to look in the other space in Penelope's room!"

"Agreed," Phil said. "Let's go check out the rest of Penelope's room and then get home to call Aaron's mom." He walked out the door with Darla following.

Aaron hung back and walked up to Steve. "Just so you know, none of this would be happening without you and the kindness you showed me. So, as of now, you own half of what is in my room, and I *won't* take no for answer. It's mine to give away and I want you to have it. No objections! Now, let's go check out *our* stuff!"

Steve tried to speak, but his words wouldn't work. He grabbed Aaron in a big hug as he gathered his thoughts. "I love you, too. Thank you!"

Aaron squirmed and gasped out a "you're welcome."

They walked over to Penelope's room with on arm on each other's shoulders.

"Holy crap!" Steve yelped when they reached the room.

"Yep, that's exactly what I said when I first saw it!"

Darla and Phil waited patiently. Well, Phil was patient. Darla was dancing around a bit by the ladder. Aaron made a beeline for the ladder as his excitement picked up again.

"We felt it only best and right that you should get to go down the ladder first, Aaron," said Phil, "and we will wait patiently until you say we can come down. Right, Darla?"

"Umm, yep. Patiently waiting," Darla confirmed sarcastically.

Aaron grabbed hold of the ladder and looked down into the hole. There was no light on down there, and he could not make anything out.

"Here goes nothing!" Aaron said as he descended into the darkness.

14

A VAULT INSIDE A VAULT

Step by step, Aaron climbed down the ladder until his feet hit solid ground. *It's pitch black in here. I can't even see my own hand in front of my face.*

He outstretched his arm, feeling for something to hold onto before letting go of the ladder. His hand found a wall, then a small switch. He flipped it.

"Ahh!" Light blasted into every inch of the room. Once Aaron had blinked a few times, he could see that a giant moss chandelier hanging from the ceiling was the source. The room—another small square cut out of stone—had two main sections. One side had a giant rootwood cabinet covering the wall from floor to ceiling, each cabinet labeled with its contents. A giant, round metal door in the middle of the right wall dominated the other side. It was flanked by two figures, both dressed in a blue armor.

Just like the armor Penelope is wearing in the painting! Aaron thought as he examined the regalia.

In the middle of the room was a table with a sign that read *USE THESE THINGS ON YOUR JOURNEY.* Aaron walked up to it to see what else was there, and a handful of blue bracelets at the center caught his eye first. Beautiful blue scallop seashells, ink pens, a few small bottles filled with a blue liquid, and another note filled out the rest of the table. On the floor below were several blue duffel bags. Aaron picked up the note.

Take these items on your journey.

1. The blue bracelets, when worn, grant the user almost all abilities a natural shimmer would have. These are made of a special blue seaweed found only in Seaweed City. BE CAREFUL who you give these to. These abilities include:

- *Underwater breathing*
- *Faster swimming*
- *Fish eyesight*

2. Shimmer shell badges act as translators. They give the wearer the ability to speak to any ocean creature. You won't be fluent in all dialects of dolphin—there are too many vulgar words in that language—but you will know enough to get by.

3. Squid pens can write underwater on any surface. These are made of blue coral reef and a special squid ink found only in Seaweed City.

4. When drunk, the Tears of Titan potion creates an impenetrable bubble of protection directly around the user for ten seconds. This comes from a local brew shop in the market at Seaweed City.

5. Once filled, shrinkweed satchels can be made to shrink by sprinkling water on the outside. They are waterproof and made by a special tailor in Seaweed City.

Remember to only give these items to people you absolutely trust.

P.

Aaron stared wide-eyed at the table for a minute, then read and reread the note.

This is amazing! What is Seaweed City? Wait . . .

The rolodex of information in his head began to spin through its files. *I know this! That's the name of the shimmers' home city!*

"Aaron? Umm, how's it going down . . ." Darla's voice brought Aaron back to the present.

"Darla, leave the boy alone," Phil said from further back. "Give him a few more—"

"Y'all, come on down," Aaron cut in.

Darla raced to the ladder. She squeezed her wings tightly to her back to make it through the opening. Phil followed right behind her.

"Oh, sweetheart! This is amazing!" Darla said as she walked around the room, taking in every facet. "I just *knew* Penelope would have the best room."

"Wow, this is cool!" Phil said as he stepped off the ladder.

"Yeah. It's nuts, right?" asked Aaron, who was about ready to pinch himself. "So, this table right here had this note on it."

He handed the note to Darla. She read it quickly, then stared at the table wide-eyed, just as Aaron had. Phil tapped her on the shoulder and gestured for the letter. Without taking her eyes off the table, Darla handed him the notecard.

"Aaron, this is simply astonishing," Phil said.

Darla, who finally could form words again, picked up each item individually study them. "Yeah, this is . . . just . . . wow," she mumbled.

Aaron smiled at how excited his favorite history buff was. He looked back at the supplies. "Looks like we have enough for everyone on the trip. We only need five of those bracelets and badges, and there are plenty of pens. There are six potions, which means one for each of us!"

Darla and Phil looked proud of how Aaron was handling his new treasures. He hadn't even considered keeping them all to himself.

"Dude, this place is awesome!" Steve screamed from above as he looked through the main room's contents.

"Come down here!" Aaron yelled up to him. Steve stuck his head in and peering around.

"There's more!?" He climbed down the ladder. "Aaron, this is a lot of stuff. Are you sure?"

"Of course, man," replied Aaron.

Darla and Phil looked at each other curiously, then at the boys. "What are you two talking about?" Phil asked.

"Oh, I told Steve that half of the stuff in my room was his. Penelope left so much stuff. I just figured—Oof!"

Darla had swooped Aaron up in giant winged embrace. "I am just so proud of you!" she squealed as she squeezed him.

Phil joined in. "Me too, son!"

"Don't forget me!" Steve bounded over to join them.

"I guess wait for me, too." Vee was back from the mall and halfway down when she spoke. "What? I can join y'all. No one's going to see down here."

She ran over to add the final piece. They all stood there together for a few moments, just savoring their time. Vee sniffled, which caught the others by surprise.

She stepped back before any other signs of emotion could escape.

"Anyway . . . Mom said to meet here. So, when I saw the door open and heard y'all down here, I just came down. Dude, Aaron . . . sweet digs." As Vee began walking around the room, the rest of the Dimeters released their hug.

"Okay, we have *a lot* to see, and we still need to get home and give Aaron's mom a call to make sure we can even make this trip," Darla reminded them. "What else do we need to do here before we leave? Aaron, it looks like we haven't looked at the cabinets or the wall safe. It looks like there is a scanner like the door for the wall safe, so why don't Phil, Vee, and I look at the cabinets and you boys go check and see what's in the safe? Once we have a good idea of what all is in here, let's talk in ten minutes about what to take home with us. Everyone know what they are doing?"

The others nodded. The dragons moved over to the giant cabinet on the left side of the room and started going through the drawers and cupboards, while Steve and Aaron eyed the metal door. On its left was another genetic hand scanner, just like the one on the outside door.

Aaron looked at Steve. "Here's hoping there is something cool inside."

He placed his palm on the scanner, which gave off a slight hum at first. *CLICK!* The safe door swung inward to reveal yet another room. With all kinds of jewelry, gems, and gold, it looked like a pirate's treasure trove!

"Dude," Aaron said stone-faced.

"Dude," Steve replied.

They turned to face each other, then started screaming and jumping around over the sight. Aaron stepped through the doorway and into the smallest room. Steve followed, and they slowly turned to take in everything around them.

"I can't believe this!" Aaron said. "How is this my life?"

"That's a lot of Geks!" Vee interrupted. She had come over to their side once she heard the boys' excited cries. Looking through the round doorway, she could see why they were excited.

Phil and Darla arrived to see what all the excitement was about. Vee stepped back so they could both peek inside. Phil put his wing around his wife and leaned his head against hers. They stood like that for a moment, just watching the boys reveling in their discovery.

"You ain't kidding, Vee! It's not only a lot of Geks—that's a lot of gold!" Phil exclaimed.

Aaron, hearing the others, came back down to reality. *I now have more money than I have ever had before. No more poor kid Aaron!*

"This is crazy!" Steve said.

"It really is!" said Darla, whose eyes were as wide as Phil's breakfast biscuits.

"Umm, y'all love me, right?" Vee asked as she tried to slide a couple gold bars into her bag. "Could I maybe just have, say, one or two of these bars? I mean you don't need *all* of them, do you?"

"Put it back!" Darla commanded. "I am sure the boys can figure that out later, but for now put it back."

"Ugh, fine!" Vee whined and returned the two gold bars to their place.

"Why don't you boys come on out?" Phil suggested. "Let's close this door. There's no need to let anyone find out how much is actually in there."

After Steve was out, Aaron pressed the door closed until its lock clicked.

"We found a few interesting things over in the cabinet," Darla announced. "It seems to be like a huge filing and storage system. There are several very rare items in these cabinets. It could be a great resource."

"Well, y'all saw what we found," Aaron replied. "Just a bunch of treasure, it looked like. No special notes or instructions in there."

"Okay. What do we think we need to take with us before we head home?" Darla asked the rest of the family.

"I think we should pack all the stuff from the table over there." Aaron pointed to the collection of blue items.

"I would like some of the books from up there as well," Darla said. "There are so many fascinating titles along that one wall."

"We should also maybe go ahead and grab some extra Geks from the safe to help with all the travel costs," Phil reminded them.

"Absolutely. Anything else we can think of?" Darla asked

Met by silence, she spoke again. "All right then. Aaron, you get the Geks from the safe. Take one of the satchels under the table and fill it up. That should work to get it home. Vee, you and I will load up the rest of the contents of that table into the other bags there. Steve and Phil, take one of the bags upstairs, but be careful. Grab some of the letters and photos by the desk. We'll all meet upstairs in the main vault room in five minutes."

She looked around for disagreement or uncertainty, but found none. "Break!"

After a few minutes of heavy lifting, they regrouped in the main vault.

"Okay, do we have everything?" Darla asked her family as they all stood in front of her, each one carrying his or her assigned items.

"I think so," Aaron said, adjusting the bag on his shoulder. "These Geks are a bit heavy, though."

"Yeah, my bag is heavy, too," said Vee.

Steve, who was holding two bags full of letters and photos, shrugged. "Eh, it's not too bad. I'm good."

"Didn't the note say something about using a sprinkle of water to shrink these or something?" Aaron recalled. He rolled his mental rolodex for shrinkweed bags. Sure enough . . . *DING!* The information flooded to the forefront.

"These bags are made of shrinkweed and will shrink down to a smaller size once sprinkled with water," Aaron blurted out in an almost robotic voice. "The contents do not get crushed when shrinking, and in order to return it to its normal size, you just need to pull slightly on the zipper at the top to break the seal."

"What was *that*?" Steve asked.

"I don't know. I think that was the journal knowledge coming up again. It seems if I ask myself a question, and the information just appears if it has to do with shimmers or people of The Table that Penelope would have known."

"Let's give this a try then, shall we?" Phil said.

"Darla. do you have your water bottle?" His wife never left home without at least a small one.

"Yes, it's right over there," she replied, pointing to her bag in the corner of the main vault room. He walked over to the purse, took the water bottle out, and sprinkled some of it on the shrinkweed bag he was holding. *SNAP!* The bag shrunk to the size and shape of a fanny pack, belt band with a clip and all!

Phil picked it up and clipped it around his waist. "Wow! This is going to be amazing on the trip. We can carry so much more! Do we have enough for everyone to have one?"

"Sure do!" Darla said, counting them out. "We even have one extra!"

"Hey, can I try it?" Aaron asked Phil, holding out his hand patiently for the water.

"Of course! Here you go." Phil tossed Aaron the bottle.

Aaron set his bag on the ground and sprinkled a few drops. *SNAP!* He picked up his miniature bag and put it back on. "That's much better. You can't even feel the weight! How do they come up with this stuff?"

The others took turns shrinking their bags. They were shocked by each transformation. After a few minutes of excitement, Darla got them moving. "Okay, let's get home to get packed. We also have a surprise for this evening."

"I love surprises!" Steve said.

"Then let's get home so we can show y'all!" Phil prodded.

As they traveled back out onto the stage, it looked

like the other two families had already left. On the short walk home, each Dimeter's excited thoughts and theories tumbled over the others', with nothing but joy on their faces.

15

CALLING MOM

Back at home, the boys headed off to pack. When Aaron got to his room, he realized he hadn't packed *anything* for a trip like this when he left his house in the overworld. He only had a few pairs of clothes, at best, with him.

Man, what am I going to do?

"Hey, Aaron, did you want to try to give your mother a call really quick?" Darla asked.

"Oh! Yes, please," Aaron replied.

"Come with me then. We can use the wall phone in the kitchen."

"Do phones work the same here as they do in the overworld?" Aaron asked as he followed her.

"Yes and no," said Phil, who was sitting at the kitchen table as they walked into the room.

"You see," Darla said, "the way we get service down here is by splicing into the phones lines that are already buried in the ground. We then have our very own Table switchboard that helps direct the call. So, to make a call here, you dial 0 for the operator and then tell them what number you want to be connected with. Calling the overworld from The Table is considered 'long-distance calling,' and the switchboard charges an extra fee for every minute we stay on the call."

"Oh, so just like in the overworld with that part! When we call my grandma, who lives in Dallas, we only do it during the day when the rates are lower for long-distance," Aaron said.

"Yeah, like that, but we don't need to worry how long we are on this call to your mom. We just want to make sure she is happy and knows you are safe. That is a mother's biggest worry. Okay, so what number are we calling?"

Darla pressed the Speakerphone button, which blared out a loud dial tone. She then pressed the 0 button for the operator. The phone rang a couple of times, followed by a nasally voice crackling across the speaker.

"Operator. Where can we transfer your call?"

"Could you please connect us with 830-555-4257?" Darla asked her.

"We would be happy to help. Were you aware of the extra charge for completing a long-distance call like this one?"

"Yes, we accept all charges," Darla replied.

"Connecting you now."

The phone speaker went silent, then rang three times.

"Hello?" Aaron's mother's voice came through.

"Hi, Mrs. . . ." Darla looked at Aaron in a slight panic. She didn't know his last name! He never told her.

Aaron, reading the look in her eyes, realized the same thing. "Hi, Mom," he butted in. "This is Mrs. Dimeter. Mrs. Dimeter, meet my mom, Mrs. Wright. . .

. Mom, my friend Steve from school invited me to stay over at his house tonight. He is on my baseball team, and we wanted to practice a little extra before school started."

"Hi, Mrs. Wright! Your son is a great kid. Steve is having some friends over for the last weekend of summer. I told them I would call you and ask, as we have not met before."

"Well, it's nice to meet you," Mrs. Wright said with a chuckle. "Sounds like they have concocted quite the plan. I am sorry for how excited Aaron can get. He is a handful sometimes. Where all will you be going this weekend? Just so I know where Aaron will be."

"Of course," Darla said. "We plan to just hang around the house. We live just down the road. Aaron found us down at the river swimming earlier today, and Steve wanted to see if he could join the fun."

"Well, I don't see any reason he can't enjoy the last weekend with his friends. Aaron, you behave and listen to *everything* Mrs. Dimeter says, okay?" Aaron's mom requested. "Be safe, sweetheart. I love you!"

"Love you too, Mom!"

"I promise we will keep him safe and have him home by Sunday afternoon, if that works for y'all," Darla added.

"Sounds good. Thank you," Mrs. Wright replied, and the phone call ended.

"Yes!" Aaron shouted loud enough to startle Phil, then began dancing around with joy. "We are going on a real, live adventure!"

Darla smiled, seeing how excited the boy was, and gave him a quick hug. "All right, now let's go get you packed."

Aaron's face paled. "But I didn't bring any clothes with me for the trip. I didn't know . . ."

"Don't worry about that. Do you remember how I said we had a surprise for you?" she asked.

Aaron nodded and looked up at her.

"Well, Phil and I were talking, and we thought it might be fun to use some time today to go to the mall to buy you and Steve some new clothes and stuff for the trip!" she said, trying to hold back her own excitement.

Those words felt like a stone in Aaron's stomach. *New? I can't afford new . . . Wait. Yes, I can!*

His thoughts exploded from his mouth like a volcano. "Oh gosh, the safe! I *can* get new stuff! . . . Umm, Darla, I've never done that. How do we do this?"

Darla scrunched her eyebrows, both confused and concerned by that fact. Then, she shook it off as a thought for another time. "Well, we figured we could head down to the mall in the shopping district and start there. We also thought it would be fun to have a family meal out this evening to celebrate. You and Steve can pick!"

Aaron stood there, still processing that all of this was in fact really happening—and to him, of all people.

"So . . . go ahead and change into the clothes I set out for you on the chair, then we will get going." Darla smiled and gently pushed him toward his room.

16

HEADED TO THE MALL

"Looking good, bro!" Steve said as he walked by Aaron's open door. Aaron had just finished changing into the clothes Darla left for him—a blue polo shirt with the shimmer insignia, some khaki shorts, and a pair of tennis shoes.

"Not looking too bad yourself," Aaron replied, noticing Steve was wearing a similar polo shirt, blue shorts, and red Converse. They both wore their Elfwater hats, of course.

Aaron held up his hand for a high-five, but Steve did not high-five him.

"Come on, don't leave me hanging," Aaron said.

"Umm, hanging from what? Why are you holding up your hand?" a confused Steve responded.

"You don't know what a high-five is?" Aaron asked, incredulous.

"A high what?"

"A high-five! Look, here is what I mean: Hold your hand up like I am mine." Aaron held out his hand for Steve to high-five.

Steve held out his hand, and Aaron immediately smacked it with his palm. "Like this!"

Steve was a little taken aback by the gesture. But once he caught on, he was all in. "Oh, I get it! High . . . five!"

Steve held up his hand again. As Aaron went to smack it, Steve smacked Aaron's hand first. *SLAP!* The noise echoed through the house.

"Oww!" Aaron howled.

Darla came running in from the hall. "Is everything okay? We heard a scream!"

"I'm sorry! It's all fine. Just don't high-five Steve," Aaron mumbled while he shook the pain out of his hand.

"Don't what?" Darla asked.

"Nevermind. It's just a greeting we use in the overworld. Sorry again about the yell," Aaron replied.

Darla smiled. "Well, let's get loaded up since you two look ready. We are out in five minutes!" she said as she walked back to the living room.

"Sorry, buddy. I thought I had it," Steve said once Darla had left.

"Oh, you definitely did, man. I just have to remember how strong you are. We will work on it, and it can be our secret handshake." Aaron smiled to show his big friend that he was going to be okay.

"I've never had a secret handshake with someone," Steve confided.

"Me either!" Aaron added.

As they entered the living room, Vee sat on the couch wearing what looked to be a uniform for a fast food restaurant, specifically Harold's Hot Dogs. Her little hat had a hot dog on top.

"Bahaha! What are you wearing?" Steve asked.

"Shut up, Steve!" Vee yelled, exasperated. Her red and yellow uniform looked good against her green skin, but she hated wearing it.

"Leave your sister alone," Darla commanded. "She took a job at Harold's to make some extra money for a car, and she starts today. We are going to drop her off before we start shopping. You should be proud of her and what she is doing, not laughing at her."

"Congrats on the new job," Aaron said, trying semi-successfully not to smile every time the little hot dog on Vee's hat flopped around.

Vee threw up her hands and stormed toward the front door. "Ugh! Even Aaron thinks it's ridiculous. I will be in the car."

Aaron's smile quickly faded. "I'm sorry! I didn't mean to."

"It's okay, son," Phil chimed in. "She is already gone, and it is hard not to smile when that hot dog wiggles like that. Deep down, she knows you didn't mean anything by it."

"Yeah, she is just mad that her fancy friends might see her dressed like that," added Steve.

"No matter the reason, she is clearly sensitive about it. So, let's try to be nice, okay?" Darla requested. "Now, let's go to the mall!"

She herded them into the hall. They headed down the elevator, to the parking garage, and into the Suburban, where Vee was waiting for them.

"Took you long enough!" Vee snapped.

"Calm it down a bit, young lady," Darla replied.

Once they were all loaded up, Aaron turned to Vee. "Hey, I am sorry. I like your uniform, and I am super proud that you are working hard to get a car."

Vee looked back at him and cracked a small smile. "You know, you're okay, Aaron."

Just as quickly, she wiped the smile off and turned to stare out the window.

Aaron looked out his own window and dreamed of all the things he could buy at the mall. He wasn't sure how many Geks he had or what all they could afford, but from the way everyone else reacted, it was more than he would ever need. He had never been to a store where he could buy anything new, much less anything he wanted.

This is going to be amazing! Oh, and I can buy some presents for Darla and Phil and Vee! I wonder what they might like. I bet I could find some cool stuff for everyone!

"Here we are!" Phil's voice and the Suburban coming to a halt brought Aaron out of his daydream.

"That was quick," Aaron said.

"Yeah, the mall is just down the road from the apartment. We normally would have walked, but we thought we might have quite a few things to carry. Bringing the car made the most sense," Darla said.

Aaron opened the door and stepped into a parking garage similar to those in the overworld. In the far corner, a sign reading *THE MALL OF MAGNIFICENCE* had a giant red arrow pointing down the stairs.

"So, I am guessing it's that way?" Aaron asked as the rest of the Dimeters climbed out of the vehicle.

"Yes, but slow down just a little," Darla replied. "Let's make sure we have everything before we head out."

"Umm, can I just go to work please?" Vee asked,

still annoyed.

"Sure, honey. Be safe and have a good first shift!" Darla said as she tried to reach for Vee, who was somehow already halfway across the garage.

"Bye, hon!" Phil hollered toward her, which made Vee cover her face and pick up speed.

"Boys, do we have everything? Here is an empty shrinkweed bag for each of you to fill up," Darla said. "Aaron, did you bring the bag of Geks?"

"Yep, it's right here!" Aaron unclipped the belt for the bag around his waist and set it on the seat in the Suburban. "Okay, it said that you just pull on the zipper—"

HISS! SNAP! The bag popped back to its original size, with the Geks inside making a loud thud as it happened.

"Wow, that works so well!" Darla exclaimed.

Aaron unzipped the bag the rest of the way and grabbed a stack of cash. He split it between Phil and Darla, then grabbed another stack for Steve and one for himself. "That should be enough, right?"

Darla and Phil stared at Aaron. "Yeah, a thousand Geks should be enough for each of us. But we can't take this," Darla protested. "It's yours and Steve's. We have money. You don't need to do this."

Aaron pushed the money in her outstretched hand back toward her. "You're right. I don't have to. *I want to*. Now let's go shopping!"

He turned and ran toward the big red arrow. Steve took off right behind him. Darla and Phil held hands and casually strolled along behind them.

17

NEW CLOTHES

Aaron slowed down as he reached the stairs, waiting for Steve and the parents. "So, what all do we need to get?" he asked when the dragons walked up.

"Well, you boys need clothes for the trip. That means at least one week's worth of clothing. We might be gone longer, but we'll figure out a way to wash them as needed," Darla began. "Make sure you get a jacket, definitely a swimsuit, some new underpants, and maybe some new hiking boots. We don't know where all we will be going."

"Oh, and see if you can find a good bottle for water. We'll need a few new tents and sleeping bags to fit all of us," Phil reminded them.

"Well, the camping supply store is on the other side of the mall, and the clothing store is on this side," Darla mused. "Boys, why don't you come with me to the clothing store. Phil, you take care of the camping supplies, then we can meet in the middle at the food court for dinner."

The boys nodded and started walking. Phil motioned for Darla to stay back a moment.

"If we use the extra money Aaron gave us, we could get a Traveler's Toolkit!" Phil whispered once the kids were out of earshot. "We never could have afforded one, but with this extra from Aaron, we can! And it would make the trip so much easier. What do you think?"

"That would be a dream, but they are so expensive," Darla said as she stared off into space.

"Darla? Darla?" Phil prepared himself for disappointment, but asked one more time. "So, should we use the extra funds to get one?"

"You know what? Let's do it!" Darla said.

"What can we do to help?" Aaron shouted from the lower level.

"Nothing, boys! All good up here," Phil said, then turned back to his wife. "I want to keep it a secret until we are packing. I bet Aaron is going to lose his mind when he sees it!"

They walked down the stairs to where the boys were waiting in a long corridor. It was about twenty feet wide and just as tall.

This is massive! thought Aaron. The walls were covered in a dark purple carpet, accented with rootwood trim. Every six feet or so, there was an archway of rootwood logs. The bark was so dark red that it almost looked maroon compared to the light red hue of the bare wood.

Aaron found what looked to be a map mounted on one of the walls. *WELCOME TO THE MALL OF MAGNIFICENCE*, it read above a diagram of the building. The mall was shaped like a rectangle. Just like the malls Aaron had been to in the overworld, the mall was two levels with stores down each side. He spotted the *YOU ARE HERE* sticker, but it was more confusing than helpful.

"Are we inside the wall?" Aaron asked since the sticker was firmly planted on the line for the walls.

"Yeah, kind of," Phil replied with a chuckle. "We are in the express walkway right now. It's a track that goes around the outside of the mall, and there is one on both levels. If you need to get some shopping done but don't want to deal with all the people trying to sell you stuff, it has several spots like this where you can enter or exit close to your destination."

"Wow! I don't think our malls have that." Aaron was impressed.

The map showed a store called CampWorld to their right. "There!" Phil said. "All right, I know where I am headed. I will meet y'all in what . . . an hour? At the food court?"

Darla nodded, and he vanished through a door from the express walkway.

"Okay, we need to go to . . . ah, right there!" Darla said as she pointed to a group of stores on the left and began walking in that direction. The corridor went on for about thirty feet, then curved to the right. As they passed the turn, Aaron could hear the sounds of the mall—jazzy music, laughter, sales pitches.

The exit door included a porthole that revealed the mall. The mall was huge, but otherwise pretty normal. The walls and floors were made of a polished black stone with silver metal trim outlining the panels. The stores he could see looked pretty similar to the overworld's.

Yep, almost identical to Grapevine Mills, Aaron thought. *So, this is going to be . . . normal?*

The familiarity instantly comforted him, so much so that he almost ran right into a minotaur. *Okay, maybe it's not just like home. Close enough, though.* he thought with a smile.

Darla paused and pointed toward a store at the end with *JMART* emblazoned on it in big red letters. "We are going to Jmart first. They should have some good clothes for the price. Steve, you have plenty of clothes at home, but why don't you get two to three sets of new ones and some new shoes? Aaron, you are a different story. You're going to need at least seven sets of clothes, a pack of underwear, socks, tennis shoes, boots, a jacket. . . . You know what? What size do you wear?"

"Umm I don't know. Large, maybe?" Aaron said, embarrassed that he wasn't sure.

Darla smiled warmly. "Turn around."

Once he did, she pulled the tag up from the neck of his shirt. "Yep, large it is, like those polos at home. I am going to check the back of your shorts now, okay? Just to see the size."

"Yes, that's fine. Thank you for that!" Aaron said, a bit relieved to have help.

"Medium shorts," Darla said, "and what about your shoes?"

"Umm, 9E or 9 wide," Aaron said. That one, he was confident on.

Darla nodded. "You two go pick out your clothes and shoes, and I will go get the extras."

Steve patted Aaron on the back and pointed him in the right direction.

18

LUNCH TIME

"Find everything, Dimeters?" Darla's voice cut into the giggling coming from the fitting rooms in the boys' section.

"Yup," Aaron blurted out from behind a door on the left end. "I have four pairs of gym shorts, three pairs of jeans, seven sweet T-shirts, and an awesome pair of sneakers! They even have a pump in them to help me jump!"

"And I have three T-shirts, a pair of jeans, and a pair of gym shorts," Steve boomed from the right end. "Oh, and we got matching shoes!"

"Okay, okay. Shh," Darla said with a chuckle. "I know y'all are excited, but try to keep your voices down. Does everything fit?"

Both boys replied with a simple "Yep!"

"Everything?" Darla asked pointedly.

"Yep!" Aaron replied quickly, but Steve was quiet.

"Even the jeans, Steve?" Darla knew he hated trying on pants.

"Ugh! But Mom, I know what size I am!" he complained.

"Try them on. You are both growing boys, so you

never know when your size might change."

"Fine!" Steve lamented.

Aaron could hear Steve stomping and shuffling things around as he walked out of his fitting room holding a pile of clothes and hangers.

Darla hurried to his side, grabbing some of his pile and putting it in their shopping cart. "Let me help you."

She methodically put his items back on the correct hangers, then hung them neatly over the side of the cart. It took her a few minutes, which gave Steve enough time to change into the jeans.

"Mom, they fit. I think," Steve hollered. "I mean . . . yeah, they do."

"Well, just come on out really quick and let me take a look," Darla replied.

"Really?! Come on!" Steve said as he slowly opened the door.

"Well. look at my handsome boy!" Darla howled as soon as she could see him.

"You see? All good." Steve turned to go change.

"Hang on. Is the length good? Turn around and show me the back."

Steve turned around a few times, then stormed back into the room and closed the door. Aaron giggled when the door smacked closed.

"Aww, honey you look great! I think those will work," Darla confirmed.

Once Steve was back in his own clothes and out of the fitting room, Darla helped him rehang and fold his stuff, too. "Now, who's hungry?" she asked.

"I'm so hungry I could eat a horse!" Aaron said.

Darla and Steve paused and turned to eye him

quizzically. "Huh?" Steve said.

"I mean ... me! I'm hungry."

Darla led them to the register. Checkout went smoothly, other than the pit in Aaron's stomach when he saw the total. He started to sweat as she counted out the Geks.

While the cashier bagged up their purchases, Darla glanced over to the boys. Aaron's nervousness caught her eye, and she rubbed his back to reassure him. "It's fine," she whispered to him. "We have plenty to cover this, and you deserve to have nice things."

Aaron smiled up at her, and the three of them headed toward the food court. It was smack in the middle of the mall. Before long, he could smell some the of tasty dishes available.

For a second, he flashed back to the Blackwings' attack while they ordered food at The Originals Festival. *No! Bart is gone, and it's safe to be here. No one is going to attack you,* he reminded himself. He took a deep breath in through his nose and was back to the present.

The air buzzed with chatter. Much like other food courts he'd seen, restaurants wrapped around the outside in a semi-circle, and every twelve feet or so would be a different restaurant. There was Ted's Taco Truck, Risk it for the Brisket, a couple Asian places, and Paul's Pizza Palace.

Mmm, pepperoni! Aaron's brain took over as he headed toward the neon blue lights at Paul's that read *KING OF PIZZA*.

"Hey, gang!" Phil shouted from a table right inside the entrance to the food court. They walked over to him and unloaded their arms.

"Wow! Looks like we got a few things," Phil teased, eyeing the mountain of white and red plastic Jmart bags.

"Yeah, but we got everything we needed, I think," Darla said. "What about you? How was CampWorld?"

"Great. We're all set," Phil said as he pointed to a few bags on the table next to them. "Boys, you can go grab some food. And don't worry about saying hi to Vee. I tried, and the results were not great."

"Pizza time!" Aaron shouted and ran off toward Paul's.

"I want some barbecue!" Steve said and headed that way.

"Well, you want some tacos?" Phil turned to where Darla had been standing, but she was already in line at Ted's and waving for him to join her.

When they met back at the table, there wasn't much talking. The food was delicious, and no one wanted to stop eating.

"Ugh, I can't finish that," Aaron said, setting down the crust of his last piece.

"Same. I am stuffed," Phil commiserated.

BURP! "Excuse me," Steve said as he waved his hand in front of his mouth.

Aaron and Steve cracked up, and Phil and Darla even let out a chuckle. They sat together quietly for a few more minutes, enjoying the peace that full bellies and good company could bring.

SMACK! Aaron's tray went tumbling to the floor as a young male dragon bumped their table.

"Oh, sorry!" the dragonkin said with a laugh, not sounding sorry in the least.

"Back off, Garrett!" Steve barked as he stood up from the table and blocked Aaron protectively. "We don't want any trouble!"

"Trouble?" Aaron said, confused. He hadn't noticed the newcomer until Steve spoke up.

"Aaron, meet Garrett. He's Bart's nephew," Darla said.

Aaron's eyes widened, and he stood up behind Steve. *Bart's nephew? Bart, the dude who tried to kill Steve and left me to die? . . . Wait. Garrett isn't Bart. Give him a chance.*

After a few long seconds, he reached out his hand. "Nice to meet you, Garrett."

Garrett scoffed. "I would never shake hands with you! You are an abomination!"

"Okay then. That's a no on the handshake," Aaron replied. *Well, nevermind. He is a jerk, too.*

"You don't deserve to be here," Garrett snapped. "Bart should be king, and you aren't even a full-blood shimmer! Why should you get to rule? Huh?"

He moved forward one step too far and bumped into Steve's chest. Garrett bounced off the giant, then eyed him up and down. The dragon apparently decided it was a good idea to step back before his next sentence.

"Aaron, no one wants you here. The Blackwings are going to make your time here miserable," Garrett continued.

"Well, I've got some good news for you. We are leaving tomorrow for his journey!" Steve said proudly.

Garrett smiled. "Tomorrow, huh? Interesting. Well, just stay out of my way, Dimeters!"

He walked away from their table and disappeared

into the mall crowd.

"Wow. That was . . . something," Aaron said, turning to the others for more information.

"I'm sorry, Aaron. I asked the others not to tell you about Garett yet," Darla said. "I was going to tell you once we left the city. Garrett is the new leader of the Blackwings."

"What's left of them," Steve said.

"Yeah, there are not many, but the few that still remain are not happy with you and the fact that you are half-human. They believe you can't be a part of the 'royal bloodline' with human blood," Darla explained.

"Well, that kind of sucks," Aaron said, self-doubt creeping in. *I mean, he isn't wrong. I am half-human.*

"Hey, don't worry about little ol' Garrett," Phil said. "If he shows his face again, I will give Steve full permission to defend you."

Steve smiled as he balled up his fist. "And I will happily take care of him."

That helped put Aaron at ease, and he snickered at Steve.

"Let's head to the car so we can pack and get enough sleep," Darla suggested.

Aaron smiled and shook off any lingering worries about the Blackwings. "Yes! I am so pumped to see the shimmers' home!" he said, louder than he intended.

A few groups around them got quiet and turned toward Aaron.

"Sorry!" Darla said to their neighbors as she ushered her crew out. "Boys!"

19

PACKING

So, maybe shirts in this bag, and the other stuff in that one? Aaron considered his options as he shuffled his new things between the shopping bags on his bed and the shrinkweed bag.

"Aaron, you can just get your personal shrinkweed bag packed," Darla said from the doorway. "Give me the clothes you bought. I want to make sure you and Steve have all the things you need in your travel bags."

He looked up and let out a deep breath. "Thank you so much! Do I look as lost as I feel?"

"Yeah, probably." She laughed, and Aaron joined in. "Also, I have a video call later with Horace to pick the best lava link path to get us as close to Seaweed City's location as we can. Then, we will travel the overworld to the exact coordinates."

Darla picked up most of the clothes and headed to her room to pack.

Well, that definitely makes things easier. Aaron laid down on his bed next to the empty shrinkweed bag and considered what he wanted to bring with him. *My journal, Penelope's pen, and all the other items we brought from the vault. I should grab some extra Geks, too.*

Aaron twirled the small blue shimmer stone on the end of his new necklace. He drifted off to sleep, lost in thought and too comfortable to stay awake.

As Phil walked down the hall, he caught sight of Aaron fast asleep next to his empty shrinkweed bag. He pulled a blanket over Aaron and turned off the light.

"Sweet dreams, son," Phil whispered as he closed the door.

20

TAKING OFF

“Okay, adventurers, it’s time to get up!” Darla’s voice rang through the apartment.

What time is it? Aaron wondered as he yawned. The room was still pretty dark, but he could see the light from the hallway beneath the door. Darla’s voice called out again from the other side as she walked toward the kitchen.

“Steve, Aaron, wake up! We’ve got to get moving.”

Aaron smiled as climbed out of bed. Today was the beginning of the journey of a lifetime. *I can’t imagine what all is in store for us. Who will we meet? What will we see along the way?*

“Honey, are you up?” Darla’s impatient voice came with a knock this time.

“Morning, Darla! Yes, ma’am, I am,” he replied. “I will be right out.”

“Sounds good! Breakfast is on the table, and then we are on the road and heading toward Midtown Lake in thirty minutes!”

Thirty minutes? I haven’t even packed yet. Okay, umm, what do I need again? The journal, some extra money, and umm . . .

BOOM! BOOM! Aaron jumped at the sound.

"Hey, buddy! It's, uh, Steve. Can I come in really quick?"

"Come on in, dude."

Steve shuffled into the room holding his shrinkweed bag and his journal, looking uncertain. He closed the door behind him and looked to Aaron.

"I think I need some help," Steve said.

"Of course. Whatever you need," Aaron assured him. "What's up?"

"Well, umm, I don't know what to pack. Like, what do I take? Mom packed all the clothes, extra shoes, food, camping gear, and anything else you might think we could need on this trip. She has been up all night filling up the Traveler's Toolkit."

"Travelers Toolkit?" Aaron repeated.

Steve smiled. "Whoops. Forget I said that, please. Mom and Dad want it to be a surprise, so no more questions, okay?"

He looked over to Aaron, who nodded. Aaron smiled at the thought that the Dimeters were waiting to surprise him and decided not to press the subject.

"Thank you," Steve said. "Anyways, what are you packing? Because I really don't know what else to bring besides, like, myself and this journal thing?"

"I don't know either. Darla said to make sure I am ready to go, but then I think she packed it all already," Aaron replied.

As Steve pondered, Phil's voice floated in from the hallway.

"Do, do, do! I am excited to go on this here trip

with you!" Phil sang in a fun sing-song voice as he walked.

"I've got it!" Steve said as he opened the door and pulled Phil inside. "Dad, quick question!"

"Woah! Everything okay?" Phil asked, a bit shaken up.

"Yeah, sorry. Aaron and I don't know what to pack because it seems like Mom already packed it all, but she keeps telling us to make sure we are ready. We don't want to upset her."

"Your mother has indeed already packed most everything you need," Phil said. "I would say you need to make sure you have your journals and any special items you want to bring on the trip. Other than that, your mother has it ready to roll. And anything we forget, we can pick up once we get to Seaweed City."

Hearing Phil saying the city's name gave Aaron chills.

"Sounds good to me," Aaron said. "That will leave room for treasures I find along the way."

"Same!" said Steve.

"Now, let's get some breakfast!" Phil said as he opened the door and went back to his singing.

"Race you!" Steve yelled as he tore out of the room.

"No fair!" Aaron hollered as he scrambled after his giant friend.

"Slow down in the house!" Darla's sharp tone told the boys she wasn't messing around, and they both calmly made their way to the table.

Aaron couldn't believe what had been laid out for breakfast. "Are those kolaches? Like the sausage-in-a-roll thingies?" he asked.

"Yep," Phil said. "These are a big deal down here."

"Yes! "Aaron said with pure joy. "They are my favorite!"

"Mine, too!" Steve added.

"Before you dig in, pay attention," Darla warned. "The ones on the right have jalapeño in them, so they might be too spicy for Aaron. The donuts are a mix. Enjoy, but be ready to roll in fifteen minutes, okay?"

The boys and Phil nodded and added food to their plates.

"Oh, look what the dragon drug in!" Darla said sarcastically as Vee entered the room.

"Yeah, yeah. Mom, why do I even have to be up right now?" she lamented as she sat at the table.

"We are headed out for a week or maybe longer," Darla replied. "Just because you have to stay and work doesn't mean you can't see us off. Plus, you need the car, and we need you to bring it home from the lake."

"Ugh, fine. At least I get some jalapeño kolaches out of this!" Vee snatched a kolache out of Steve's hand with her tail and stuffed it into her mouth.

"Mom!" Steve whined.

"Venus Anne Dimeter!" Darla hollered. "Apologize to your brother!"

"Geez! Sorry, Steve. I love you and will miss you, okay? I am going to be here bored and alone while y'all are off having a huge adventure," she began, then corrected herself. "Umm, I mean, or maybe I won't. I am mature enough to have my own place anyway. I am going to go do my hair."

"Don't worry about her," Darla said as Vee sauntered off. "She is just upset that she has to work.

She isn't enjoying that part of growing up so much. She will be fine. I will go check on her while you boys finish up. Please put the dishes in the sink when you are done."

Both boys agreed, even though they had not stopped eating during Vee's appearance.

"I'll make sure they are ready, hon," Phil said. "Thank you for checking on Vee."

The trio ate as quickly as they could, so there wasn't much room for conversation between bites.

After a few more minutes, Darla's voice came from the living room. "All right! Let's get this rodeo on the road!"

The boys and Phil cleaned up their mess. Darla smiled as they walked into the room.

"Perfect timing. Let's roll!" She opened the front door and led her family toward the elevator.

"Shotgun!" Vee yelled as soon they arrived at the garage level.

"Dang it!" Steve hollered.

"Too slow, bro!" Vee yelled back as they headed to the Suburban.

"Did y'all forget that both your parents are going on this drive? There's no open front seat," Phil said with a laugh. He got buckled in, then maneuvered the vehicle out of the garage and out onto the main street.

"So, boys," Darla said, turning to face them, "we haven't fully discussed how we are getting to Seaweed City."

"Oh yeah!" Both boys responded, a bit surprised they had forgotten that part.

"We only have a few minutes now that we are on

the highway, but I wanted to try to explain a little." Darla said. "Phil and I spoke with Horace last night and came up with a route. The best bet is everyone using the lava links to get to the overworld exit near South Padre Island, Texas."

"Wait, Seaweed City is near South Padre?" Aaron interrupted excitedly. "I know where that is! I went there when I was younger. I can't remember the trip, but my mom told me I visited there one time when I was a baby."

"Yes, it seems the entrance coordinates have it somewhere on the edge of a small island off the coast there. It looks like no overworlders travel on it, so it sounds like the perfect spot for a secret entrance," Darla continued. "From there, it's as easy as just finding the secret shimmer entrance."

"Wait, I get to go in the lava links!?" Steve asked incredulously.

"Yep! We all do, thanks to those bracelets from Aaron's vault," Phil said.

"That's going to be so awesome!" Aaron chimed in.

"I think it's pretty cool, too, but we need to remember to be safe and follow Aaron's instructions" Darla said.

"My instructions?!" said Aaron, who was caught off-guard.

"Well, yeah. You are leading this journey," she reminded him. "We are just here to chaperone and keep everyone safe. The elders were very specific that we do not help with direction, only preparation and protection. This journey is meant to test the descendants and their leadership skills. So, we are following you, sir!"

Darla smiled at Aaron, who looked pale.

"I guess that makes sense," he said. "So, the plan is to start in the lake and take a link that will put us out near South Padre, which should be close to Seaweed City, and then I have to find the entrance?" Aaron repeated back to her.

Darla nodded, so he continued. "And everyone will be following me. What if I do something wrong? Or make a wrong turn? Or—"

"We will all be right there with you to back you up," Darla cut in.

"Yeah, buddy! We got this—together," Steve said.

"Welp, we are here," Phil announced.

Aaron looked out the window to see the sprawling lake he had come in through the day before. They were parked on the beach, right in front of the entrance to the dock. Across the street directly behind them, the buildings of downtown loomed. Everyone got out of the vehicle, and Aaron turned to check out the buildings.

"Pretty cool, right?" Phil said. "I love how downtown just ends at this lake. And look at how far down the wharf goes." He pointed farther down the shoreline.

"This place is unbelievable!" Aaron said, then walked to the back of the car to help unload the luggage.

Darla already had the back open, so he grabbed his shrinkweed bag. As he did, he noticed there was only a small, red toolbox-looking thing left back there. It was a cube, about two feet long on each side, and it looked brand new.

"Should I grab this thing and bring it with us? Where are the rest of the bags?" Aaron inquired.

"Oh, that?" Phil asked with a grin as he picked up the metal cube with ease. "That is a Traveler's Toolkit! I am so excited to show it to you. Come grab it and set it over there on the ground away from everything. It needs at least four feet of space on all sides. After you step at least four feet away, clap twice."

Aaron looked unconvinced.

"Just do it," Phil assured him. "You're going to love this!"

Aaron took the toolkit from Phil. *Holy cow! This thing is lighter than a regular toolbox.*

He walked over to an empty spot in the parking lot, set down the box, rushed away, and then looked over to Phil. He motioned for Aaron to clap twice.

"Okay, I'll do it." He clapped twice.

SNAP. CLICK. CLANK. CLACK. The red box unfolded over and over and over again. Aaron couldn't keep up with the panels switching places as it grew. Before he knew it, an oversized armoire had appeared. The large doors on its front had silver handles, and there were six large drawers below them. Each had a letter sticker on the front.

"*That* is a Traveler's Toolkit!" Phil announced.

"*That* is epic!" Aaron shouted.

"Right! And look inside," Phil added as he ran over to open the doors. Inside on the left was an area for hanging clothes. The right side was a stack of six drawers from top to bottom. Each drawer had a letter sticker that matched the ones on the lower drawers.

"We each have one drawer on bottom and one up top, and they hold a ton of stuff," Phil explained. "All the things Darla packed are in this toolkit."

Aaron stared in amazement. "How does it work, though? Like, none of the items inside are broken or anything? And how is it so light?"

"I am a sanitation specialist. I don't know the how," Phil said. "I just know it works on some sort of magical physics . . . and it's super cool and helpful. Thank you so much for those Geks earlier. That gave us enough to get this."

"Wow, that is cool!" Liz's voice came from across the parking lot.

"Hi, Liz," Darla said with a wave. "Just bring your bags over here and we can consolidate like we talked about earlier."

Liz made her way over to where the others were admiring the toolkit and set down her things.

"Why don't you boys head down to the water and get things ready there? Make sure everyone gets their supplies. One shrinkweed bag, a bracelet, a shimmer badge, and we each need one of Penelope's pens. I will stay here and get the toolkit packed with Liz's stuff and then Emily's when she gets here."

"When I get where?" Emily's voice boomed from the other side of the parking lot.

"And there she is! Hi, Emily! Come on over!" Darla replied to their dwarven friend.

"Y'all, this is going to be awesome!" she exclaimed as she set down all her stuff near Darla.

The boys said quick hellos, then they headed down to the beach to find where they would be taking off.

Some of Emily's entourage had already headed down there as well, as had some of Liz's family.

"Okay, let's see how this thing works," Phil said as the boys got close to the water's edge. He put the bracelet on his arm, which made his ears pop and his eyes feel dry. He then clipped his shrinkweed bag to his waist and pinned the shimmer badge to his chest. As the badge hit his chest, he briefly heard a small whine, like a radio being dialed in.

"That was something! Now, what happens when I . . ." He ran out into the wake, dove into the water, and disappeared.

Aaron and Steve scanned the surface feverishly. After what felt like several minutes, but was actually just a few seconds, Phil shot into the shallow water and stood up.

"That's so much fun," he said as he wiped water off his face. "Come check this out!"

The boys ran over, and Steve slid on his bracelet. He scrunched his face as it activated.

"Weird, right?" Phil said.

Steve nodded, then put on his shimmer badge. He again scrunched his face.

"The whining noise will stop," his father said. "Just give it a second."

Steve shook his head, then smiled. "I think it stopped," he said.

"Now clip your shrinkweed bag to your waist and go for a swim," Phil said. "But be careful—you swim *really* fast with these bracelets. Watch where you are going."

Steve waded into the water cautiously, but curiosity

quickly got the best of him. He dove face-first into the water and took off like a missile. Aaron could see the crest of the waves his giant body created as he made figure eights in the middle of the lake. Aaron clipped his bag to his waist and took off to join his friend.

"Hey, wait for me!" Phil hollered. They met up and sped around the lake.

"Woohoo!" Steve shouted out under the water as he came to a stop. "Wait! I heard myself. Wait! I am talking underwater. And I am breathing underwater."

"Cool, right?" Aaron said as he slowed down and floated next to Steve.

"It's more than cool," Phil said as he shot by and then came back to join them. "Thank you for sharing this with us."

"Of course! I am excited to be able to show y'all. I am still trying to figure it out, so having family out here is just the best," Aaron said.

"Race you to the beach!" Steve said and took off.

"No fair!" Aaron said as he chased him back to the shore.

"Be careful coming into the bank!" Phil yelled after them.

Both boys swam as fast as they could toward the sandy beach where Darla and the girls were waiting. They were so focused on who would win that neither slowed down in time to stop.

THUD! THUD! The abrupt stop sent them tumbling into a pile of sand.

Aaron and Steve stood up, slightly bewildered, and tried to shake off the sand and seaweed stuck to them.

"I told you to be careful," Phil said as he stepped

out of the water, laughing. "Y'all okay?"

"Yeah," they groaned.

"Oh, I want to try that!" Emily said excited as she saw the wake they left in the water.

"I will admit that looked like a blast," Darla agreed. "Other than the crash."

"Yeah, it did!" Liz added.

Darla and Emily looked at Liz, apparently surprised to hear excitement in her voice.

"What? I like fun stuff, too," she said, somewhat offended, then turned to Aaron. "So how does it work? Darla said you had some things that we need for the trip that would help us swim. What are they? Does it do *that* to us?"

Aaron stammered a little as he held out the bracelets and badges. He started to explain them, but apparently wasn't quick enough for Liz. She snatched a bracelet and badge and headed toward the water.

"So, you just . . . what? Put them both on?" Liz put on the bracelet and then, at almost the exact same time, slapped the badge on her chest. *WEE!* Her ears rang with the sound, and she fell to one knee. She quickly recovered, though, and gave a thumbs up.

Liz then dove into the water and took off. *SPLOOSH!* She rushed past, just as the boys had earlier.

"Oh heck yeah!" Emily yelled as she grabbed her badge and bracelet out of Aaron's hand, then tossed them on as she ran to the water. She slowed for a few seconds as the side effects took hold, then shook it off. "All right, let's roll!"

"Well, now I want to go," Darla said as she pulled her gear from her pocket.

Phil met her at the water's edge. "Hey, it's a bit . . ."

Before he could finish his sentence, Darla had already slipped the bracelet over her wrist. She froze in her tracks, trying to orient herself. She looked at Phil with fear in her eyes.

"I was trying to say it's a weird feeling, but you already had the bracelet on," Phil said with a chuckle. "Once you put the badge on, it will feel like your head is tuning into a radio station. It only lasts for a few seconds."

Darla nodded and pinned the badge to her chest. She shook her head after a few seconds. "Just like you said." She waded into the water and then dove in after the others.

"I am going to go grab the toolkit and get us ready to launch once they get back," Phil told Aaron and Steve, then went back to the Suburban.

"Man, I can't believe we are going to see where the shimmers come from," Aaron said. "I am so pumped!

"Me too, dude. . . . Umm, but I have a question that I wanted to ask you without my parents around," Steve said, looking a little nervous.

"Sure. What's up?"

"So have you thought about who your shimmer parent was? I mean, it had to be your dad, right?" Steve asked. "I'm sorry if this is too personal. I just can't stop thinking about the fact that I have a family out there somewhere, maybe, and that I might get to meet them. We just had not talked about it, and thinking about my stuff made me think about yours. And I don't want to bring up talking about parents with mine around because I don't want to hurt their feelings. Phil and

Darla raised me, and they are for sure my mom and dad, but who are my birth parents?"

The color drained from Aaron's face as his thoughts spiraled out of control. *Wow! Why didn't I put that together? So much has taken place these last few days, I hadn't even thought about it. Was my dad a shimmer? I mean, my mom sure isn't. She hates swimming. So, yeah. Wow. I just—*

THUD! Emily smacked into the shoreline almost exactly where the boys had. "Totally tubular!" Emily yelled as she sat up in the sand pile. "These things are awesome!"

Darla and Liz walked in from the shoreline behind her. "They really are!" Darla added.

Emily dusted herself off, and the three women walked back toward the group.

"We can talk about it later," Steve whispered quickly to Aaron before they got too close.

Aaron nodded blankly, still not over Steve's revelation. *So, what actually happened to Dad? What was his tragic accident? Is this why none of my family knew much about him or could give me any information?* he wondered as he put on a smile for the girls.

"Where is Phil?" Darla asked.

"Oh, he went to get the Traveler's Toolkit ready," Steve said.

"Gotcha. Girls, here are the other two pieces of equipment you will need." Darla picked up the two empty shrinkweed bags and demonstrated how they worked. She then handed one to each, along with one of Penelope's pens. "The pens will write on any surface and underwater. Please be respectful of these items and take good care of them. *All* of you."

As she said the last part, she turned to stare at Aaron and Steve in a way that said, "I mostly mean you two."

"Darla! Hey Darla!" A female voice came from the other end of the beach.

Liz looked over. "Hi, Mom," she said to the woman.

"Darla, I just want to make sure that you are safe with my baby, just like we talked about on the phone!" Liz's mother said as she walked up.

"Of course, Mandi. Liz will be perfectly safe and, as we discussed, Phil will be finding a place to make a call home each night we are gone. He will call the main elders' chambers and give them a report. Parents are welcome to be present for that call. Just make sure and check with the elders, okay?"

Mandi relaxed her shoulders. "Yes, I know. I'm just worried about my little dragon."

"Mom, seriously? I am seventeen . . . almost eighteen. Can we please stop calling me little?" Liz said.

"Don't forget my daughter!" a dwarven man in a wheelchair said as he rolled up to the Suburban.

"Sup, Dad!" Emily said as she walked over to him and leaned down for a hug.

"Darla, you make sure my daughter comes back a glorious warrior! Any battles she can get in, push into it! She is my strong gladiator and the champion of The Table! She deserves a challenge!" The dwarven man coughed as he got a little too excited. "Why, if I hadn't lost my legs in that accident . . ."

He looked to the clouds as he recounted the tale for the thousandth time.

"Hi, Dale," Darla said. "Yes, we remember how you tragically lost your legs. Again, sorry to hear it. Also, there will be no intentional fighting on this trip. We have no clue what might take place, but it's our goal to stay away from that."

"But what glory is there in that?" Dale huffed.

"She will be fine, I promise. You too, Mandi. Liz will be fine," Darla said. "Now why don't you all say your quick goodbyes and we will get going? We are burning daylight!"

Liz walked over to the rest of her family with her mother, and they began their hugs. Emily's family did the same, except theirs sounded more like a chant followed by a football team breaking their huddle.

"Hey, can I have a hug or whatever?" Vee's voice came from behind them. She looked a bit wistful.

"Aww! Of course, sweetheart!" Darla wrapped Vee in a giant wing hug.

"Group hug!" Steve yelled as he piled onto the women. Aaron and Phil joined, too. Once the hug broke, the boys said goodbye to Vee and headed back toward the water.

Darla hung back. "If you need anything while we are gone, you call—"

"Aunt Alison, who lives down the hall," Vee said, completing the sentence. "Obviously. I don't need you to quiz me."

"We trust you. Just be smart, okay?" Darla said.

"I will be. I promise," Vee said in that tone she uses when she is actually being serious.

"Deal," Darla as she wrapped up her daughter once more.

"Hey, leave me some," Phil said as he waited to say goodbye to his daughter.

"Love you, dude," he whispered to Vee. "Be good and don't do anything stupid, cool?"

"Cool," she replied.

Phil walked over to the toolkit and clapped his hands once. The toolkit flipped and snapped and cracked until it was shaped like a backpack.

"It turns into a backpack, too?!" Aaron shouted from the shore.

"Yep, that's the traveler's part of its name," Phil said as he put the backpack on. "One clap, and it changes to the backpack. Two claps opens and closes it."

"It's never going to get old how cool it is here!" Aaron said.

"Well, just wait until we get to Seaweed City!" Steve added. "I bet it's even cooler than we can imagine!"

"Then let's get going!" Emily said as she and Liz walked up to the group again.

"Aaron, this is *your* journey," Darla said somberly. "Horace told us to follow the orange glow sticks and that the trip should only take ten to fifteen minutes at most to get to our exit."

She pointed across the lake. "He said the entrance is on that end, toward the middle of that cliff face."

"Got it," Aaron replied, then took a deep breath. "Okay, everyone, just follow me across the lake and try not to run into each other. The tubes are really only meant for single file-traffic, so try to keep in line if you can."

He paused for a minute, trying to think if there was anything else he needed to explain. He couldn't think of anything as he looked back at the others, who were watching him for direction.

"All right then. Let's go," he said timidly.

"Let's try that again," Emily demanded. She put her hand out flat, like she was about to break a huddle.

"Come on, y'all. Descendants on three, okay?" She glanced at the others to join, and they all stacked their hands on top of hers.

"One, two, three, descendants!" They all hollered and threw their hands in the air in excitement.

"That's more like it. *Now* we can go, Aaron," Emily said with a smile.

Aaron looked at Darla and Phil, who both nodded to him. Their confidence in him squashed any lingering doubts.

He held his hand to his chest, where he could feel the shimmer stone through his shirt. Touching the stone seemed to calm him. *You are a shimmer, Aaron. You got this!*

He took a few steps forward, dove into the lake, and headed toward the cliff face. As he swam, he looked back to see that he had created a small current in the water. Behind him was Liz, then Darla, Emily, and Steve, with Phil as the caboose. The current seemed to make it easier for them to follow him.

Aaron turned back to the front and searched through the rushing water for the orange glow that would light the entrance they needed. *There!*

The glow stick was coming up fast, so he slowed down and ensured the others followed suit by putting his hand out flat back toward them. The entrance resembled a tiny cave in the side of the rock face with a small beacon attached to the top.

"Here we go," Aaron yelled to the others, and he entered the tube. He swam a bit slower than usual to give the others time to acclimate to the new sensation. He came to a stop and just floated in the tube until everyone was inside.

"All good back there?" he asked. Each replied with a yes or a thumbs up.

He smiled and took off a little faster. The others had no trouble keeping up.

This is going to be awesome! Aaron thought. *This trip won't be hard at all!*

After a few minutes of swimming in a fairly straight line, the tube made a big turn. *SMACK!* Aaron ran into a pile of stones closing off the link. He turned around to the others, who had piled up behind him after the abrupt stop.

"Sorry, y'all. I'm not sure what to do now. The entire link is blocked," he explained.

KABOOM! The side of the tube exploded into several pieces and sent water surging out. The pressure change sucked the travelers out of the tube, along with rocks and other debris.

What the heck just happened? Aaron thought as he regained control of his direction. He tried to open his eyes, but his vision was blurry from the blast. He shook his head a bit and blinked a few more times. The devastation was all around him.

He and the others found themselves floating in a large body of water that the lava link apparently ran below. Aaron spotted a giant hole in the top of the lava link, then remembered his fellow travelers.

Where is everyone else? He scanned the water for his family. In the distance, he saw three dark figures in what looked like scuba gear swimming away. He swam after them, but then spotted Liz, lifeless.

Aaron dragged her toward the surface, propelled by adrenaline. They were a long way down, but he could eventually see a few shadows on the surface as he continued up.

Yes! It's the others! The sight pushed him to swim even faster toward safety. His eyes were still a little blurry, and he felt himself beginning to fade as he crested the water near the shadows.

He was almost there, but the energy in him had run out. As his eyes closed and the darkness set in, he saw several hands reaching through the top of the water to grab him and Liz.

After that, only darkness.

21

STRANGE PLACE

Where am I? Aaron thought as his eyes opened. The hammock he found himself in wobbled as he studied the small room. Another hammock hung directly above his. Wooden planks of a familiar pink hue, secured with black bolts, lined the walls. Light peered in through a small circular window on the back wall and illuminated the space a bit more.

Is that rootwood? This whole place seems to be made of it. So, I'm still somewhere in The Table. Think, Aaron! He remembered Liz was on his back when he blacked out. He panicked and quickly sat up, forgetting he was in a hammock.

CRASH! "Oww!" Aaron yelped as he tumbled to the ground.

"Ugh, could you keep it down? I am trying to sleep." Liz's groggy voice drifted down from above him.

Aaron scrambled to his feet. "Oh good! You are okay!" he said, relieved, as he grabbed the edge of the top hammock and shook it excitedly.

"Whoa there!" she replied. "Calm down before you make me fall. Wait. Where are we? Umm, and do you remember how we got here?"

"I don't know," Aaron replied. "I just woke up, too. Last thing I remember was pulling you to the top of the water, seeing shadows, and then hands pulling me out of the water."

"You carried me?" Liz asked, slightly confused.

"Umm, yeah, kind of. I mean, I don't know that I made it all the way to the top," he said awkwardly.

"Thank you so much—seriously. Thank you." Liz sounded both grateful and shaken.

"No big deal. You would have done the same for me. We should go find the others. It looks like there is a door over here." He approached the door and peered through its round window.

"Oh, you're awake now, are ya?" A man with a large, round face, blue eyes, and brown slicked back hair appeared in front of the window.

"Ahh!" Aaron jumped back.

"Oh, I'm just kidding with ya." The tall, heavy-set man laughed as Aaron watched him walk off. "Hey, Phil! These two are up!"

"Aaron? Liz?" Phil's voice came from the other side of the door as Aaron heard his footsteps pounding toward it.

"Yes, it's us!" Aaron shouted as the door burst open and Phil wrapped Aaron in the biggest dragon hug he had experienced yet. He quickly set Aaron down and turned to Liz.

"Are you okay?" Phil asked her. "I have been worried sick about you both. First of all, everyone else is okay. You two were the last of us to wake up. Darla is up top with Steve and Emily getting some food. We have been taking turns watching your room for any signs of change. I was just in the other room across the corridor when Bill yelled for me."

"Bill?" Aaron asked. "Who is Bill, and where are we? What happened to us? What is 'up top'? Was everyone knocked out?"

Aaron couldn't stop the word vomit. Phil held up his hands.

"I promise we will get all these questions answered, but we need to take them one at a time. First, Bill is a friend of mine from back in high school. His proper name is William the Wise, but he goes by Bill. He was the first shimmer I ever met. After high school, he went off to be a commercial fisherman. This is the first time I have seen him in years, but he is a very good person and can be trusted. To answer your second question, we are on his ship . . . well his ship-house."

"Umm, ship-house?" Liz said questioned.

"You know, why you don't both follow me and see for yourself?" Phil walked out into what he had called "the corridor."

It had a small, horseshoe-shaped wall on one end of the home, with a flat wall opposing the arch of the horseshoe. Aaron counted four other doors. The corridor had the same pink wood and black bolts as the first room.

That's definitely rootwood, Aaron thought as he followed Phil across to a door on the opposite wall. Phil opened it and motioned for Aaron and Liz to go in front of him.

"This is a ship!" Aaron yelled back toward Phil as he stepped out onto the deck. He gazed up at the large rootwood mast that stretched into the sky.

"Umm, Phil?" Liz asked.

"Are we sailing?" Aaron asked as he and Liz stumbled toward to the edge of the ship.

"Well," Phil began.

"Nevermind," Aaron replied, his disappointment clear as he looked over the railing. All he saw below him was sand and rocks. He turned his head toward the other end of the ship, and it became clear just how huge this vessel was. He could see the ocean, but it was a little way off in the distance. *We're hanging out on a wrecked ship!*

"Yeah, she ain't on water, but she is still my pride and joy!" Bill said as he crossed the walkway that went above and behind where the corridor and rooms were.

"Aaron and Liz, meet Bill. Bill, meet Aaron and Liz," Phil said as the old sailor walked up to them.

Bill stuck his hand out. "Pleasure to meet ya both!"

Aaron shook his hand. "Nice to meet you as well, sir!"

Liz gave a small wave. "Hello!"

"Welcome to the Savvy Seal!" Bill said with a giant grin. "She holds a lot of stories. Once she was wrecked, I couldn't bring myself to leave her, so I made her my home."

"Aaron, I know you still have plenty of questions, but let's get some food in you first," Phil said. "We also need to let the others know you two are okay."

"Follow me to the galley," Bill said. The kitchen and dining area were in the belly of the great vessel.

"Aaron!" Darla's voice deafened all the others as they walked in. She ran to hug Aaron, with Steve right behind her.

"Sweetheart, I am so happy you are all right!" Darla exclaimed. She then grabbed Liz and hugged her, too.

Emily walked up next. "Glad to know y'all are good to keep going," she said, then went back to eating.

Aaron took a look around the kitchen, which was more modern than he expected. Other than the plank walls, all of the kitchen items, including a large two-door refrigerator in the corner, seemed pretty up-to-date. In the center of the room was a large steel table surrounded by several metal stools. Massive plates of finger foods—mini sandwiches, dips, meats and cheeses, crackers, chips, and more—filled the table.

"You are welcome to whatever you would like," Bill said.

As soon as he heard that, Aaron darted for an empty stool and began feverishly loading up his plate. Liz was not far behind him. The adults chuckled as they settled in.

"Okay, now that Liz and Aaron are here, let's talk about what happened, where we are, and what we are going to next," Darla announced.

Everyone stopped eating and looked at her.

"So, let's start with what happened. From what Phil and I can tell, someone was trying to sabotage us by blocking the tunnel so that they could blow it up with us in it. We don't know who it was or why, and none of us saw anything. What about you two? Did y'all see anything?" Darla asked.

"Umm, I remember seeing someone in the distance in what looked like a wetsuit or scuba gear of some sort. There were three of them, and they swam away as I was coming to after the blast." Aaron recollected.

"Oh, wow. None of us saw them, but that tells us it was sabotage!" Darla said. "Did either of you see anything else?"

Aaron shook his head no. Liz stared at the ground.

"Liz?"

"Umm, nope. I don't remember anything," she stammered. "I just remember being in the tube, then the explosion, and then waking up in the hammock."

"Okay. Sorry to bring that up so soon, but thank you two for trying," Darla said. "We obviously have an idea of who it might be, but we're not one hundred percent sure. We spoke to the elders earlier on a phone call that our lovely friend Bill here facilitated. We told them and your parents everything that happened. They all agreed that it was important for the descendants to battle through any trials they encountered on this journey. As long as no one was hurt and we are more careful in the future, they agree that we should keep going to Seaweed City."

She paused there to see watch for reactions. Each traveler glanced around the room at the others, awkwardly waiting for someone to break the silence.

"Well, I still want to go," Aaron said quietly.

"Me, too," Steve added with a little more confidence.

"You know I am in! The more fighting, the better!" Emily added.

They all looked at Liz, who smiled. "And I am in, too! Onward we go!"

Everyone at the table cheered, and laughter broke out for a moment as the tension lifted. Once they had all calmed down again, Darla continued.

"Then it's settled. We keep going. That brings me to the next topic: Where are we and how did we happen upon a friend at the beach? I believe that was the next question we had to tackle, right?"

"Yep!" Aaron said in between stuffing his face with ham and cheese.

"Yeah, what is that all about?" Liz asked.

"The explosion blew Phil, Steve, Emily, and me up toward the surface. Phil and I never lost consciousness, but Steve and Emily were out cold for a few. I grabbed Emily, Phil grabbed Steve, and we started swimming with them to the surface. When we got there, we were met by Bill's crew. By the time they had us out of the water, Aaron came up just below the surface with Liz on his back, and they grabbed you both as Aaron lost consciousness. They had heard a large boom off the coast of this island and headed out to see what it was. They saw the wake in the water and came over in their fishing boat to investigate. They brought us up here to Bill, as he is the owner of the fishing operation on this island. Well, he actually just owns the entire island," Darla explained. "And as far as location, we are in the middle of the Gulf of Mexico. What is the island's name again, Bill?"

"Rieler. It's Spanish for shimmer," Bill said with a twinkle in his eye. "We're off the tip of Tampico, Mexico."

"Yes, Ray . . . Ray-lar." Darla said, trying to roll her R the way Bill did his.

"Yes, something like that," Bill said with a chuckle.

"Well, at least I tried. So, how do we get back on track from here?" Darla asked, but did not wait for an answer. "We need to hurry since we are in the overworld. The longer we are here, the more chance we have of getting spotted, and we don't want that. Bill and Aaron blend in, but the rest of us sure don't. First, we thought boating was a good idea, but it takes too long and is too out in the open. I think it's best if we swim. We will get there three times faster, and we would be underwater most of the time."

"But how will we know where we are going?" Liz asked.

"The shimmer badges!" Aaron burst out. "We can ask the fish for directions, but remember that Penelope warned us not to trust dolphins."

Darla smiled with him. "That's right! Love that idea!"

"As long as you stay along the coastline and head north, you should get to South Padre with no issues," Bill said. "But yeah, dolphins are terrible sometimes. You can absolutely trust a tuna, though. They are great with directions! I don't use the powers much anymore, but I still have 'em."

"Cool. Anything else we need to figure out? No? Then let's get going!" Emily interrupted from the other side of the table. "I'm ready for some more action. All this talk is boring."

"I agree we need to get moving quickly," Darla said. "I just want to make sure we have a good plan, and it sounds like we do. So, everyone, get your bags and meet me on the north beach in fifteen."

With that, the other stuffed the remaining food into their mouths and ate as quickly as they could. Once they were finished and the table was cleared, each traveler headed down the beach to the launch point Darla had selected.

"Phil you still have the toolkit, right?" Darla asked.

He patted the red metallic pack on his back. "Yep! All good!"

"Everyone have their shrinkweed bags, badge, bracelets, and pens? We don't want to leave anything here on accident." Darla paused to watch for nods. "Good. All right, Aaron, we are following you. Now the coordinates are a latitude of 26.11 and a longitude of -97. That puts the location somewhere in the middle of the Gulf of Mexico, about ten miles east of South Padre. Once we get there, you are on your own to actually find the island. It's not on any map, from what we can tell.

"Okay, I got it," Aaron said. "We need to follow the shoreline north until we hit South Padre Island, then go east ten miles or so to find the entrance. And if we get lost, we ask tuna, not dolphins." As he said the last part, he looked to Bill for confirmation.

"Yep, tuna are the best," Bill confirmed. "Octopus also have a great sense of direction. They are a bit hard to keep focused sometimes, though. They need to keep all eight arms busy and can get distracted easily by shiny objects."

"Adding octopus to the helpful list," Aaron replied with a slight smile. "Let's get going, I guess."

He started walking calmly toward the water's edge.

"Have I taught you nothing?" Emily bellowed from behind him. "Come on, everyone. Hands in. Descendants on three!"

She smiled at Aaron. He smiled back and put his

hand in. The others quickly joined them. "All right, shimmer boy, count us off."

He chuckled, then began. "One, two, three . . ."

"Descendants!" They chanted.

"Okay, now we're ready!" Emily announced.

Aaron turned and dove into the gulf. He headed straight out until the water was about thirty feet deep. *That should be deep enough to keep everyone out of sight as we follow the bottom.*

The deep blue darkness enveloping them was stunning. As he saw the drop-off approaching, he slowed his swimming, and the others did, too. They all worked seamlessly together as a group, even though their partnership was still so new. They eventually came to a stop and floated in a small circle.

"Okay, here is the depth I want us to keep. From here, we head north, which is that way," Aaron said and pointed. "I confirmed it with Bill before we left. Everyone all good?"

Everyone nodded, so Aaron began swimming again. He knew that from Bill that this leg of the trip would take about an hour. He aimed to set a swift but comfortable pace. Once they were all up to speed, he turned over on his back as he swam so he could check on those behind him. The wake he left pulled everyone along. None of them seemed to be struggling, more just enjoying a leisurely ride.

Nice. That means my plan is helping, he thought with a smile. He had been feeling like he wasn't good enough for all of this, but seeing his shimmer powers in full force was pretty convincing.

22

THE SWIM

The voyagers swam for about thirty minutes, just cruising along close to the bottom. Aaron could still hear random oohs and ahhs from behind him as they took in the magnificent scenery. He was just as thrilled as his friends, both with the sights and the company.

"Did you see that fish?" Emily asked Liz. "It was *huge*!"

"I saw a silver fish!" Steve added in from behind them.

"I didn't see that, but did you see the entire school of red fish? They just whooshed by!" Liz replied.

Phil and Darla had changed up the line so they were both in the back, chatting as the kids led the way.

"Y'all, let's check the shoreline and take a quick breather," Aaron said as he slowed to a halt. Once stopped and floating, the conversation turned to gushing about all the things they had seen.

"Seriously, those red fish were so cool!" Liz started off, "and just this entire thing is so cool. These bracelets are amazing!"

"Yes, this is absolutely just wonderful," Darla added.

"And it seems like as long as we stay in Aaron's wake, it makes it very easy to swim. I am not nearly as tired as I should be!"

"Agreed! I am having a blast!" Phil said.

"Me too!" Emily and Steve said, almost in unison.

"I know! I am still getting used to it all as well. These gadgets Penelope left us are the best. Speaking of, think this a good time to try speaking to a fish?" Aaron asked.

"Yes, dude!" Steve said.

"I'll do it! I'm not scared," Emily said.

"Since we all want to try it, why don't we each find a sea creature to give us directions? Then, we can compare and follow the best option," Aaron suggested.

"Why don't you four do that?" Darla replied. "I think this is a great time for you all to take the lead. Phil and I will remain here and wait for you. It shouldn't take long, right? There are creatures everywhere."

The descendants nodded and then took off to find their informant.

I need to find a tuna . . . or what was the other one Bill said was good? Aaron thought as he swam toward a boulder surrounded by seaweed and grass. He wanted to check whether any creatures were hidden there.

PLOP! A tentacle smacked Aaron straight in the face.

"Ahh!" Aaron yelled as he swiped it away.

"Sorry, sorry, sorry," a garbled voice said.

Aaron followed the arm back to its owner—a purplish-blue octopus. His big, bulbous head and a few of his arms floated freely in the water as he sat on top of a smaller rock.

"Sorry, sorry, sorry," the voice said again as more of its arms reached out to smack Aaron.

"Woah! Hey!" Aaron yelled back while blocking most of the slaps with his hands.

Wait! Octopus was the other one Bill said.

"Sorry, sorry, sorry," the octopus repeated as it went for another round of playful attack.

Oh yeah! It needs to have its arms busy so it can focus, and it likes shiny things, Aaron remembered as he defended himself.

He reached into his pocket, grabbed a few coins, and held them out toward the octopus. He closed his eyes and waited to be slapped, but the barrage stopped. The octopus picked up coins, one by one.

Aaron looked down at his hand and noticed there was only one coin left, but three arms left to deal with. He quickly grabbed two of them—one in each hand—and held them away from his face. The octopus picked up the last coin from the sand, and its demeanor immediately changed.

"Hello!" the octopus said, surprising Aaron.

"Umm, hi? My friends and I need directions," Aaron said. "Do you know where South Padre Island is?" He wasn't sure if he was even talking correctly. No one gave him a how-to book on chatting with sea creatures, or at least he hadn't discovered it yet.

"Yes, I do," replied the octopus.

Aaron waited for it to tell him, but it was silent.

"Okay, so which way is it?" Aaron asked slowly.

The octopus used all eight arms to point in the direction they had already been swimming, then it floated back down to its resting place.

"Thank you." Aaron turned to swim back to the group.

"You're welcome," the octopus called.

When Aaron met up with the others, they were eager to share how their interviews worked out.

"Well, I found a tuna who didn't know a ton of words, but it understood me fully," Liz reported. "It pointed that way."

"I found a giant fish that called himself Gary the Grouper. He wasn't super talkative, but he also pointed that way," Steve said, pointing in the same direction as Liz.

"I met a couple dolphins, but I can't repeat what they said," Emily added.

"Yeah, we were warned that might happen with dolphins—" Aaron replied.

"Hey, I had to see if it was true," Emily interjected. "Plus, it sounded like a challenge, which has been seriously lacking around here."

Aaron shrugged, then continued. "But it sounds like all the others pointed the same way we were already going, so it worked out well!"

"Yes, it did," Darla confirmed with a proud smile.

"Is everyone good to keep moving? I don't plan to stop again until we get to South Padre Island. It should be about twenty or thirty minutes north still." Aaron paused for a second. "Cool, then let's go. . . . Umm, I mean, hands in!"

Everyone smiled and stacked their hands on his.

"One, two, three . . ."

"Descendants!"

Aaron turned and began swimming. *We are almost to*

Seaweed City and the answers to all my questions.

He got lost in thought as he swam, and the time passed quicker than he realized.

"Hey, Aaron! You good?" Steve shouted.

Aaron slowed down until everyone was once again floating together.

"Sorry, y'all. I kind of zoned out there, just thinking about all that has happened and such," Aaron said.

"No worries, dude. You were just cruising, and I noticed we had been swimming for around thirty minutes. You said that was where we needed to stop, so I stopped you," Steve said proudly.

"Thank you, man!" Aaron said as he rushed to the surface to determine how close they were to his ancestors' home. He broke through the surface of the water and searched for something that would confirm where they were. His eyes landed on a long shoreline with several white buildings. He dipped back under the water and headed down to the others.

"There's a strip of land up there, but I also just realized I don't know what I am looking for. Is there any sort of landmark that tells us whether it's South Padre?" Aaron asked Darla and Phil.

They shrugged.

"Oh, right. You can't help us. So, descendants, how do we know when we are there?"

"Maybe we ask some more fish?" Liz suggested. "It seemed to work well last time."

"Good idea! I keep forgetting we can do that," Aaron said with a small chuckle. *You have to remember that you can talk to fish, dude. You're the leader here . . . and the shimmer.*

GURGLE! Several fish dashed right through the middle of the group like torpedoes. "Sharks!" one of them shouted.

Aaron turned around to see a giant bull shark headed directly for his group.

"Y'all, it's a shark! Swim!" Aaron screamed.

Everyone shot off in different directions, scattering just barely enough as the shark blew right through where they had been. The shark kept going, but then stopped shortly after.

"What is that delicious smell? It is like shimmer flesh, but also smells human. I haven't had either in ages!" a deep, vicious voice rumbled.

Aaron and the others rushed back to each other to regroup.

"What do we do?" Liz shrieked.

Phil and Darla swam between the group and the predator that was speeding back toward them.

"Yum, yum, yum!" The shark's tone was terrifying.

"You're going to have to go through us first!" Darla screamed.

"Sounds good to me!" the shark replied as he opened his giant jaws to eat the adults.

"Everyone, get close!" Aaron yelled as he motioned for Darla and Phil to come to him. "Hurry!"

Steve grabbed Liz and Emily by the hand and pulled them all together in a tight circle.

Aaron reached into his pocket, grabbed the blue potion bottle, and chugged it quickly.

POP! As soon as he finished, a brilliant blue force field bubble snapped closed around all of them. The shark smashed directly into the giant ball of people with such force that sent it them flying off toward the shoreline. The bubble shot out of the water and slid up onto the sand.

POP! The bubble shield disappeared, and they fell out onto the beach. Everyone laid there for a moment, panting.

"That was . . . awesome!" Emily said with more joy than one should have about a shark attack.

"What was that?" Liz asked.

"Is everyone okay?" Darla asked. As she looked around, heads nodded. "But yeah, what was that, Aaron?"

"So that was the shield bubble from the blue potion bottles from Penelope's vault. It's made for personal use, but I didn't know what else to do. I figured it might work if we all got close enough, and it did!" Aaron replied.

"That was cool, man," a new voice said from behind them. Everyone turned quickly to see who was talking. It was a large sea turtle with a beautiful swirling caramel and yellow pattern on its shell.

"Uh, hello. I am Aaron. Who are you?"

"What's up? My name is Tonka," the turtle replied. "What you did to that shark was pretty sweet. I didn't think they let shimmers come this close to land, though."

"You know the shimmers?"

"Oh yeah, of course. Most of us sea turtles are born in Seaweed City," Tonka said.

"Sweet! So you know where it is!" Aaron was overflowing with excitement at hearing someone else say the city's name. "That means you can take us there!"

"Hold on. I didn't say I knew where it was, just that I was born there. I have never gotten to see it," Tonka said.

"Well, can you at least tell us if this is South Padre Island?" Aaron asked, deflated after the previous answer.

"Oh yeah, man. This is definitely South Padre." Tonka pointed his fin toward the white buildings. "There are a ton of humans over that way, so y'all might want to steer clear of there."

"Thank you, Tonka," Darla said. "We are trying to get to Seaweed City, and I know you said you don't know its exact location, but I figured you might have a general idea."

"We think it is about ten miles that way." Aaron said and pointed to the east. "Does that sound right at all?"

Tonka followed his hand. "Yep, that sounds about right. All I remember from being a baby turtle was swimming up onto this beach from that direction. The older turtles knew where it was, and they would make trips there, but no one ever told me. But every time they left and returned, it was from that way."

"Thank you! This helps a lot!" Aaron replied with renewed excitement. "But how will we get to the city with that shark still out there? He's probably watching us right now, waiting for us to get back in."

"I can help with that one!" Tonka said. "You can use the currents. Sharks hate being in the current when they are hunting, so we turtles use them to move around without being bothered. It starts right over there."

He pointed his fin to a decrepit wooden dock a little farther down the beach. "As a shimmer, you should be able to see the current lines in the water. As long as you stay in the current until you are a few miles out, you should be good. Sharks are not lazy, but they won't follow you that far."

"Perfect!" Aaron said. He turned to the others, who seemed less enthusiastic. "Y'all ready to go?"

"I am ready," Liz answered. "The shark was scary, but if we made it this far, we should keep pushing."

"Yeah, that was a blast! I am in for sure!" Emily said.

"That was horrible, and I am so happy everyone is safe," Darla said. "I am in, but solely based on the fact that I think the safest place for all of us now is getting to Seaweed City as quickly as possible."

"I go wherever my bro goes," Steve said, shooting a confident look to Aaron.

"Yeah, I agree with Darla. The safest place for all of you right now is Seaweed City," Phil added.

"Well, we're going to take off. Thanks for your help, Tonka!" Aaron said, then led his friends toward the dock.

He looked over the edge into the clear blue water. *I do see them! This is so cool!*

He watched the wavy purplish lines in the water, almost like lines on a map.

"I see it, y'all! Keep your potions on you in case you need them, but I think this is going to work! On three?" he asked with a smile as he put his hand out flat for the others to join him.

"One, two, three . . ."

"Descendants!"

"Let's go!" Aaron said excitedly. "It's not far now. I am going to go a little slower so we can watch for signs and things, but it should only take us a few minutes to get there."

He looked to the others, then dove into the current below. As soon as he hit the water, the force sucked him in and pushed him toward the open sea.

Whoa! This is already moving too fast. He slowed down even more than he planned and scanned the area for any signs of an island, a cave, a ship-house . . . anything. They swam for a few more minutes, and still nothing unusual showed up.

Who knows what I'm even looking for? Frustrated, he decided to stop and check in with the others.

"Anyone see anything?" Aaron asked.

"Sorry, sweetheart. All I have seen is ocean," Darla replied. "I haven't even seen many fish."

The others didn't have anything to report, either.

"Why couldn't they just say, 'Hey, it's right here, Aaron'?" he said as he rubbed his temples. "I feel so dumb. Why am I even here? Just like they said, I am half-human. I don't belong here."

Aaron cried from the mix of anger and self-doubt.

Phil and Darla swam over and wrapped him in a hug.

"Son, you *are* a shimmer through and through. You do deserve to be here, and I promise we will figure this out," Phil said.

"You are being way too hard on yourself," Darla added. "We love you no matter what, okay? Don't worry. We will find it together."

The parents held him for a few more seconds as he

sobbed. Once he was able to collect himself, he looked up at them. "Thank you both so much. You don't understand how much you mean to me."

He pulled back and got to thinking. *There is something you are missing here. What did Penelope say in that letter again? Man, if my heartbeat could slow back down, I could hear myself think. Wait, that's not my heart!*

He reached into his shirt and grabbed the shimmer stone hanging around his neck. Sure, enough the rock was glowing and pulsing. *The rock will guide you if you will let it,* Penelope's words from the letter ran through his brain. *I wonder if . . .*

He held the rock out in front of him and let it float in the water. The rock slowly tilted and pointed directly down until the silver chain was taut around Aaron's neck. The shimmer stone pulled slightly, and Aaron swam in the direction it pulled. The rock's pull became stronger as he dove deeper. Aaron raced after it, with the water flying by as he picked up speed.

Down, down, down, down, down, down, down, down deeper it pulled him. The ocean that was light before was now almost pitch black because of the depth. Only the light of the shimmer stone remained. Aaron could only see a few feet in front of his face, but he pressed on. He could feel that he was on the right track, and he wasn't going to stop until he arrived.

Suddenly, the sandy ocean floor came into view, but he was moving too quickly to stop. *SMACK!* He hit the sand and rolled to a stop.

Ouch! Anything feel broken? . . . No, all seems good, he thought as he righted himself. The sand that had been stirred up when he crashed began to settle, and Aaron couldn't believe what he saw once it had cleared up. In front of him, only a few feet away and half-buried in the ground, was a door that looked just like the rootwood plank door from Bill's ship-house. He couldn't see much else, but it looked like the door went directly into the ocean floor.

"Aaron!" Steve hollered from the darkness.

"Hey! Y'all, I'm over here!" Aaron called out.

"Aaron, is that you! We can see hardly anything down here," Darla said.

"Yes, Darla, it's me!" Aaron replied. "I think I found the entrance!"

"On our way, sweetheart!" Darla yelled back, obviously thrilled at the news.

After a few seconds, Aaron saw four small balls of light headed toward him, but he could not tell what they were.

"Oh, there you are!" Darla sounded relieved.

The lights got closer, and soon Aaron could see that it was the glow from each of their shimmer badges. The badges glowed blue, just like the shimmer stone.

Once she got close enough, Darla grabbed Aaron and hugged him. "Thank goodness you are okay."

Right after the hug, she lightly swatted him on the arm. "But don't ever leave us like that again. That was terrifying. You just took off, and none of us could keep up. Please don't do that again. Deal?"

"I am so sorry, Darla, and to all of you. I felt drawn here, literally, and I just didn't want to miss it."

"We're cool, Aaron, but miss what? There is nothing here," Emily said as she gestured around them to all the darkness.

"I didn't want to miss *this*!" Aaron said as he turned around so his shimmer stone illuminated the door.

"Whoa! I didn't see that there!" Emily shouted.

"That looks really old," Liz said as she swam over for a closer look.

Everyone else made their way over to the door, speculating on how they should open it. Emily was the first to try. As soon as she got near the handle, she yanked on it. It didn't budge.

Seeing that Emily couldn't open it with her strength, the others decided there must be a lock or a mechanism. They inspected the door for a place to put a key, but could not find one. They checked around the edges for any sign of a button or trigger.

Aaron floated above the door, staring at it. *It will guide you if you will let it*, Penelope's words repeated in his head again. Just below the knob, there was a blank space where a lock would normally be. He swam down to it, and the shimmer stone shone brighter. He touched it to the blank space.

CLICK! The door swung inward, creating a huge whirlpool. They all tried to swim away, but the vortex was too powerful. The door slammed closed, and the ocean was quiet once again.

23

THE ENTRANCE

Aaron tried to grab on to something, anything, to slow his descent. Nothing was there. He was in a tunnel just like the lava links, only this one went straight down. He looked up and could see the others all falling, too. He turned back around to see where they were headed. A small light came into focus, then kept getting bigger in a hurry.

PHOOMP! He shot out of the tube like a cannon and landed in a deep body of water. He swam straight down to try to get out of the way of the others, but luckily it wasn't an issue. With different sizes and weights, each had a different trajectory. Aaron swam back up to the surface to check in with his friends.

"What was that?" Liz asked as she bobbed at the surface and tried to catch her breath.

"I think it was the entrance," Aaron replied.

"That was fun!" Steve bellowed as he floated on his back.

"Is everyone okay?" Darla asked as she righted herself. "Everyone here?"

They all nodded, answering her first question as she counted their heads. "Yep, all five of you. Phew!"

"Hey, do y'all think we should head that way?" Phil pointed to the other side of lake. A large rootwood dock with a ladder at the end jutted out into the water. The banner above it read *WELCOME TO SEAWEED CITY!*

"Definitely!" Aaron said excitedly as he raced toward the dock.

Once they had all climbed up, they could see that the dock led directly to a grand entrance with two massive rootwood plank doors. The doorway was cut directly into the black stone wall of the great cave that held the lake. In front of the doors were two large guards wearing shiny blue armor that almost looked like it was made of glass. Aaron walked toward the guards, who eyed him with suspicion.

"You there! What business do you have in Seaweed City?" the first guard yelled out.

Aaron froze, then quickly found his nerve again. "Hi, I am Aaron. I am a shimmer from The Table here to fulfill the journey set before me by my ancestor, Penelope the Peaceful," he said, loud and proud.

Hey, I am getting good at this, he thought and smiled.

"I'm sorry, did you say Penelope the Peaceful and that you are a descendant from The Table?"

"Umm, yes?" Aaron replied, slightly less sure of himself.

"Open the gates! He is here!" the guard shouted toward the sky. The doors creaked open, and both guards knelt as they motioned for Aaron's party to head in.

Aaron looked at the others, and they all seemed impressed.

"Awesome! Here we go," Aaron said as he walked through the doors.

The scene that lay before him was unlike any he had even imagined. They were on top of a hill with a cobblestone street that fed into a highway. As he followed the highway to the horizon, it entered an impressive city in a giant domed cavern, just like The Table! This one did not have nearly as many skyscrapers, though, and seemed to have lakes surrounding it and rivers going through it. Moss and seaweed covered many of the buildings.

Other than all the seaweed and stuff, this place looks like pictures I have seen of that floating city in Italy, Aaron thought to himself as the city seemed to beckon him. It felt almost identical to the first time he had seen The Table.

"Wow!" Darla exclaimed. "It looks so similar to home, except with more water."

"Yeah, *a lot* more water, and everything is so green," Phil added.

"This placc is fantastic!" Liz said as she walked farther down the street.

"Howdy there, y'all! Welcome to Seaweed City!" a tall, broad-shouldered man said as he ran up to them. The man, probably in his mid-twenties, was wearing blue jeans, cowboy boots, a brown belt, and a paisley pearl snap shirt. His ensemble was topped off with a black Stetson cowboy hat.

"My name is Justin, and I am here on behalf of the royal family to welcome you! We heard news that the shimmer descendant had been found, but that's all we had heard. We had hoped you would come to get the box and see your shimmer home," Justin said, then dropped his voice to a whisper. "Wow, you look just like him."

"Hello, Justin. My name is Aaron. I didn't hear you at the end there. What did you say?"

Justin smiled quickly. "Oh, nothing important. Just that you look like an old friend. Sorry about that."

"Ah, gotcha. Well, we are excited to be here. Also, you said something about a box. What box?" Aaron asked.

"Well, the box Penelope left you, of course."

Aaron's eyes grew wide. "Yes! That's what we came for. I am so excited to see this place, and now I can't wait to see what is in that box!"

Darla stepped forward. "Hi, Justin. I am Darla, and this is my husband, Phil. We are the chaperones along for this trip. If you don't mind me asking, how did y'all hear about Aaron?" she asked. "We have had a few mishaps on this trip. I just want to know that the kids are safe and that we can trust you. No offense."

"I understand completely, ma'am. The shimmer community is very close-knit. We heard about Aaron within thirty minutes of them unlocking the vault. My cousin Ted lives right down the street from the vault park and called me to give us the news. It spread like wildfire around this city after that. You see, most of Seaweed City knows of The Table, and a lot of them have been there. Even though we like to stay hidden from the world, the world can't hide from us," he said with a chuckle.

Darla nodded. "That makes sense, but please remember this: You hurt my kids, and I will hurt—"

"Whoa, honey," Phil cut in before she could finish. "I am sure everything will be just fine. We don't want to offend our new friend here."

"It's quite all right, Phil. I truly appreciate how much she cares for these kids. I promise that y'all are safe. We want you to feel at home here. Mi casa es su casa!" Justin said.

"Sorry, what was that?" Steve asked.

"It's Spanish for 'My home is your home.' Please enjoy my city. We are happy you are here," Justin replied. "Let's get you all to The House for some food. How does that sound?"

"Sounds great to me," Aaron said.

"I can always eat," Steve added.

"Yes, I think we're all pretty hungry and could use some rest," Darla said.

"We will take the royal wagon to the house," Justin said.

He clapped twice, and a long white limousine drove up the cobblestone street from down the hill. It stopped right beside them, and the driver got out to open the door for the group.

"Hop in," Justin said.

They all squeezed into the limo, with Steve being the last one in.

Justin waited until everyone got comfortable. "To The House, please, John."

"Wow, this is fancy!" Aaron said as he eyed the charcuterie plate in the corner.

"Go ahead, Aaron. This is all for you," Justin said, which made the boy blush.

Aaron was used to always being the one that people

made fun of, not the one people actually wanted around. He grabbed a few snacks and passed the plate to Steve.

"So, about this box," Aaron said between bites of the cracker sandwich he had assembled. "What is it?"

"It's a box," Justin replied.

Emily and Liz giggled, which in turn made Aaron giggle at the question he had just asked.

"Okay, yes. But do we have any idea what is in it?" He tried to reframe his question.

"No idea," Justin said. "All I know is that Penelope brought a box to the king of Seaweed City years and years ago and asked that the royal family protect it until the day her descendant came to claim it. She did not know when it might be or who it would be, but that someone one day may come for it. And if they did, they are supposed to be given royal treatment and shown the entire city. She also stated that once they are given the box, we should help and assist them in any way needed to complete their journey. My father was king until ten years ago, when he died unexpectedly. So, now I am in charge, along with our elder council. I was only thirteen when Dad passed, but I have decided to continue using the elders as advisors even as an adult and to run things as a more of a majority-rules society. The people here in Seaweed City have really appreciated the change."

"Aww, Justin, I am so sorry for your loss," Darla said.

"Yeah, sorry man," Aaron added. "I know how bad it sucks to lose a parent."

"Thank you, but I have done my grieving," Justin said as he stared out the window for a moment. "But, umm, we need to get you familiar with Seaweed City. . . . I have an idea! John, can you slow down a little and drive us into downtown?"

"Can do, sir," the driver responded, and he directed the limo to an exit ramp that curled underneath itself and onto the street lined with the few skyscrapers they had.

Justin reached over to press a button; the sunroof slid open above them. "I thought you might enjoy a closer look," he said.

"For sure!" Aaron said. "I've always wanted to do this!"

Aaron stood up so half of his body was out of the sunroof, and he waved his arms in the air as they drove. "Yahoo!" he shouted, long and loud, as they drove.

Downtown included many of the familiar stores he had seen in The Table and some others he hadn't. Some of the blocks included what Aaron assumed were family-owned businesses, based on their unique names and mossy exteriors.

He closed his eyes for a bit, just enjoying the wind blowing in his face. It felt like a few seconds, but he must have been up there for a while.

Justin tapped his leg. "Okay, pal. We have to pull in and park."

"That was crazy!" Aaron said as he sat back down.

"You think that was crazy? Wait until you see The House," Justin said.

"What is The House?" Liz asked.

"Check it out for yourself. We just arrived!" Justin said excitedly as the limo came to a stop and the driver hopped out to open their door.

"This way, please, ma'am," John said to Liz as he held out his hand to help her exit. As she stepped out, Aaron heard her gasp.

He scrambled out after her, ignoring John's hand, then froze. Before him was a massive white marble pool the length and width of a football field. Thick, tall trees provided privacy, and several fountains lined the sides. The car had pulled into what looked like the drop-off area a hotel might have, except there was no building—just a small, white pagoda.

Everyone else piled out behind him, and they looked as shocked as Liz and Aaron. The pool was so massive and the water so crystal clear that it was mesmerizing.

"This is beautiful!" Aaron finally said.

"Just wait," Justin replied. He walked over to the wooden pagoda and motioned for the others to join him.

Once everyone was standing on its platform, he pressed his thumb to a scanner on one of its poles. "Keep your hands at your side as we go down, please!"

The platform shuddered to a start and descended into the ground.

24

THE HOUSE

The platform came to a halt in front of a simple wooden door with a black handle.

"After you," Justin said to Aaron as he opened the door for his guests. "Welcome to The House."

When Aaron saw what was on the other side, he couldn't find the right words. He just stammered for a minute as he walked into the massive modern mansion. The foyer had two grand staircases going up either side of the room, just like in Hollywood movies. In the center hung a sparkling chandelier made of fantastic blue stones.

Is that all shimmer stone? Aaron thought. *It must be incredible to be part of the royal family.*

The first floor of the house continued on through a hallway in between the staircases.

"I can show you the lower floor later, but upstairs is the coolest part," Justin said as he headed for the left staircase. He ascended the stairs while the visitors stared blankly around the home, transfixed.

"Are y'all coming up?" he hollered down to them.

"This place is *huge*," Steve said as the rest of them started up the stairs together.

"Right? I mean, just look at that chandelier!" Aaron said.

"And it's all underground!" Darla gushed.

As they reached the top of the stairs, they were again caught off-guard by the magnitude. They were standing level with the bottom of the pool from above. The only thing keeping the water from them was a glass wall. Justin tapped on it twice, and the wall transformed to create a glass hallway in the center of the pool.

Justin smiled as Aaron's jaw dropped. "It's not done yet. Come with me."

He walked down the new hallway.

Aaron was so excited that he nearly ran into Justin as he tried to keep up. He was completely fascinated with the water falling down the outside of the glass around them. A doorway in front of them opened up into a large room.

As they entered the room, Aaron realized it was the bottom of the pool in the dead center. *So this room was here the whole time? I didn't even notice it from above!*

Four doors lined the wall across from where they entered. In the middle of the room was an entertainment center with a television and a few couches. On the left end, there looked to be a full kitchen.

"Welcome to the guest quarters. We have these four rooms available for y'all," Justin said, addressing everyone but Aaron. "You can make several modifications to your rooms using the panels on the front of each door. They work with this new technology called shimmer panes. That's what all the walls in here are made of. It's like glass, but can change shape and color. It's made with the same technology as your traveler's kit."

Phil, Darla, Emily, Liz, and Steve headed over to the four doors. Liz took the far left one, Emily went in next, then Phil and Darla, and finally Steve to the room on the far right. They all messed with the panels on the front of the doors, seeing what they could customize.

"Aaron, come with me. I will show you to your room," Justin said as he turned to walk back downstairs.

"Oh, I don't need my own room. I can just bunk with Steve, I bet. It won't be a problem," Aaron replied.

Justin didn't stop, so Aaron followed him anyway. They went downstairs and then turned around and walked down the middle corridor. The walls there were made of shimmer panes and would flicker and change to all the colors of the rainbow as they walked by.

"I will never get used to that," Justin said as he saw Aaron admiring the panes.

"These are so cool!" Aaron replied. "Oof!"

He ran directly into Justin, who had stopped beside a small hand scanner. Justin put his hand on it.

BEEP! The wall next to them slid open.

"Welcome to your room, Aaron," Justin said as he stepped back so Aaron could walk in.

"Wow" was the only word that Aaron could muster. Before him was a twenty-by-twenty room with dark blue glass walls that almost looked mirrored. The floor was a beautiful white marble that gleamed with a fresh coat of polish. In the center was a California king bed with a dark blue comforter and blue pillows. The walls were adorned with many photos and paintings. On a white table right in front of the foot of the bed was a simple wooden box.

Aaron slowly entered the room. As he looked around, he could see that each painting had a name under it.

"There is Penelope!" he said as he saw her painting on the right wall. He ran over to get a closer look. He smiled and turned around to face the small box.

"So that's from Penelope?" Aaron said as he pointed toward the white table.

"Yes," Justin said, "but that is not all there is to discover here."

Aaron cocked his head to the side and eyed Justin. His host smiled and gestured to a painting across the room. Aaron focused on the portrait, and his entire world came to a screeching halt. He felt like his eyes were lying to him. It looked just like him, but much older. The placard below read *KING DONALD THE DUTIFUL*. Aaron ran over and stared at portrait for what felt like an eternity.

That looks a lot like me! Wait . . . is that my dad? It looks like the photo I have!

"Aaron, that is your father. He is also my father," Justin said.

Speechless and wide-eyed, Aaron looked to Justin.

"He told me that I had a half-brother out there somewhere in the world, but swore me to secrecy," Justin continued. "He was never able to tell me who you were, or where you were, or any of that—just that I had a half-brother and Dad had plans to one day come find you and reunite the family. When we heard of the descendant, I got so excited that there might be a chance that you were my long-lost brother. The minute I saw you, all doubt was gone. You look so much like Dad. It's uncanny. I look more like my mother, who unfortunately passed during my birth."

"So, wait, you're telling me that my dad didn't die in a tragic accident?" Aaron asked, feeling both overwhelmed and confused.

"Oh, sweetheart!" Darla's voice came from the doorway. "Are you okay? We heard everything. Come here. I got you."

She swooped him up. Aaron melted into the familiar comfort of her arms, his head spinning.

My dad was here, and that's my brother. I have a brother. Why didn't he come find me? How did Dad die? What all does this mean?

The question tsunami continued hammering the shores of his mind. He sobbed into Darla's shoulder as she held him. Phil, who was just behind Darla at the door, joined in on the hug.

"Hey, buddy. Sounds like we have some new family to meet, huh?" Phil said with a laugh to try to ease some of the tension in the room.

Aaron let out a muffled chuckle, then walked over to the painting of his father once more.

"So, you're my brother?" Aaron said, looking back at Justin.

"Yes, I do believe I am," Justin replied.

"And my dad was Donald the Dutiful?"

"Yes," Justin replied calmly.

"Okay. Okay." Aaron paced the room, trying to organize his thoughts.

"Wow, that is a lot to take in," Darla said.

"You said my dad . . . umm, Donald died here unexpectedly? I was told he died in a tragic accident, but no one ever told me anything about his death," Aaron said. "So, like, how did he die then? Was it an accident or what?"

Justin sighed. "Yes, Dad died here, and it was very unexpected. You see, before you were born, Dad would go on monthly trips to the overworld to check in on society and make sure Seaweed City stayed up on the latest overworld news. One day, he began to make weekly trips, then it became daily and or every other day. He never told me why until the very end—just that it was 'official king business.' He began going so often that people here started to question it. However, it only lasted a few months, so no one ever really looked into too much after that."

He stopped to clear his throat. "Dad got extremely sick very suddenly. He had a rare and aggressive form of brain cancer that, from what the doctors have told us, was dormant until it wasn't. It was such a quick decline. He was healthy one day, then gone the next. From the diagnosis to when he passed was only three days."

Aaron stared at the painting, trying to comprehend it all.

"So, he didn't die in an accident," he finally muttered. "He was here the whole time?"

"He didn't tell anyone about you until the day he passed away," Justin said. "All he told me was that you existed and one day might find your way here. He made me promise that if you did, I would protect you and love you as family. He wouldn't tell me any more in fear that I might endanger myself trying to find you. Remember, I was only thirteen at the time."

Justin walked to a panel on the wall and pressed it. A cabinet door opened out of the blue glass wall. Inside it was a small aquamarine box with the shimmers' symbol on top. He took the box out of the cabinet, closed the door, and turned around to Aaron.

"He also gave me this to give you if we ever did meet," Justin said as he handed over the box.

Aaron cradled the box in his hands. *I am holding a gift from my dad.* He had never been given anything of his father's, let alone something his father had left just for him. He glanced to Phil and Darla for support, and each gave him a warm smile.

Okay then. Let's see what's inside.

25

THE BOX

The lid opened easily, and Aaron surveyed the box's contents. The only items inside were a shimmer stone on a chain necklace and a small, tattered envelope. As Aaron picked up the stone, it glowed aquamarine, not the brilliant blue like other shimmer stones he'd seen.

"Wow, I didn't know there were two!" Justin said. He reached into the collar of his shirt and pulled out a necklace that looked almost identical. The stone shone brightly, just like Aaron's.

"Dad gave me this when I was born, and I have always had it on me," Justin said through tears. "I had no idea another one existed."

Aaron slipped the necklace around his neck and then pulled out the envelope. He was excited about the shimmer stone, but was more focused on reading what his dad had to say. He tore open the envelope and quickly unfolded the paper inside.

Aaron,

As I write these words, I dream of a world where I get to see you grow up, although now I know that it is not possible. Please know that I love you with all of my heart and would have done anything to change things. I am writing this letter to explain some things to you. If you are reading this, then you have already figured out a ton on your own, as I knew and hoped you would.

Aaron's eyes filled with tears as he read the words. He had to take a few deep breaths before he could keep going.

Coming home yesterday from visiting you, I realized my abilities were depleted for some reason. I fainted once I got back to The House. I was taken to the doctor immediately and told that I had cancer and not long left to live. This type of cancer is particularly aggressive for shimmers, and mine has already spread so much that my abilities are now gone forever. I cannot come back to see you, as my body is already too weak to move. As I lay here, I think of the things I wish I had done differently. One of the main ones is that I should have told your mother about this place and who I really was. I only wanted to protect the shimmers and the city. I tried to live two lives, but it was a foolish decision, and I am sorry. In this box is a shimmer stone that is only like one other in the world. Justin, your half-brother, has the other. Once the two have touched, they will forever be connected and will be drawn to each other. That way, you two will never lose each other again.

Aaron looked up, smiling through his tears, at Justin, who was smiling right back at him. He continued reading.

There are so many things I want to say, but I can tell that I don't have much time left. So, I will just say this: Aaron, I love you so much and I am so proud of you. I regret many of my decisions, but you were never one of those regrets. I wanted so badly to teach you to fish.

Love,

Dad

P.S. Listen to your older brother. He is smart and one of the best people in the world.

As he finished the letter, he sat on the bed and put his head in hands. Darla and Phil sat down on either side and put their arms around him as his body shuddered with sobs.

"We love you, Aaron," Darla said.

"Yes, we do," Phil agreed as they held him. They sat there for a few minutes, just letting him cry.

Justin walked over to him. "I am so sorry about how overwhelming all of this is. I get it, I promise you. Last week, I wasn't even sure you really existed. I had given up hope. Then, I heard of this shimmer boy who was half-human but also a descendant of Penelope and that he was headed here. It was the best feeling in the world to know that there was a chance that I still had family out there. It's a lot to process for me, too."

Justin turned and stared wistfully at the painting of their father.

"Yeah, it is," Aaron mumbled from Darla's shoulder. That brought a small chuckle to each of them, and Aaron sat up.

"Man!" he said as he wiped the tears from his eyes. "I really don't know what to say."

"You don't need to say anything," Darla replied. "Why don't you get some clean clothes, take a shower, and then meet us over in the guest area for some food? Will that help?"

"Yeah, I think it might," Aaron replied.

"Sounds like a good idea to me," Phil added.

"There is a private shower through the back door there in the corner," Justin said as he pointed to the blue panels on the back wall.

"Umm, I don't see a door," Aaron said.

"Oh yeah, sorry. Let me show you. It can be tricky to see if you don't know where to look." Justin walked over and pressed on a panel. The door clicked and swung into the room. "There should be soap and towels in there, but just let me know if you need anything."

Justin walked out the bedroom door.

"Are you sure you will be okay?" Darla asked as she and Phil headed stood to leave.

"Yeah, I will be. It's a lot to take in, but yeah," Aaron said. "Wait, I don't have any of my clothes in here."

"I will grab them from the toolkit and drop them on the bed," Darla said.

"Thank you."

"You are most welcome. We love you." She walked out with Phil and closed the door behind them.

What just happened. How? What? Where? The questions and new information bounced around his head like bingo balls as he walked toward the bathroom, forgetting all about the pink box that was holding another giant secret.

26

THE OTHER BOX

"There he is," Phil said playfully as Aaron walked back into the guest quarters common area, freshly showered and ready to eat. "Justin made burgers and hot dogs!"

Phil, who was situated on the couch with a cheeseburger in hand, pointed across the room toward the kitchen.

"Hey there! How do you like your burgers?" Justin called out to him.

"Medium, please," Aaron replied. "It smells amazing!"

"Well, thank you. I will get you one medium burger coming up."

"How are you feeling, Aaron?" Darla asked from the door that led to her and Phil's room. She walked over to him for a quick hug.

"I'm good. Still trying to understand it all, but I have had a lot of mind-blowing things and traumatic events come up recently, so I am getting better at dealing with it," Aaron said with a snicker.

"Yeah, I can see that," she replied. "Well, make sure you tell us if you need anything, okay?"

"Of course."

She walked over and snuggled up to Phil on the couch.

"Hey, buddy!" Steve's booming voice came from the other end of the room as he ran to hug Aaron. "Mom told me about the stuff with your dad. Sorry about what happened, but it's also really cool that we got a new brother out of it!"

Steve walked over to Justin and wrapped him in a bear hug. "Yep, you're stuck with me now, too. Wherever Aaron goes, I go," he said as he squeezed.

"Sounds great, but can you ease up a little, pal?" Justin squeaked.

"Sorry!" Steve released his grip. "Just excited."

"Not a worry," Justin replied as he returned to the burgers. "I am excited, too. It's pretty cool having a family again!"

"It's wild that you are basically a prince now," Emily said as she followed her nose to the food.

"Yeah, sorry about your dad, though," Liz added as she walked with Emily.

Aaron furrowed his brows, then turned to Justin. "Wait, am I a prince?" he asked, smiling now.

"Yep," Justin replied. "I mean, we don't use those titles really anymore and, like I said, we are changing the way things are done here to be more modern. But you are shimmer royalty."

Emily and Liz made their way over to the smaller couch and sat down.

"Dude!" Steve said, and Aaron raised his hand for a high-five. Steve looked confused for a minute, then caught on. "Oh yeah, the secret handshake!"

He slapped Aaron's hand excitedly. Aaron grimaced from the impact, but kept a smile on his face.

"Yep, you're getting the hang of it. Just slightly softer next time, cool?" Aaron said through gritted teeth, shaking his hand out.

"Totally," Steve said.

"So, Justin told us that the other box in the room is from Penelope. Did you want to maybe take a look at it?" Darla asked.

"Darla! We agreed that we would let him eat before we asked about it," Phil said with disappointment in his voice.

"I know, but we have to wait for the food to be done anyway," she replied.

Oh yeah! Penelope's box is at the foot of my bed! Aaron's mind raced and he ran to the bedroom. He grabbed the pink box and rushed back to the commons. He set the box in front of Phil and Darla on the small white coffee table between the couch and the TV.

"Could I sit between you two while we open this one? Who knows what we might find out this time."

The dragons scooted over so he could sit with them on the couch, and he plopped down.

"Justin, you ready?" Aaron asked as he looked over at him.

"Let me grab this last burger off the stove, and I will be right over," Justin said as he put Aaron's burger onto a plate he had prepped with a bun, fries, and all the fixings. He walked over and set the plate of food next to the box.

"Here, this is yours," he said to Aaron. Justin and Steve pulled chairs from the kitchen table and sat down to watch.

"Here we go," Aaron said as he picked up the small box. He unlatched the small hook holding the lid shut and opened it up. Inside was a small, folded piece of paper and a small leathery journal. After a quick look around at the others, he unfolded the paper and read it aloud.

Hello, my champion,

I hope you are enjoying Seaweed City and our people's origins. As you know, there is an item you need to retrieve and bring back with you to The Table. You will need to complete the Shimmer Trials to earn your Shark Sigil.

"What?!" Justin burst out. "No, no, no! That's not possible. I won't let Aaron do that!"

Aaron stopped reading and looked at Justin. "Why?"

"You can't get that. It's too dangerous!" Justin said as he started pacing.

"Let's calm down," Darla interjected. "What's so dangerous, Justin? What are these trials?"

"Aaron will get hurt if he does this, no matter what. Y'all don't understand. The Shimmer Trials are a test of Seaweed City's strongest and bravest warriors. Many who attempt them end up badly injured—or worse."

"What are the trials exactly?" inquired Phil.

"The biggest test of a shimmer's abilities, and there are three parts. First, you have to go to the seaweed fields north of the city to retrieve a rare blue seaweed," Justin said.

"Like the stuff our bracelets are made out of?" Aaron asked.

"Yes, exactly that blue seaweed."

"That doesn't sound so hard," Emily added from

the other couch.

"Well, to get to the seaweed, you have to get through the hammerhead sharks that protect it. As you can see, it's clearly very powerful, and they are sworn to protect it from being misused. They will attack anyone who tries to take any," Justin explained.

"Oh, yeah . . . that's a little more difficult for sure," Emily said with a sigh.

"Yeah, and that's just the first part! For part two, you need to retrieve a saltwater crocodile's tooth! They always travel in groups, so any crocodile you find there will be with at least two others. Are you catching on now? It's way too dangerous. Y'all, I just found my brother. You can't ask me to put him in that kind of danger." Justin was falling apart at the idea of Aaron going with through the challenges.

"That is a lot," Darla said nervously.

"Yeah, I don't know about this," Phil said with a sympathetic look toward Aaron.

Aaron's face was solemn and focused. He stared at the box. "What is the third trial?"

Justin sighed. "The third part involves a deadly underwater chamber below the city center. It will be opened once you bring the two items you collected to the entrance. But very few shimmers have ever completed the trial. In my lifetime, I have seen hundreds compete, but only a handful finish and receive the Shark Sigil. Most endure injuries or worse, as I said before."

"People have died in this trial?" Liz asked, incredulous.

"Unfortunately, yes. These trials are not for Aaron,"

Justin said. "The chamber itself is a giant death trap. It was designed to be the most difficult test of a shimmer's strength. I think Penelope assumed that Aaron might be an older shimmer who had mastered his powers, but this would be a tall task even then."

"Okay, but to be clear: To complete this journey and retrieve the item Penelope sent me after, I need to complete the trials, right? Is there any other way to get a Shark Sigil?" Aaron asked.

"No, there is no other way," Justin answered. "You can't even use money to buy one, as it would dishonor the others who fought to get one."

After a few seconds of contemplation, Aaron locked eyes with Justin. "Then it seems like I have to do this."

"No way! Not happening, brother. I will do everything in my power to stop you if needed. I am not losing you, too!" Justin's face turned red, and tears streamed down his cheeks.

"If I don't, then I can't go back to The Table and I can't complete this journey!" Aaron was getting angry.

"Whoa, boys," Darla interrupted. "We need to calm down. You both have good points, but Aaron . . . honey, Justin is right. This seems way too dangerous."

Aaron looked hurt. "Darla, I *have to* do this. It's my destiny."

"How about we take a few and let this information sink in?" Phil piped up. "Darla and I will give the elders a call to update them and see what their thoughts are."

"The elders can give all the thoughts they want! It's not going to change my mind!" Justin said as he stomped down the hall toward his room on the other side of the house.

Aaron stood up to go after him, but Darla grabbed his arm.

"Give him some space, sweetheart. He will calm down. Why don't you kids head to bed a little early and try to get some sleep? I know that we will find the best solution. Phil and I are going to go chat with the elders, and we will follow up with you in the morning. Sound good?"

"Sleep sounds great!" Emily said.

"Agreed!" said Liz. "Night, y'all!"

Both girls headed to their rooms.

"Steve, is it okay if I sleep on the floor in your room?" Aaron asked his best friend.

"Umm, Mom?" Steve turned to his mother with a hopeful, toothy grin.

"Aaron?" Darla asked.

"I just don't really want to be in the big fancy room all by myself right now. I kind of just want to be me for a night," Aaron said. He sounded exhausted.

Darla smiled gently. "That's fine with me then."

"Yes! Sleepover!" Steve bounded off to get a spot ready for his buddy.

"Are you sure you are going to be okay, sweetheart?" Darla asked Aaron once they were mostly alone.

"Yeah, I think so," he replied.

"Night, bud," Phil said with a quick hug.

"I almost forgot my hugs!" Steve shouted as he ran out of the room to wrap his parents in a tight hug. "Love y'all! . . . Let's go, dude. I found some extra blankets, so we can make a fort!"

The Dimeter boys ran to Steve's room and closed the door behind them.

27

I AM A SHIMMER

Aaron rubbed the sand from his eyes as he looked around the unfamiliar space. *Oh yeah, Steve's room.* His mouth felt dry, so he tiptoed out of the room without waking his friend.

As he headed over to the kitchen for some water, he noticed the light on in Phil and Darla's room. He could hear them talking to someone.

"I don't care what the elders say! I am not letting Aaron begin these trials!" Justin whisper-yelled. "He is too young, and they are too dangerous. If they won't allow him back, that's on them."

"Justin, please," Phil said. "I agree with you, but the elders said that if he doesn't at least attempt to retrieve the sigil, then it is only fair then he has to give up his claim as the descendant of Penelope and all of the contents of the vault. The others may have potentially dangerous journeys, too, and the elders believe it is part of becoming a leader to experience these types of things."

Aaron moved closer to the open door so he could hear better.

"I don't want him to go any more than you do, but

I also want to give him the choice," Darla argued. "It should be Aaron's decision."

"No! He isn't even a full shimmer! How can we think that he will get through this? I will not risk my brother's life to impress your elders. I will let the guards know in the morning that Aaron is on lockdown here until we can think of a real solution," Justin said, then stormed out of the room.

Aaron froze in the darkness of the common room as Justin walked out the door and toward his wing of The House.

"What are we going to do?" Phil asked just before the door closed.

I would have to give up everything I just got if I don't do this? Justin underestimates me, but I know I can prove him wrong. Aaron ran through the possibilities as he finally made it over to the sink for that drink.

Justin said that I would be on lockdown tomorrow, so the only chance I have to do anything is tonight. I have to do this. I have to prove that I am a real shimmer. No one will question it ever again once I have the Shark Sigil!

He chugged his water, then headed to his room to grab his things. He picked up a pen from the bedroom's side table and tore a blank piece of paper out of his journal.

Dear all,

I am sorry I left without saying anything. I knew you some of y'all would try to talk me out of this. I have to attempt the Shimmer Trials and get my Shark Sigil. I will prove to everyone that even though I am half-human, I am a real shimmer and I belong here. I promise I will be as safe as I can, but this is something I must do. Thank you all for the kindness and love you have shown me, I truly appreciate it. I love you all.

Love,

Aaron

He set down the pen and folded the paper, then placed it on the pillow of his still-made bed. He slipped into his blue swim trunks and a white T-shirt, then grabbed his shrinkweed bag and clipped it to his waist. *Okay, let's get out of here.*

He tiptoed down the hall and under the stairs to the front door, thankful there was no troll or creaky floorboards on his path this time. He gently turned the black handle on the front door until it clicked, stepped into the lobby, and then closed the door behind him.

When the elevator reached the top, Aaron stepped out from the pagoda into the yard where they had first arrived at The House. *Okay, what do I know? Let's see . . . my journal knowledge says the citizens of Seaweed City are generally kind and enjoy helping others. Not much to go on, but I can manage. I didn't think about traveling around the city. I guess I will walk toward the shops and see what is there. I bet someone there can help direct me to the right fields.*

He headed down the sidewalk that ran next to the line of trees and the pool. The House was set back in a cul de sac; it was the only residence there. Aaron could see the lights of downtown from the street, so he walked in that direction.

After a few minutes, a giant neon sign glowing on a storefront came into view. *PASSING GAS,* it read in bright letters above what looked to be some normal gas pumps.

Perfect! A gas station attendant will know directions. He

picked up his pace and headed toward the store, which looked very similar to old dinosaur gas stations he had seen signs for in a garage back home. The store walls were all white with a light green trim around the edges of the big bay windows up front.

RING! RING! A bell on the front door alerted the staff that he was there. Aaron walked over to the counter.

"Sorry! I am coming," a young voice with a small lisp came from behind him.

Aaron turned around to see a young shimmer man hurrying out of the restroom door in the back corner. "Welcome to the Passing Gas," the attendant said. "How can I help you?"

"Hello, sir. I am looking for some blue seaweed, and I think it's somewhere north of the city," Aaron said with a hint of awkwardness.

The man looked confused. "Umm, okay. We don't have any blue seaweed here . . . just gas and such. I would think you might have better luck across the street at the potion shop. He pointed out the window at a wooden sign across the way that read *BOBBY'S BREW WORLD* and had a small potion bottle on each end.

"Right, that makes sense," Aaron said. "Thanks for your help anyway."

"No problem," the attendant said. "Come back if you need to fuel up."

The potion shop was a small storefront like any he might see back home. Red brick made up the front of the store with two windows, one on either side of the large wooden door with black hinges. Aaron reached out to open the door, but didn't have time.

THUD! The door swung open in front of him, and a well-aged, lanky man appeared. He was dressed in a light blue suit with a golden name tag on his left lapel that read *BOBBY.*

"Welcome to my shop!" Bobby's shrill voice cracked with excitement.

"Hello. I am looking for some blue seaweed," Aaron said. "I believe it's found north of the city."

"Why would a kid be looking for that stuff? It's incredibly dangerous to get and very expensive. If I had some of that here, it would sell out in minutes," Bobby said.

"You know where it is, though?" Aaron asked.

"Well, yeah. But ain't nobody stupid enough to risk their neck, so it don't matter," Bobby replied.

"What if someone was stupid enough and would give you some if you helped him get to where it is?" Aaron asked.

The old shopkeeper pondered this for a minute, then looked back at Aaron. "Aren't you awfully young to be out here doing this stuff—and all alone?"

"That may be, but do you have anyone else offering to bring you any?" Aaron countered.

"Fair point. And if something happens to you, I will just tell them I never saw you and go about my life," Bobby replied. "You can get to the seaweed fields by taking the express links north to the exit marked for the seaweed fields. Once there, you are on your own."

"How do I get to the express links?" Aaron asked.

"You really aren't from around here, are you?" Bobby said. "Once you head out of the store, take a left and head to the express stop. It's a two-minute walk from here to the entrance."

"Thank you so much, sir!" Aaron said excitedly as he turned toward the door.

"Don't thank me. Just bring me back some seaweed!" Bobby yelled after him.

Aaron saw a sign on the corner that read *EXPRESS LINKS ENTRY/EXIT—DONALD AVENUE.*

Remember that: You entered at Donald Avenue.

As he got closer, he could see that the sign pointed to a manhole cover in the ground. A small button dominated the sign, which read *PRESS TO OPEN*.

Only one way to find out how this works, Aaron thought. He pressed the button, and the manhole cover slid open to reveal a small ladder going down. He took a deep breath and then peered over the edge. The ladder went down about ten feet and ended at a large metal grate. Below the platform was rushing water. He gripped the ladder, took a deep breath, and made his way down.

Looking left and right, he could see this passage was a large cement tunnel. On the right wall was an illuminated map of the city with several lines running across it. *I think this is like the lava links, just bigger tunnels. These look like what subway tunnels look like on TV,* Aaron thought to himself. He smiled as the familiarity made him feel more comfortable about this crazy trek he was on.

Aaron scanned the map. *There!* he thought as he spotted *SEAWEED FIELDS EXIT* in purple. He followed the purple line all the way back to the star icon showing where he was currently. *It's a straight shot north, then the purple exit.*

He looked over the edge of the platform below at the rushing water. "Okay, how do I do this?"

"Excuse me! Ugh, tourists," grumbled a tall, blonde shimmer woman. She pushed right past him and hopped off the edge into the stream.

"I guess that's how," he said as he leapt off the platform and grabbed his legs. "Cannonball!"

Under the water, an intense scene laid before him. The express links had to be more than one hundred feet deep, and there were signs everywhere. Dozens of shimmers swam at different depths in different directions. It seemed like the direction or speed would change every twenty feet or so, like it was a superhighway for shimmers. The walls even had billboards on them advertising products from local stores. Aaron floated there for a second in shock and amazement.

"Hey, move it or lose it!" someone yelled as they sped past him.

Aaron realized he was sitting still in the middle of the highway. He took off in the direction of the seaweed fields, trying to keep pace with traffic. The others moved much faster than he was used to, but he was beginning to get the hang of it.

See? I can do this!

To his right, the exit sign for the seaweed fields was coming up. He slowed and moved over to make his exit, like he had seen his mom do in the car. He took the right for the exit, where the water made a sharp bend.

PHOOMP!

"Ahh!" Aaron hollered as he fell through the air.

SPLASH!

Aaron landed in a new body water and scrambled to the surface to see where he was. When he cracked the surface, he could hear laughter.

Aaron spotted the express link's end, a spout that poured him out into a small lake. Behind him was a wooden dock with a ladder up from the water. The laughter was coming from the two travelers in front of him that heard him yelp.

Red with embarrassment, he swam to the ladder. He wasn't sure what he expected to see when he got to the top of the dock, but it definitely was more than a large stone wall with a small door. Above the door, a sign read *EXIT TO THE SEAWEED FIELDS*. Another one below it had big, red letters. *CAUTION: HAMMERHEAD SHARKS ARE VERY AGGRESSIVE.*

Oh boy, he thought. *Time to man up! You are almost there. Don't give up now.*

He reached out for the handle and twisted the knob.

CLICK! BOOM! The door opened up with a rush of water, sucked him in, and closed back in a flash.

28

THE SEAWEED FIELDS

Aaron closed his eyes and shook his head to gain his bearings. When he opened them again, he could see miles of seaweed floating in front of him on the ocean floor. Red, orange, purple, yellow, white, black. *Where is the blue?* He scanned as far as he could see, but there was not a single blue seaweed in sight.

Okay, so they are rare. Maybe I should swim around a little, but I need to watch out for the hammerheads. What do I know about them? He flipped through the rolodex of shimmer info in his mind. *Hammerhead sharks are strong and agile, but not the brightest. They have terrible eyesight. Don't ever try to fight one head-on. Use brains, not brawn. . . . Umm, I'm not sure what exactly to do with that. I will just try my best to be quiet and not run into any of them.*

He swam close to the ocean floor, slowly and silently. The seaweed crops were beautiful, and it was hard not to get distracted. He searched for anything blue, but came up empty.

"Hungry!" a deep voice called out somewhere in front of him.

Aaron dove into the seaweed to hide. As he looked

up, the shadows of three humongous hammerhead sharks cast him in darkness. Two of them grumbled out the same word: "Hungry!"

Aaron's panicked breathing sent a steady stream of bubbles up, and one shark paused to look around. Aaron quickly plugged his nose and held his breath until the hammerhead continued on his way.

He watched the sharks until he was sure they were gone. He swam up and out of the seaweed, trying to keep his cool. His eyes darted across the landscape, desperately searching so he could get out of there.

In the distance, something caught his eye. *Please tell me that's blue seaweed!* He swam closer to investigate. *Yes! And it looks like there's plenty!*

Aaron zoomed toward the patch of blue and pulled plant after plant out of the ocean floor as fast as he could.

"No, no, no! Hungry!" a deep, gravelly voice shouted from behind him.

Aaron turned around just in time to see a giant shark begin swimming right for him with its jaws wide open. Squeezing the precious plants tighter in his hands, the shimmer put his feet firmly on the ocean floor and launched himself up and out of the path of the shark missile.

"No! Hungry!" the shark boomed as its dorsal fin smacked into Aaron's leg, leaving a nasty welt.

Aaron rushed toward the exit, ignoring the throbbing in his leg.

"No, no, no!" the shark bellowed again as it chased after him.

Even swimming at his fastest, Aaron could see the

shark was going to catch him before he would get to the door. *Think, Aaron! Oh, the potion shield!*

He reached for the small bottle in his pocket, but it wasn't there. *It must be in my other shorts!* He could see the wall and the door in front of him, but the shark was too close. Even if he got there first, the shark would get him before he made it through.

What did the journal say about hammerheads again? Strong but stupid. . . . I've got it! He swam as fast as he could directly at the door, screeched to a halt directly in front of it, then turned to stare at the shark as it charged him. *One . . . more . . . second!*

SMACK! Aaron rolled from in front of the door like a matador would from a bull as he twisted the doorknob.

BOOM! The door snapped open, sucked them both in, and snapped shut again. Aaron found himself back on the dock where he came in.

"Hey! Me thirsty. Need water," the shark complained from his left. He looked over to see the hammerhead lying belly-up on the dock, still snapping at him. Aaron couldn't stop himself from cracking a smile at seeing the big, bad shark helpless. His humanity got the better of him, though, when he noticed the predator drying out and becoming lethargic.

Aaron moved his harvest to one hand, stepped to the side of the door so he would not get sucked back in, and pressed the button once more. The door snapped open, sucked the shark back in, and closed with a large splash.

"Dang! That was a little *too* close!" Aaron let out a

huge sigh and laid down. He rolled over and spread out the seaweed he had clutched in his hand. *Looks like four plants—not bad!*

He unclipped his shrinkweed bag and pulled on the zipper. *HISS! SNAP!* The bag returned to its normal size, and he unzipped it the rest of the way. He placed the blue seaweed inside, then closed it again. He wiped some of the water off his arm and flicked it on the bag. *SNAP!* It shrunk back down, and he clipped it back around his waist.

Okay, next thing: Where to find a saltwater croc's tooth. Do I already know something? He asked the rolodex: *Where can I find saltwater crocodiles?*

Just like that, he had the information. *Saltwater crocs can be found in the swamps to the south of Seaweed City.*

All right then, he thought as he looked around at the dock. He spotted a sign pointing to an elevator that read *TO THE EXPRESS LINKS*. He got up off the ground, dusted himself off, and pressed the button to go up. When the lift stopped, he was on another grated platform out over the rushing water. He looked at the map on the wall and followed it south, hoping to find an exit for the swamps. *Yes!* he thought as he spotted the green words.

He followed the green line back to his current location. *It seems the trip to the swamps will take about twice the amount of time as it did to get here.* He confirmed the route, then turned toward the south and dove into the water.

This time, he blended into traffic almost like he had been doing it his entire life. No close calls, just merging right in and getting moving. *It's a straight shot south. I wonder how fast I can really swim.*

He had yet to try to swim fast, he realized. He had always been finding his way or making sure the others could keep up. The only time he had not was when he found the door on the ocean floor to Seaweed City. *Let's push it a little,* he thought as he sped up.

Before he knew it, he was passing other shimmers like they were standing still in the lane. *WOOSH!* He swam right by an older male shimmer, a little too close, and he yelled at Aaron.

"Slow down, you crazy kid!" the man shouted.

"Sorry!" Aaron yelled back as he slowed down and noticed a sign for the swamps. He made his way into the exit lane for the swamps. Traffic in the lane slowed a good bit, and then the lane turned off into a tube in the wall. *Prepare for the fall, and try not to yell like last time,* he told himself as he turned into the tunnel.

PHOOMP!

"Ahh!" he yelped as he hurtled through the air and splashed safely into a lake of light green water inside a stone cavern. There was a wooden dock on one end of the lake, similar to the previous exit. He broke through the surface of the water to again hear some locals on the dock in front of him giggling.

"I was expecting a fall, not to be shot out of a cannon," he grumbled as he swam to the ladder and hauled himself onto the dock. Just as before, this dock led to a stone wall with a wooden door with a black handle and hinges. The sign above it read *THE SWAMPLANDS* in white letters. Then, just below it, there was a sign with big red letters: *CAUTION: SALTWATER CROCODILES ARE VERY DANGEROUS.*

What if they are right and I am not strong enough for this? I could really get hurt messing with a croc. He shook his head and knocked away the doubts.

No, you can do this! he told himself as he gripped the door handle, ready to be whipped into the swamplands.

CLICK!

It opened like a normal door. *Umm, what?* Aaron thought as he peered through the opening at what looked to be a pretty typical swamp on the other side.

He cautiously crossed through the doorway and into the green moss-covered territory.

29

CROCS AND SUCH

If there was a crocodile heaven, it would look just like the swamplands. The tall trees jutting into the sky reminded Aaron of Caddo Lake's bald cypresses, draped with a darker version of Spanish moss. An eerie fog rolling along the ground provided the perfect cover for the ancient predators.

Now that I have checked another embarrassing entrance off my list, how am I going to get the tooth? Aaron wondered as he peered into the depths of the swamp. *I could punch one. No, that wouldn't work. It would just make it mad.*

"Well, you look delicious!" a deep southern voice drawled from his left.

Aaron turned just in time to dodge the creature lunging at him. He rolled out of the way, then turned again to face his attacker.

The reptile, which was at least twenty feet long, used its scaly tail to smack the swamp water as it stared Aaron down.

Is that a saltwater crocodile? It's humongous! Aaron searched his mind for a plan as the croc sprinted in his direction, its jaw agape and ready to snap him up.

I know I can't outrun it, but I've got to do something while I think of a better plan. Aaron turned to take off, but he heard a familiar shout before he could move.

"Leave him alone!" Steve's voice blasted through the swamp as the giant ran to intercept the threat. His oversized right fist smashed directly into the croc's jaw, sending teeth flying.

HISS! The angry, injured crocodile dove into the shallow water and sped away.

Aaron looked over at Steve with an ear-to-ear grin. "Holy crap, dude!"

"I didn't know I could do that," Steve replied. "But, dude, why didn't you tell me you were going? I would have come."

"Why didn't you tell any of us?" Darla demanded from the entrance.

"Aaron, how could you do this?" Justin asked as he walked past Darla.

"I'm sorry—I truly am—but that is why I left you the note. That way, you knew," Aaron said.

"Yeah, but you still left us and almost got yourself killed!" Justin said, pointing to where the croc had been.

"Hey, did we need some crocodile teeth or something like that?" Steve asked as he bent down and picked up a pointy one off the lily pad to his left.

The others looked at Steve, who held up the tooth and smiled.

"Yes, dude! That's exactly what I needed!" Aaron exclaimed.

"Hey, don't think that changes the fact that you should not even be here," Justin muttered.

"Okay, Justin, we get it. I am upset, too," Darla

said, cutting him off. "Seeing that we have the tooth, let's just get out of here first. Then, we can get into this once we are safe back at The House. Let's go, everyone—now."

Aaron and Steve nodded and headed toward the door. Justin was obviously frustrated, but relented. Once they were on the other side of the door with it securely closed behind them, Aaron walked toward the expressway ladder.

Justin stopped him before he reached it. "We have a royal express tunnel that runs from one end of the city to the other. It's over there and can only be accessed by members of the royal family," Justin said and pointed to a small hand scanner in the corner. "We can use it to get directly back to The House. That's how we got here so quickly."

Aaron walked over to the scanner and placed his hand on it. The scanner turned green, and an oval rock slid open in the floor next to the scanner. Inside, rushing water filled a lava link.

"Okay, everyone, straight back home. Aaron, you meet us in the common room to discuss what we do next," Darla commanded.

30

IN TROUBLE

Aaron stared nervously at Darla and Phil, who were seated across from him on the other couch in the common room. *What are they going to do to me? You messed up huge this time, dude. You shouldn't have done that!* Fear and doubt overran his mind.

Darla finally broke the silence. "Aaron, sweetheart, don't ever do that again, okay? Seriously, never again, please. I don't ever want to be that worried ever again in my life."

"We understand why you did it, but not the fact that you actually did it," Phil added. His voice was firm but caring. "That should have been—and will be in the future—the type of decision you talk to us about. No exceptions. Got it?"

Aaron smiled at them through tear-filled eyes. "Got it!" He jumped up and hugged them both around the neck. "I am so sorry. I promise!"

"I get it, too, and I am sorry for anything I said that offended you," Justin added from the other side of the room. "I was just worried about you. I have not had family in so long, and I don't want to lose you."

Aaron ran over to his brother and wrapped him in a

hug. "I am so sorry, Justin. I just wanted to show you I could do it."

"No, I am sorry. I clearly underestimated you and will never do that again," Justin said. "The three of us have discussed it. We agreed that if you want to attempt to finish the trials, you can."

Aaron was in shock when the words reached his ears. "Are you sure?" he asked as he looked back at Darla and Phil, who both nodded.

"Thank you, thank you, thank you!" Aaron yelped as he hugged Justin before running back to Darla and Phil to embrace them again.

"Well, there are some stipulations," Darla added as he hugged her. "First, you will never run away like that again. Promise me."

"I promise," Aaron replied with a solemn nod.

"You also have to promise that if there is anything in that chamber that is too dangerous, you will turn around and leave, knowing you have attempted it." Darla continued.

"I figured that you were going to try to attempt the last part, no matter what we did to try to stop you," Justin said. "You also showed a ton of drive and determination with what you already have accomplished. You are doing your shimmer heritage proud. Dad would have been so proud of you"

Justin choked up a little at the end, then cleared his throat.

Aaron beamed with pride and hugged his brother. "Thank you so much!"

Aaron reached into his shrinkweed bag and pulled out three blue seaweed plants. "Oh yeah! Can you get these extra plants to Bobby?"

"Sure, but how do you know Bobby?" Justin asked.

"He gave me directions in exchange for my extras."

"Of course he did." Justin chucked and shook his head.

"Well, what's next?" Phil asked after a few seconds of silence.

"Well, the chamber entrance is at the center of the city," Justin replied. "It's about a ten-minute drive from here. I can have John take us there whenever Aaron would like. Aaron will present the tooth and seaweed to the guards, and they will open the gates."

"That's it?" Darla asked, sounding skeptical.

"Yep, it's pretty straightforward from here," Justin said. "Aaron attempts to complete the last part of the trial. If . . . I mean, when he does, Aaron will have completed what he needs to for the elders at The Table. Word has already spread around Seaweed City that he is attempting the final part . . . and I may have tipped them off that he was the long-lost son of their former king, so there might be a few people there to cheer us on."

Justin smiled in his brother's direction. "The entire city is behind you. They are excited that you didn't back down. You stood tall in your shimmer abilities and faced the tests head-on."

"How did anyone know what he was doing?" Darla asked.

"Darla, the shimmer trial is famous here. With people seeing a tourist yelp as he came out of the links in two of the trial locations, as well as knowing Aaron was headed here from previous news, people put it together."

That seemed to appease Darla, so she turned her attention to Aaron. "Well, it's up to you. Are you sure you want to do this?"

"Yes, more than anything!" he replied.

"High-five!" Steve hollered and held up his hand for Aaron. Aaron smiled and slapped his friend's open palm.

"Did I do it right?" Steve asked.

"Yep," Aaron confirmed with a light chuckle. "Perfect."

"That settles it then. Let's get ready to roll, y'all!" Phil said excitedly.

"Grab your bags and meet at the elevator in ten?" Darla asked with a smile.

"Yes!" Emily hollered from the doorway of her room, where she had been eavesdropping. She pounded on the wall between her room and Liz's. "Liz, we are going! Aaron is gonna try it! Get ready to go!"

"I need to grab a couple things from my room," Aaron said. "I want to make sure I have everything I could possibly need."

Once there, Aaron took stock of what he had. *Hmm, what do I need? Oh, the shield potion things! And Penelope's pen, and all of this,* he thought as he stuffed the items into his shrinkweed bag.

He looked over at the portrait of his father and smiled. "We got this, Dad. I know I can do this!"

Aaron headed back down the hall to the elevator, where the others were waiting.

They piled into the limo, which wound its way through town as supporters lined their route.

"We are almost there. That's the park where the

entrance is," Justin said after a few minutes as he pointed out the window.

The band of adventurers watched the lush green meadow come into view. It was similar in size to Central Park in New York, Justin told them, but it had large lakes and ponds throughout, with small rivers of blueish-green water connecting them. There were some trees, but not nearly as many as Aaron expected, given all the water.

"Can I roll the window down?" Aaron asked.

"Of course!" Justin said. "John, can you please roll all the windows down?"

John pressed the buttons on the driver's-side door. Wind whipped in Aaron's face as he thought about what he might encounter.

You can do this. You are a shimmer, and a prince on top of that, he reminded himself as the nerves started getting to him.

Darla noticed Aaron's demeanor had changed. "Aaron, are you sure you are okay?" she asked, sounding a little worried.

"Yeah, I think so," he replied, though not convincingly.

"Well, that's good because we are here!" Justin said as he excitedly pointed out the windshield.

As the car came to a halt, Aaron couldn't believe the sight in front of them. Where Justin had pointed, he could see what looked like a shimmer stone, except it was the size of a small shed and jutting out of the ground.

Surrounding it had to be at least a thousand people holding signs and cheering Aaron's name. There also was a group of what looked like soldiers or guards standing in a ring around the crystal to keep people away from it.

He could hear the crowd's chants coming in through the open car windows. "Aaron! Aaron! Aaron!"

"See? I told you the people are behind you!" Justin yelled over the now-overwhelming crowd noise. "John, could you roll up the windows, please?"

As the windows closed, the sound died down, though it was still pretty loud.

"Everyone ready? Aaron?" Justin asked as he glanced around the vehicle. Everyone nodded, so he continued. "From here, you take the items with you and walk up to the stone shard entrance. Place them on the ground in front of you, then place your hand on the stone. The entrance will then reveal itself and you can enter. I had some of the Royal Guard meet us here to keep the entrance clear while you are attempting it. They will make sure no one bothers you."

"Okay, so I just put them on the ground, like, next to it?" Aaron asked, a bit skeptical.

"Yes. From what I know, the crystal should then open and allow you to enter the chamber," Justin confirmed.

"From what you know?" Aaron asked. "I thought you would have already done this."

"No, royals aren't required to complete it, and Dad always warned me about the dangers."

Welp, here we go. Dad, please help me! Aaron thought to himself.

"All right, let's do this!" He opened the door and hopped out of the limo.

31

TRIAL TIME

"Okay, dude, this is it," Steve told Aaron. "Have fun, be safe, but most importantly, come out alive. . . High-five?"

He held up his hand for Aaron to complete their new ritual.

"I will. I promise you!" Aaron replied as he high-fived his pal. He turned to look at the giant crystal shard jutting up in front of him.

"Good luck, son," Phil said as he wrapped Aaron in a quick hug. "I know you can do this. Remember, though, that we don't need a sigil, but we do need an Aaron."

"Thank you, Phil!" Aaron replied, but it was a bit muffled by the wings.

"I am serious about you being safe," Justin said sternly from behind them.

Aaron broke the hug with Phil and smiled at Justin. "Yeah, yeah, big bro. I got this."

"All right . . . you got this, kid!"

"Be careful!" Darla said during her turn to smother Aaron with a quick dragon hug.

"Just don't be stupid," Emily said. "And kick some

tail in there!"

"What they said," Liz added from the other side.

Darla loosened her grip. "Okay, we need to just let you go. I love you, Aaron."

"I love you, too!"

She stepped back to join the others off to the side. Aaron smiled at them, then turned back to the stone shard. He unclipped his shrinkweed bag, set it on the ground, and pulled on the zipper. *HISS! SNAP!*

He retrieved a piece of seaweed and the saltwater croc's tooth and set them to the side.

"Hey Darla, could I use your water bottle really quick?" Aaron said as he realized he needed to close the bag again.

Darla smiled and tossed him the small water bottle from her purse.

SNAP! With a sprinkle of water, it was travel-size again. He tossed the bottle back to Darla, clipped the belt back to his waist, and knelt down to place both items at the base of the stone. After standing back up, he took one look back at his family and placed his hand on the shard.

The ground shook slightly as a piece of the crystal slid down into the earth to reveal a small doorway leading into a dark hallway. The crowd roared with excitement, and the Aaron chant broke out again.

He glanced back at Darla, who smiled at him lovingly. *You can do this,* her face assured him. He returned the smile, then walked through the doorway.

The hallway was cold as he entered. He had barely made it five feet in when the door slid shut behind him in one quick motion. He jumped farther away from the door, worried he might be crushed.

Wow, it's dark in here! Aaron thought as he tried to look around the space without the light from outdoors. He spotted a small green light shining a few feet in front of him. He took a few steps forward, feeling the way with his hands along the wall to make sure he did not trip over anything. He reached for the green light and determined it was actually a small button on the wall in front of him.

CLICK! It depressed into the wall at his touch. Aaron braced for whatever was coming next, but nothing happened. He stood still for a few seconds, then relaxed and stepped closer to the button to see whether there was something else he needed to do.

CRASH!

"Ahh!" Aaron screamed as the spot he had just stepped on fell away and dropped him into a small pond in a room below. He shot to the surface to see where he was, noticing a small dock with a ladder in front of him. *Another dock . . . must be the way.*

Once he reached the top of the wooden ladder, he could tell the cave was almost identical to the express link exits: A small, dark cave with a pond at one end and a dock at the other. A wooden door with a black handle, cut into the cavern wall, awaited him.

Aaron crossed over to the door, which had a wooden sign with a navy shimmer seaweed symbol on it. He reached for the door handle, not sure what to expect.

"All right, Aaron, you got this," he reminded himself as he turned the handle and tensed with anticipation. The door squeaked as it opened up and . . .

that was it. No snap or strong force.

A normal door! He smiled as he walked through. The next room was a much larger cavern that held a massive lake. Most of where the cave floor should have been was just deep, dark blue water.

The small beach of smooth rocks Aaron found himself on was just a few feet wide, but it had enough room for a simple wooden table to the right of the door. Aaron picked up the only item on the table—a book—and opened it cautiously.

Hello, champion!

Congratulations for making it this far in the Shimmer Trials! Be warned that the journey forward could be fatal, so please be careful. This trial is meant to test all of your shimmer abilities completely. Rely on your heart and head to guide you.

Completing the trial is simple. At the bottom of this body of water, there is a large shimmer stone. It is an extremely rare and powerful one. You must retrieve a piece of it and place it on this table. BE WARNED: The water is filled with all sorts of dangerous sea creatures, and the stone itself is protected.

Aaron closed the book and laid it back on the small table.

Looks like I'm going swimming . . . not surprising, he thought as he moved to the water's edge. He peered into the water and now could see that it was a straight drop-off. There was no gradual decline. It had to go down at least a hundred feet!

Before he could chicken out, he dove headfirst into the water. As he cracked the surface, his shimmer powers took over. It was like someone turned on the lights underwater. The scene that lay before him was like something out of a nature documentary.

Aaron was floating in a much bigger body of water than he thought, and it was salty. He could see for hundreds of yards in every direction. In the far-off distance, he saw the gleam of a colossal green shard jutting out of the sand. It had to be three hundred or four hundred yards away, but he could make out its shape.

That has to be it. Wait . . . what is happening?

Aaron's thoughts were hijacked as the shimmer stone around his neck started pulling at him to go toward the green stone.

Why is it doing that? Is it the same as the stone in my necklace? Is this where Dad got it?

Aaron's thoughts raced as he stared down at his keepsake.

It's too green for that, but I still need to get it, he reminded himself, trying to stay focused. He shook his head to clear his thoughts and stared at the shining stone in the distance. He took off swimming, not wanting to waste any time. The closer he got, the brighter the light from the shard was. He could see it more clearly with every kick. There was something around its base that looked like a large pipe or rope of some sort.

Is that moving?! Aaron thought as the "rope" slid away from the stone.

KABOOM! It slammed down into the floor right next to him, causing a massive cloud of sand where it landed. Aaron followed the rope back into the depths to find it was attached to a massive octopus. The creature had to be at least twenty feet long and eight feet wide. Its bulbous head was a dark purple that blended into the water surrounding it like a natural camouflage. Its giant yellow eyes peered through the darkness at the young shimmer floating in the water. The other seven arms flailed about behind it, casting horribly eerie shadows on their surroundings.

"Who dares touch my stuff?!" the enraged monster bellowed.

Aarons rushed away from where the giant arm smacked the ground. "Sorry! I didn't mean to."

"A shimmer?! It was the shimmers that put me here!" the octopus roared as it pushed itself up on six of its arms and snapped the others in the water out of frustration.

At that moment, Aaron could see that the giant creature had some sort of metal belt around its middle and four large iron chains connecting it to the ground. The creature was restrained, but not enough to keep it away from the stone.

"Get away from my stone!" the octopus demanded, and two of the unchained arms smashed down on either side of the stone.

Aaron swam up next to the stone, using it as a shield of sorts. "I'm sorry," Aaron hollered again without even realizing it.

"Sorry? I have been chained here for hundreds of years by you shimmers, and all you can do is apologize? Grr!" It slammed its arm down in anger on the stone as it tried to get at Aaron.

SNAP! A part of the stone splintered off into the water.

Yes! That's all I need! Aaron thought as the piece floated in the water away from him. He made a move toward the shard, but the monster was too fast. It snapped him up in one of its free arms, squeezing the breath out of him.

"No!" Aaron screamed out silently as the monster's slimy arm cut off his air supply.

It raised him up to eye level and stared him down. From that height, Aaron could see the full contraption holding back the beast. It looked like some sort of pulley system.

"Yes, I win! I may not eat you just yet, though. It's nice having someone to talk to," the monster mused, then let out a deep laugh. It loosened its grip on Aaron as it laughed, allowing air to flow back into Aaron's lungs.

Aaron took a deep breath and tried to come up with a plan. *How can I beat this thing? How did Penelope think anyone could? She must have left a way to beat it. What did the journal say about octopus again? Oh yeah! They get distracted easily!*

He glanced around the room quickly while the monster was still caught up in its own joke.

What could distract it? Something shiny? . . . There! In the corner, he spotted a glimmer off of something. A large, shiny blue shield was embedded in the rock, but it stuck out slightly.

Almost like a button! I just need to get free from this grip.

As if on cue, though, the monster's grip tightened. It had stopped laughing.

"Okay, *now* I will eat you," it said as it moved Aaron toward its mouth.

Now what do I do? Think. Aaron, think! How do you usually distract people? . . . A joke! The idea hit his brain like an atom bomb.

"Hey, hey, hang on!" yelled a panicked Aaron, "Do you like jokes? I bet I have some you have never heard, being down here all by yourself."

The monster didn't stop, so he kept going in one last desperate hope it would work. "How do you make a tissue dance? Put a little boogie in it!"

"Hahaha!" the monster's laughter echoed throughout the water. "A little boogie! Hahaha!"

Just as Aaron had hoped, it loosened its grip once more. This time, he was ready. He darted away from the beast and into the open water. The monster stopped laughing abruptly.

"You tricked me! Now, I'm *really* angry!" the giant screeched in fury as it raised its arms to smash Aaron.

He quickly swam over to the shield button and tried to push it into the wall. *It won't budge!*

"I will smash you!" the giant octopus shouted and swung at the boy, who rolled away just in time.

The creature's arm smashed the shield into the wall. *CLICK!*

"No!" it screamed as the floor opened and the chains attached to the creature pulled it toward the edge.

"No, I want out!" the creature shrieked as it lashed out, trying to grab onto anything it could. Aaron barely dodged a wild arm flailing as it tumbled into the darkness below. The floor closed back up with a slam.

32

THE SIGIL

Aaron just floated in the water for a moment, struck still by disbelief. *Did that really just happen? I did it? Wait! Where are the shards?* He scanned around him in a panic, worried they might have been washed into the hole.

There! He spotted one floating a few feet away and swam over to it. He grabbed the shard, hugged it to his chest, and headed to the surface.

He bolted for the small wooden table and placed the shard down. *CLICK!* A solid rock door he couldn't see before slid open to reveal a small room.

Well, that's neat! Inside, he found a square space cut into black stone. Glow moss growing on the walls illuminated the area. In the middle of the room was a small rootwood and leather chest. Aaron flipped open the lid to find a stack of square blue seaweed badges with a large shark tooth embroidered on the front.

He picked up a badge and held it in his hand, admiring it. "I did it! I really did it!"

Once he had taken his badge from the chest and closed the lid, the chest disappeared into the floor. He heard the same clicking noise as before, and another

stone door opened up in the back of the new room.

Aaron was excited to see his family, so he headed out right away into a long, black stone hallway. It went on for several feet, then stopped abruptly. The wall in front of him slid open, and he could instantly hear the voices of his friends and family. He sprinted through, finding himself on the other side of the shard from where he had entered.

"There he is!" Steve shouted as he ran around from the front.

The roar that came from the crowd was what Aaron thought the Super Bowl's winning moment might sound like. People were chanting his name, jumping up and down, and waving at him. He was frozen in shock until Darla snapped him out of it with a mother's warm embrace.

"Oh, thank goodness! Are you okay? Are you hurt? Did you get it? I am so happy you are alive," she rambled as she smothered him.

"I am fine . . . a little bruised, but fine," Aaron mumbled from under her wings. Phil and Justin ran over and piled in on the hug, followed by Steve, Emily, and Liz.

"So, dude, did you get it?" Steve asked, and the group hug broke up to hear the answer.

Aaron reached into his pocket, pulled out sigil, and held it high for all to see. The ground shook with the celebration that erupted from his well-wishers.

"Aaron, I am so happy you are alive, but we also need to move—right now!" Justin shouted over the noise. He pointed towards the limo, where John was standing at the back door waving them in.

"Yes, definitely," Phil yelled and pointed the group toward the vehicle. They all made a run for it and piled inside before the rowdy crowd closed in on their hero.

"Everyone in?" John asked from the front seat.

"Yep!" Justin replied as he banged on the roof twice. "Let's go home and celebrate!"

"I did it. I really did it. I got the Shark Sigil," Aaron told himself.

"You sure did, best friend!" Steve said, patting him on the back. "What did it look like in there?"

"What was the challenge?" Emily asked.

"Did you bring back any other artifacts, or maybe books?" Liz chimed in.

Maybe it was the exhaustion from what he had endured or maybe it was all the questions, but the car ride home was a blur for Aaron.

As they arrived at the house, Justin could tell his brother was in no shape to celebrate. "It's been a long day. How about we all get some rest and then chat about what is next in the morning?"

Everyone mumbled some exhausted version of a yes and headed to their respective rooms. Darlan and Phil could hear Aaron and Steve excitedly talking through the walls for the next half-hour as Aaron re-enacted the entire adventure for him.

When they finally fell asleep, everyone else could as well.

33

HEADED HOME

"Good morning!" Justin said cheerfully as he walked into the guest kitchen for breakfast. "Everyone sleep well? . . . Good, because y'all are going to need it. We spoke to the elders last night, and they want to get Aaron and the sigil safely back to The Table as quickly as y'all can."

"And I promised Aaron's mother I would get him home on time for school starting in the overworld," Darla added. "We still have some time, but the sooner we get back to The Table, the more comfortable I will feel."

"Oh yeah. Ugh," Aaron lamented. "I completely forgot. Can't we stay a little longer??"

"No, we can't. I promised your mother that you would be home safe and sound. and I will feel much better about that once we are home. Plus, the other adults agree that getting you and the sigil back home to The Table is our highest priority," Darla said. "We will be heading home in just thirty minutes. Everyone, eat up and get your shrinkweed bags packed."

"Anything that's going in the Traveler's Toolkit

should be put it in front of our door in the next fifteen, please," Phil chimed in.

"What?"

"We are leaving already?"

Steve and Aaron spoke almost in unison.

"Yep. Aaron's mother will never trust us again if we are late getting you back," Darla confirmed, then walked to her room to pack.

Both boys understood and began shoveling food onto their plates and into their mouths. As they stuffed their faces, Justin sat down beside Aaron.

"Here, this is yours," he said as he handed Aaron a small key. "This is for The House. It's yours now, too, so you can come crash here any time you—"

"My own key? To *our* house?" Aaron hugged Justin tightly. "Thank you, bro!"

"Just don't be a stranger, okay?" Justin said with a smile.

"I promise I will come visit as often as I can. You should come see us at The Table, too," Aaron said excitedly. "Wait. Sorry. Hey, Darla and Phil, is it okay if Justin comes to visit us at The Table?"

"Well, of course it is," Phil said with a heartfelt laugh from the other side of the breakfast table.

"Yes, Justin, you are always welcome to come visit our home," Darla shouted through the open door of their room.

"Well, thank you," Justin replied with a smile. "I just might have to take you up on that offer. I haven't been there in ages."

"Okay, everyone, five minutes!" Darla reminded the others.

"Be right there," Liz said from her room. "I just called my family to let them know we are headed home. They will be there to pick me up."

"Good idea," Darla said. "Emily, why don't you call your family to meet us at the main docks?"

"With the royal express links, the trip should only take an hour or so from the time you leave here. It's not long at all," Justin added.

"Man, that would have been nice for the trip here," Emily said as she went to call her family.

"I know, right?" Liz said as she joined the others in the common area.

"Everyone all packed before I close the Traveler's Toolkit?" Phil asked.

The descendants nodded, so Phil walked off to get it loaded up.

As Phil entered the bedroom, Darla came out. "Once Emily is off her call, we should be good to go," she said.

"I am all done!" Emily said as she returned.

"Phil, you almost done?" Darla asked over her shoulder.

Phil came out with the Traveler's Toolkit on his back. "Yep! Let's go home!"

"All right then! Justin, where is the entrance to the royal express link to The Table?" Darla asked their host.

"It's right down the hallway. The hand scanner is at the end, and a hatch opens in the floor." Justin pointed the way. "Aaron, remember that you will need to operate the scanner. You have the royalty genetics."

"Hey, don't give him a big head!" Steve said with a laugh.

Justin led them down the hall with his arm around his brother's shoulders.

Aaron put his hand on the scanner, and the floor slid open to reveal the rushing water of the expressway. He looked over at Justin and gave him one more quick, tight hug. "I love that I have a brother now. I promise I will call when we get there."

He let go of Justin and hopped into the water. One by one, the rest of the group followed him until they were all in the links in a single-file line rushing toward home.

34

ALMOST THERE

"Hey, look! There's a sign for The Table up ahead," Aaron yelled back to the group as they swiftly swam through the royal express link.

They had been swimming for almost an hour, so Aaron knew they had to be getting close. He slowed his pace a bit once he saw the sign, knowing that the exit would be coming up pretty quickly.

"Yes! Almost home!" Emily shouted from the back of the line.

"I am ready to get to sleep in my own bed again," Darla said.

Aaron felt excited that they had gotten to go on this adventure together, but was also relieved to know they were close to familiar surroundings. "Yeah, I am guessing the exit is only a few—"

KABOOM! A powerful explosion destroyed their lava tube and sent them tumbling into the open ocean.

Spinning and flipping in the water, Aaron tried to steady himself and clear his vision. After a few seconds, he managed to come to a stop in the water and floated upright as he looked around. The scene looked eerily

familiar to when they had used the tubes to leave The Table.

He scanned the water for the others, hoping they were all okay. To his right, he could see Emily and Liz gathering themselves. To his left, he saw Phil helping Darla.

"Steve! Where are you?" Aaron shouted as his eyes strained to find his giant friend. Out of the corner of his right eye, he spotted a dark shadow swimming toward him. He squinted through his still-fuzzy eyesight and exhaustion.

"Steve? Is that you?"

When Aaron's eyes finally focused, he saw that the figure swimming toward him was not Steve. Instead, it was a young male dragon.

Wait, is that Bart's nephew? Aaron though as the dragon got close enough for him to see that it was, in fact, Garrett.

"Oh, hello there, Aaron!" Garrett hissed through clenched teeth as he swam right up to the shimmer.

"Garrett, did you do this?" an exasperated and shocked Aaron asked, still dazed from the explosion.

"Yes, you moron! We don't want you here. This is your second warning. We tried to tell you when you left on this stupid journey, but you didn't listen. Now, give me this item you are supposed to give to the elders and go home. Then, never show your stupid face around here again!"

Garrett grabbed Aaron by the shirt and pulled him within an inch of his snout. "Give it to me!" Garrett snarled with rage in his eyes.

"Okay, okay," Aaron coughed out, struggling to

breathe through Garrett's rough grip. He reached into his pocket to grab the sigil, but his hand landed on something else that quickly changed the plan.

"Here," he said. "It was this bottle. The liquid inside makes anyone who drinks it ten times stronger than they were."

He handed Garrett the small bottle from his pocket. The young dragon laughed maniacally as he let go of Aaron and immediately drank the liquid.

"Ha! Now you don't have it and I will be ten times stronger!"

POP! Garrett was encased in a shield bubble.

Aaron took the opportunity to dart away from the dragon, who was angrily thrashing about inside the bubble.

The other travelers had regrouped and were floating together a few feet away, ready to defend their friend. Aaron—relieved to not only see Steve, but that they were all okay—swam to them before the bubble released Garrett.

POP! The bubble broke, and their adversary roared with anger.

"You will pay dearly for that one, shimmer boy!" he hissed furiously.

"Just tell me when and where, sparky!" Aaron replied with confidence. The response shocked Garrett, who then noticed he was outnumbered.

"Fine! But I will be back for you, Aaron. The Blackwings will be back, and we will avenge Bartholomew the Destroyer!" He turned and launched into the air, followed by a partner in crime who had been hiding behind a rock.

"Are you okay, sweetheart?" Darla asked as she wrapped a wing around Aaron.

"Yeah, I think so," Aaron replied, still a bit lightheaded from the adrenaline rush. "Umm, I am just a little . . ."

Aaron's body went limp, and his eyes shut as he passed out.

35

HEADED HOME AGAIN

"Aaron, honey, I need you to wake up!" Darla's voice brought Aaron back to consciousness. He looked around, discovering he was back home at the Dimeters'.

Darla stood next to the bed on his left. "Oh, there he is! Hey there, sleepyhead. You passed out after the fun little meetup with Garrett."

As she said his name, she clenched her fist.

"Aaron, how do you feel?" Phil cut in from behind her, rubbing her arm in an attempt to keep her calm.

Aaron sat up slowly and outstretched his arms. "I think I am all good. Maybe a little sore, but good, I think."

"Are you sure? You had us so scared when you zonked like you did," Darla said.

"I think sleep helped a lot. How did we get here, though? Last thing I remember was Garrett swimming off after—"

"After you kicked his butt!" Steve shouted gleefully from the doorway. "Glad to see you up, buddy!"

"Yeah, thanks," Aaron said. "But what happened after all of that? I don't remember getting home. Are

Emily and Liz okay?"

"Yes, everyone is healthy and safe. You passed out from exhaustion after an argument with Garrett. Steve grabbed you, and he swam with one hand while pulling you along. Lucky for all of us, the end of the lava link that leads to The Table was not blocked in the blast. We were able to grab you, make our way back in, and reach the exit pretty quickly. We exited at the main lake and met Emily and Liz's families on the shoreline."

"Along with the rest of The Table," Phil added.

"What?" Aaron asked.

"We can talk about it more later, but apparently the entire time we were gone, the news here was keeping up with our story," Phil explained. "My reports were being shared by the elders with The Table's newspapers. The Vendegeks are so excited and proud of you! They all showed up to welcome us back."

"Yeah, it was actually really sweet that they wanted to see you, but we didn't want to wake you," Darla said. "Vee parked the Suburban on the beach so we could come right out of the water and get into the car. The crowd wasn't too thrilled, but when we got home, I called the elders to let them know we had made it. They wanted to speak to you immediately. Once I explained all that happened on the trip home, they agreed that letting you sleep and get back home was probably best. However, you have to promise to return tomorrow after school if you can for a debrief and explanation."

"Yeah, that works for me. I don't think there is any reason I can't," Aaron said, a little less groggy by then. "Wow! Well, that's good news. I feel good to go—no

aches or anything. So what's next?"

"That's great because you have been asleep for almost twelve hours, and we need to get you home as soon as we can," Darla explained. "I don't want to upset your mother, and I don't want to give your wicked stepfather any reason to punish you any more before school starts."

"Ugh, school," Aaron complained.

Darla smiled, seeing he felt good enough to be sarcastic. "Well, grab your bag and anything you are taking with you to the overworld. Remember, this room is yours, so anything you leave here will be here when you get back. I will meet you in the front room in ten minutes. Sorry for the rush, but we wanted to let you rest as much as you could before heading home."

She hugged him quickly and left the room.

"Happy to see you are all good, son," Phil said as he patted Aaron on the shoulder and then followed Darla out.

"So, it looks like you have to jet pretty quick," Steve said with sadness in his voice.

"Yeah. Feels a bit crazy, but it makes sense," Aaron replied. "If we keep my mom happy, I can come back more often."

"I know, but it still sucks," Steve said. He walked over to Aaron and wrapped him in a big bear hug.

"I love you, buddy!" He set Aaron back down and raised his hand for a high-five.

Aaron raised his hand with a giant smile, and Steve smacked it.

"Oww!" Aaron whined.

"Haha, yup. That's so you won't forget me!" Steve

said as he ran out of the room, giggling at his own prank. Aaron smiled as a tear escaped his eyes.

This family is amazing.

He looked around the room to decide what he should bring home with him. *I want my lucky hat and my shimmer stone. I think everything else can stay. Plus, it will be hard to explain a shrinkweed bag to Mom.*

He neatly packed everything into the chest of drawers there and made his bed. He turned off the light, closed the door, and headed down the hallway lined with portraits.

"Ready to roll, Aaron?" Phil asked.

"Yep, I think so," Aaron replied.

"Hey, I know I wasn't there with you on this journey," Vee piped up from her spot at the kitchen table, "but the news here in town told us everything that happened. It was pretty cool, kid."

Aaron smiled her way, then walked over to wrap her in a hug. "Aww! I love you too, sis!"

Vee tried to squirm away. "Eww!"

"But seriously, thank you Vee," Aaron said. "That was nice."

"Yeah, yeah," she murmured as she walked to her bedroom. "See ya next time, twerp."

"Let's roll," Phil said as he opened the front door. Steve and Darla each grabbed a quick hug before they left.

The drive to the exit for the lava links was as quick as Aaron remembered. This time, though, Horace was not there to greet them, and Aaron wasn't scared of the links in the least. He felt like a pro after their adventure. He hopped out of the car and walked with Phil to the

entrance.

"Well, son, it's always a pleasure to get to spend time with you. Please be safe on the way. Oh, and take this." Phil handed Aaron a folded piece of paper. "This is our home phone number. Call us when you are able to let us know you made it okay. Then, if you ever need anything—and we mean it—call us. If I need to come to the surface and deal with Rick myself, I will."

Aaron looked up at the man who was as close to a real father as he had ever had. "Thank you. Just thank you," he cried as he hugged the dragon.

After a few seconds, Aaron stood up straight and wiped the tears away. "Okay, time to go. Would you do the honors?" Aaron asked as he pointed to the vine that opened the links.

Phil nodded, then stepped over and pulled it. The small pool of water in front of them turned into a swirling vortex. Aaron looked to Phil, gave a small smile and wave, and then hopped in.

36

BACK TO REALITY

The water felt cold and refreshing against Aaron's skin as he glided through the water. This time, with the glowsticks and all the twists and turns clear, he shot out into the Vance River before he knew it. He swam to the surface and headed for the bank.

The sun was almost touching the horizon, which meant night was closing in. He made a dash for the house, hopeful that he could avoid upsetting his mother and keep Rick at bay. He ran through the woods, dodging trees and rocks as he went.

As the parsonage came into view, he spotted Rick sitting on the front porch, probably waiting to yell at him. Aaron ducked behind the fence as soon as he saw Rick, but it didn't work.

"Hey there, boy! Aren't you a little late getting home?" Rick smiled and looked to the paddle sitting against the wall.

Aaron began to stutter in fear. "Umm, nah. N-no. sir. I am on time. My mom said this afternoon, and it's not night yet."

"Oh, Aaron! You're home!" his mother said as she

hurried outside after spotting him through the window. "I missed you so much. Tell me about this new friend, Steve. His mother sounds quite nice. Where is she? Did they already leave?"

Aaron smiled a giant smile as he hugged his mother and did his best to ignore the anger on Rick's red face.

"Yep, already gone," Aaron said. "I would love to tell you all about it, Mom! Can we go inside and chat?"

"Of course, sweetheart," she replied as she hugged him and ushered him inside.

Okay, Table, goodbye until next time, he thought to himself as he walked into the house.

He shared all the fun "pretend" adventures he and his friend Steve had with his mother while his angry tyrant of a stepfather stewed alone on the front porch.

Will Booher

ABOUT THE AUTHOR

Will Booher was born and raised in south Texas and the Dallas-Fort Worth Metroplex. He now proudly calls Northwest Arkansas home.

Leaving behind his corporate job, Will embarked on a thrilling new adventure as an author and social media influencer. As he combines his talents for writing and motivation, Will aims to positively impact the lives of those who come across his work.

Despite his busy schedule, Will always prioritizes his family. He is happily married to Elizabeth, a dedicated middle school business teacher, and they share the joy of raising two wonderful daughters. Will finds immense joy in spending quality time with his loved ones, cherishing every moment they spend together. He takes pride in actively supporting his daughters in their extracurricular activities, encouraging them to pursue their dreams and reach their full potential.

Will is eager to share his unique voice and imaginative storytelling with the world. He can be found on social media platforms as JustAMotivatingDad, where he shares uplifting messages and relatable content.

With a supportive family by his side, he faces new challenges fearlessly, fueled by his passion for storytelling and his determination to inspire many, many others along the way.

ACKNOWLEDGEMENTS

To my wife, Elizabeth Booher: You are my everything, I never would have written down this story without you telling me to. I love you to the moon and back. Thank you for everything. I can't wait to see what is next for us!

To my friends Whitney, Jonathan, Azuz, and Greg: Thank you all for the constant support and interest in my writing. I truly appreciate all that you have done to help me.

To my immediate family: Mom, I love you and truly appreciate all you did for me growing up. Thank you for always pushing me to be the best I could.

To Kim: Thank you—for all of it. You are a rock, and I wouldn't have become who I am without you helping me along the way.

To Mandi: Thank you for always competing with me. It made me stronger.

To Bill and Deirdre: Without you two, none of this would be possible. Sincerely, thank you. Your constant support has been amazing. I love you both!

To my editor/coach Amber Guffey and everyone else at Book Puma: I truly appreciate you all! This book came to life with your help.

To Charles D'Amico: Thank you so much, sir, for never giving up on me and seeing my potential from the beginning. You are a great human, and Ithank you for everything again.